COMMENTARY ON
THE MAYA MANUSCRIPT IN
THE ROYAL PUBLIC LIBRARY
OF DRESDEN

COMMENTARY ON THE MAYA MANUSCRIPT IN THE ROYAL PUBLIC LIBRARY OF DRESDEN

ERNST WILHELM FÖRSTEMANN,
SELMA WESSELHOEFT,
ALBERTA M. PARKER

ISBN: 978-93-5614-507-8

Published: 1906

LECTOR HOUSE LLP
E-MAIL: lectorpublishing@gmail.com

PAPERS OF
THE PEABODY MUSEUM OF AMERICAN ARCHAEOLOGY
AND ETHNOLOGY, HARVARD UNIVERSITY
VOL. IV.—NO. 2

COMMENTARY ON
THE MAYA MANUSCRIPT IN
THE ROYAL PUBLIC LIBRARY
OF DRESDEN

BY

DR. ERNST FÖRSTEMANN

TRANSLATED BY
MISS SELMA WESSELHOEFT
AND
MISS A. M. PARKER

Translation revised by the Author

1906

NOTE

In pursuance of the plan of publishing translations of valuable contributions to the study of the Maya hieroglyphs, the Museum Committee on Central American Research has the pleasure of offering the following translation of Dr. Ernst Förstemann's important Commentary on the Maya Manuscript in the Royal Library of Dresden, generally known as the Dresden Codex.

The translation by Miss Selma Wesselhoeft and Miss A. M. Parker was made under the direction of Mr. Charles P. Bowditch of the Museum Committee.

In the original German edition, published in 1901, Dr. Förstemann used the Arabic numerals to designate the days, but in this translation, with the consent of the author who has kindly revised the translation, Mr. Bowditch has substituted the corresponding Maya names of the days, in uniformity with the general use of students in this country. It is needless to call attention to the importance of this paper by Dr. Förstemann whose long-continued study of the intricate system of hieroglyphic writing by the ancient Mayas makes all he writes of great value to students engaged in this most interesting research.

F. W. PUTNAME.

HARVARD UNIVERSITY,
October, 1906.

PREFACE.

Some of those who examine this book will say, that it is too early for a commentary on the "Dresdensis," since Maya research is yet in its infancy, and this opinion is certainly justified inasmuch as a final explanation of that remarkable monument is, of course, impossible at the present time. On the other hand the accounts of the numerous investigations and discoveries which have been made thus far are so isolated and so scattered in the shape of a hundred short magazine articles, that it is certainly desirable to have what we know and what we have still to learn gathered together under one head. This book is intended, therefore, to give an idea of the state of our knowledge in this department of research at this time, when the nineteenth century is passing into the twentieth, with the definite expectation that this work will soon be far outstripped and will possess an historical value only.

The contents of the following pages are of very little value, unless the student can compare them with an edition of the manuscript. My first edition was published in 1880 at Leipsic and the second at Dresden in 1892. The edition in Lord Kingsborough's "Mexican Antiquities" (in Volume III of that work, London, 1831) is still of practical use.

And since in this work I must premise a knowledge of the elements of the subject, I would recommend, as additional aids to the comprehension of the following pages, my "Erläuterungen zur Mayahandschrift der Königlichen öffentlichen Bibliothek zu Dresden" (Dresden, 1886), and also Brinton, "A Primer of Mayan Hieroglyphics" (in the publications of the University of Pennsylvania. Series in Philology, Literature and Archaeology, Vol. III). I would also mention the very valuable work by Paul Schellhas, "Die Göttergestalten der Mayahandschriften" (Dresden, 1897), which I follow in the designation of the various gods by letters of the alphabet.

It need hardly be pointed out, that the numerous pioneer articles by Edward Seler offer abundant instruction to the student in this field as well as in that of Aztec remains.

I wish to express heartfelt thanks to Mrs. Zelia Nuttall and Mr. Charles P. Bowditch, who have aided my work in various ways and have thus rendered possible the publication of this book.

E. Förstemann.

Charlottenburg.

CONTENTS

PART I.

PAGES 1-45.

Page 1.

As the first page is almost entirely effaced by abrasion, we know very little of its contents. Like the second, however, it was doubtless divided into four parts. The two pages have this also in common, that, for lack of space, their contents are not expressed in full, but abbreviated as much as possible.

The top section (a) of page 1 may have been filled with a sort of frontispiece, perhaps a face with a few signs around it.

The three lower sections (b, e, d,) with the three lower of the second page doubtless formed a whole. Each of these sections contained a normal Tonalamatl of the commonest kind, which was introduced on the left by five day-signs having a difference of 12 and was thus divided into five sections of 52 days each. In sections b and d, at least, these periods seem to be divided into equal halves of 26 days each. In d alone we recognize the initial week day, VII, of the Tonalamatl. In each of the three divisions there were two figures of gods, but we can recognize only the first of these in section d as the god D.

Page 2.

This page contains four much abbreviated Tonalamatls. In the following I will represent each Tonalamatl by setting down in a vertical line those of the twenty days with which the principal divisions of equal length of the Tonalamatl begin, in a horizontal line with Roman numerals the days of the week of thirteen days on which the separate subdivisions begin, and with the Arabic numerals the distance between these days. I will also remark that the position of the Tonalamatls in the "Dresdensis" is not connected at all, as in the Aztec, with certain places in the year, and that no rule for this proceeding can be found. It is curious, however, that no Tonalamatl in this codex begins with the day IX or Eb, which is the more important in the last pages of the Dresden Codex.

2a.

This first Tonalamatl has the following form: —

XIII   5 V 12 IV 11 II 12 I 12 XIII

Cauac

Chuen

Akbal

Men

Manik.

The hieroglyphs and the figures show that preparations for a human sacrifice are treated of here and that the subject is, therefore, closely connected with page 3a, where the sacrifice itself is represented.

There are but two pictures of persons, which refer, therefore, only to the first or to the first two subdivisions and which, for lack of space, are wanting for the others. On the left walks the person doomed to sacrifice, his arms are bound on his back, his head is barely visible and his eyes are apparently torn out. There is an object in front of his breast resembling a wreath. Behind this figure crouches a second, who holds an object in his hand which probably represents a rattle. The parallel passage in Cod. Tro. 2b shows the bound prisoner with an axe behind him. Then follows in Tro. 3b the prisoner without a head and behind him the black god with gory lance.

The hieroglyphs—four for each of the five subdivisions—are arranged in the following order:—

1	2	5	6	9	13	17
3	4	7	8	10	14	18
				11	15	19
				12	16	20.

Of these 9, 13 and 17-20 are wholly effaced and 14 for the most part. The very first group refers to human sacrifice, for 1 is a head with an axe affixed to it, 2 contains the hand (*i*) which so often appears as the sign of grasping, especially in representations of the chase; here it has the same superfix as on page 22a, which on pages 4a-10a and 11a, b, appears as prefix. 3 is the head of god H, perhaps given here as a symbol of wounding (serpent god?). I am unable to explain the meaning of the dot between two crosses in front of this head; perhaps the sign denotes the day Kan, which is here arrived at by calculation. We find the same hieroglyph on page 3. Sign 4 signifies the death-god A = Cimi, who appears again in 12.

In like manner 2 is repeated in 6 and 14. 7, 11 and 15 (probably also 19) are, however, the familiar cross *b*; 8 is the head of E with a prefixed knife; the intention here may have been to show that human sacrifice would be likely to have an auspicious influence upon the harvest. 10 and 16 are another unknown head. In 5 we see the familiar Kan-Imix sign, which, for the present, I am inclined to regard as denoting a feast or a sacrificial meal.

2b—c.

These two sections have something in common. First, 2b (as also 2d) is divided into but two parts and 2c into only three parts. Second, in 2b and 2c the scribe intended to draw the hieroglyphs for 10 days each, instead of 5 each, but only drew the outlines of the second five, since they could not be used for these Tonalamatls.

Third, the persons represented here are all engaged in the same occupation, each holding in his hands an object which looks like a frame for a net or web, and also a large needle with an eye through which a thread has been passed.

A very similar representation is found in the Codex Troano 34a, 33a and 23*c, and also in the Sahagun Manuscript of the Bibliotheca Laurentiana at Florence. This can hardly mean anything else than the knotting of cords, which was the only method of casting lots current among the Mayas; compare Seler, "Altmexikanische Studien II" (1899), p. 31, and "Zauberei im alten Mexiko" (1900), p. 90, by the same author. This clearly indicates the use of these Tonalamatls in soothsaying.

Fourth and last, each of the five hieroglyph groups of 2b and 2c begin with the same sign, which must, therefore, denote the casting of lots.

The Tonalamatl 2b runs thus:—

XI   34   VI   18   XI
Oc
Ik
Ix
Cimi
Ezanab.

The pictures are of three persons. At the left two sit facing one another and at the right is the god A. Of the first two, the one at the left is probably feminine, but with an old face. I am inclined here, in spite of the sex, to recall the bald-headed old god (N, according to Schellhas), whom I am inclined to consider, for the present, the representative of the 5 Uayeyab days at the end of the year. This would account for the sign resembling an 8 lying on its side, which appears on the god's head and which usually represents the change of the year (compare pages 38a, 41b, 52b, 68a and 72c). I cannot explain the person sitting facing this god further, than that from his hieroglyph he is either H or allied to H.

Of the 8 hieroglyphs

1   2   5   6
3   4   7   8.

the first, as stated, seems to refer to the casting of lots, 2 is the sign for H, 3 denotes the female figure pictured beneath it, and 4 is the sign q with the Ben-Ik on top of it. In the second group 5 is the same as 1, 6 is the cross b, and 7 and 8 are the hieroglyphs for A.

2c contains the following Tonalamatl:—

III   20   X   17   I   15   III
Oc
Ik
Ix

Cimi

Ezanab.

There are illustrations for only the first two of the three subdivisions; the two figures composing them are engaged in the occupation mentioned under 2b. At the left sits a deity, who is probably E, whose head develops into a second, which is that of an animal; on the right sits the god D.

The three groups of four hieroglyphs each are arranged as follows:—

1	2	5	6	9
3	4	7	8	10
				11
				12.

Of these hieroglyphs 1, 5 and 9 are the head already numbered 1 and 5 on 2b; 2, 6 and 10 are the cross *b*; 3, 7 and 11 are three different heads, all, as it seems, having the Akbal sign, and 11 having also the numeral 6. 4 is again (see 5 on 2a above) the Kan-Imix sign, 8 a Kin with suffix (the east?) and the numeral 16 as prefix; finally 12 is Cimi (A). Do the numbers 16 and 6 refer to the 16th and 6th of the 17 and 15 days standing below them? The beginning of this Tonalamatl III Oc seems to me to fall on an especially auspicious day (hieroglyph *a*).

2d has the following Tonalamatl:—

XIII   28 II 24 XIII

Lamat

Ahau

Eb

Kan

Cib.

This refers probably to the section devoted to women, pages 13-23. For the picture on the left is a woman sitting and holding an unknown object in one hand; on her right stands the death-god A holding in his hands what may be an apron or breech-clout; there is a similar representation in Cod. Tro. 29*b.

The hieroglyphs are

1	2	5	6
3	4	7	8.

Of these 1, 6 and 8 are one of the signs of A, 7 another, and 4 may be a third, recalling the Moan, which, as on page 14c, rests on a hand held beneath it. 2 and 5 seem to signify a carpet or other fabric (or a lying-in bed?), on the one hand suggesting the occupation of the figures in 2b and 2c, and on the other the checkered hieroglyph, which is so common in the Palenque inscriptions. Finally 3 is the woman pictured beneath.

Page 3.

We come now to the sacrificial scene proper, which practically fills the upper half of the page. The victim, a woman, lies bound hand and foot, on the sacrificial stone, just as in the Cortes. 41-42; the incision above the stomach is already made and the eyes are closed. Behind her rises the tree of life with a bird (vulture?) sitting in its branches, which holds in its bill one end of an object, resembling a ribbon (entrails) issuing from the eyes of the victim, just as in Tro. 26*a and 27*a.

This picture is surrounded by four gods, who, however, differ very much from the other four in the second sacrificial scene, page 34a. At the right above is K, who, I think, is the storm-god; the figure at the left above is almost entirely destroyed, and its hieroglyph wholly; I prefer to consider it a rain deity, so that these two gods shall signify the productive season. The two gods below may refer to the blessing upon the harvest and chase resulting from the season and the sacrifice. For, at the left below, we see the maize deity E, holding a dish of fruit, while her head-ornament contains a second head. At the right below sits the serpent deity H and in front of him is an animal with the noose still around its neck, with which it was caught.

The hieroglyphs are in the following order:—

1	2		5	6		9	10		13	14
3	4		7	8		11	12		15	16

<pre>
    1   2   5   6   9 10   13 14
    3   4   7   8   11 12   15 16

        17   18   21   22
        19   20   23   24.
</pre>

Of these, 1-5 are wholly effaced and also the most essential part of 6.

Of these hieroglyphs four (1-4, 13-16, 17-20 and 21-24) clearly belong to each of the four deities, for 15, 18, and 22 (the last again with the dot between two crosses as on page 2a) certainly belong to the picture. From this it seems to follow that Hieroglyphs 5 to 12 refer to the sacrifice itself. As a matter of fact 9 and 11, which are directly above the sacrifice, also refer particularly to that part of the representation.

I wish also to call special attention to the two signs 8 and 16 which seem to correspond to one another. They are the two which I have designated with *q* and *a*, which are met with here for the first time (aside from the *q* with the Ben-Ik, which is not in question here) and which, I think, denote the good and evil days, *q* referring to the sacrifice and *a* to its results.

In regard to the rest of these hieroglyphs, 7 and 9 are Cimi; 10, 14, 17 and 24 the cross *b* and 11 and 23 the hieroglyph *c*. 12 is the head with the Akbal eye, having for its prefix the uplifted arm, which is joined thus to the most diverse signs, and which also occurs in the Tro-Cort. 13 is a similar head, 19 again Imix, 20 the sign *o* and 21 a hieroglyph, which is without doubt a simplified head.

Here, too, we have a Tonalamatl, and one beginning on an especially ceremonial day I Ahau, which seems to play the same role in celestial affairs as IV Ahau does in terrestrial matters. On the sacrificial stone we read the days Ahau, Eb, Kan, Cib and Lamat, and I think it likely that the same days occur in the passage of the Cortes. referred to above; the passage evidently contains some errors. The subdivisions of this Tonalamatl are not known to us, for here the manuscript is somewhat confused. I propose to read it as follows:—

I 10   XI 4   II 15   IV 9   XIII 14 I,

but Cyrus Thomas, "Aids," p. 294, has

I 4   V 8   XIII 11   XI 15   XIII 14 I.

Either reading is dubious. The scribe divided the lower half of page 3 into two parts, and drew in each the outline of five days; but then he saw that, to continue his work, he needed a long surface extending from left to right, and he therefore omitted filling in these two sections.

Pages 4a—10a.

We have here a normal Tonalamatl, which, however, was evidently meant by the author to serve a very special purpose, since he divided the first section of 52 days into no less than 20 parts of 2, 3 or 4 days. I give the following arrangement here, remarking, at the same time, that in one doubtful case (between the third and fourth groups) I deviate from my former plan:—

X 2, XII 4, III 3, VI 2, VIII 4, XII 2, I 2, III 4, VII 2, IX 2, XI 2, XIII
4, IV 2, VI 3, IX 2, XI 3, I 2, III 3, VI 2, VIII 2, X.

Since the five sections on page 4a begin with the days Imix, Ben, Chicchan, Caban, and Muluc, we have resulting from this and from the intervals specified, the following days:—

X Imix, XII Akbal, III Manik, VI Oc, VIII Eb, XII Cib, I Ezanab,
III Ahau, VII Kan, IX Cimi, XI Lamat, XIII Oc, IV IX, VI Cib, IX
Cauac, XI Imix, I Kan, III Cimi, VI Muluc, VIII Chuen, X Ben.

Now, however, in the "Globus," Vol. LXXIII, in my two articles entitled "Die Tagegötter der Mayas," I have expressed the opinion that there is good reason to believe that the scribe has made a grave mistake here.

I assume that the scribe simply transferred the so-called month days from the year just past to the year in which he was writing, in doing which they were, of course, moved five days on (since 365 = 20 × 18 + 5), but he did not bear in mind, that the pictures and the hieroglyphs could then no longer correspond. Hence the days must be not

Imix, Akbal, Manik, Oc, Eb, Cib, Ezanab, Ahau, Kan, Cimi,
Lamat, Oc, Ix, Cib, Cauac, Imix, Kan, Cimi, Muluc, Chuen, Ben,

but

Cib, Ezanab, Ik, Chicchan, Manik, Chuen, Ben, Men, Cauac,
Imix, Akbal, Chicchan, Muluc, Chuen, Ix, Cib, Cauac, Imix, Kan,
Cimi, Lamat.

Let us now consider the 20 groups, disregarding the first (really zero) which has no figure and no hieroglyphs. We will leave out of the question also the first two hieroglyphs of each group, which are the same twenty times and form, as it were, merely a superscription, in which the first sign is a head, also occurring elsewhere (4b-5b), with suffix and affix, and the second is the hieroglyph *i*, which might readily denote a sacrifice. Thus only the usual four signs remain for each picture.

1. Day 15 = Ezanab; Aztec Tecpatl, flint, lance point. The figure of the god does not correspond with this at all; it is a god in a gala cloak, holding before him a serpent and bearing a quetzal bird on his back. This figure, which resembles none other in our manuscript, strongly recalls Kukulcan, who, in fact, is often placed by the scribes at the head of the 20 Maya gods (cf. Dres. 36) in which manner he appears in this place quite without reference to the day and the hieroglyphs. In this interpretation I follow Seler, in the main, who in his treatise "Quetzalcouatl-Kukulcan in Yucatan" (1898) expresses this opinion on page 403 of the separate edition. But possibly the ear-ornament may refer to Ezanab. Of the hieroglyphs, 1 and 2 are the familiar sign of the serpent deities H or I, though here they are not drawn exactly alike. They also appear together on page 6a. 3 (= *r*) I think is the sign for the week of 13 days, which recurs in groups 5, 11, 14 and 16, and hence is distributed 4 times, though not regularly, among the 4 × 13 days. Sign 4 is the death bird.

2. Day 19 = Ik; Aztec Ehecatl, wind, air, breath. The deity pictured is B, the god who is found the most frequently, and with the most varied attributes, of all the gods in our manuscript. He is the god proper of breathing and living and was, perhaps, the local god in the region where this manuscript originated. The second hieroglyph is his sign; the first, with a prefixed 9, is *p* the third *q* and the fourth *a* with the usual 3 before it; their relations to B are still unknown.

3. Day 3 = Cimi; Aztec Miquiztli, death. The deity with a black line about the mouth is certainly the bald-headed old god N, whom we shall find on pages 12c, 14b, 17a, 21c, and 37a. His hands are much deformed; perhaps indicating the bite of a serpent? Of the hieroglyphs, 1, 2 and 4 are effaced; 3 is surely the sign of the god, differing, it is true, from his usual hieroglyph, but recurring with a 4 also on pages 21c and 24. This 4 might refer to the four kinds of years, but here, perhaps, to the fourth of the five Uayeyab days, and would thus agree with the 24th day of Cumku, which should lie here (in the year 9 Kan), if I have begun the Tonalamatl correctly.

4. Day 4 = Manik; Aztec Mazatl. The significance is stag or roe, game or the chase. The first picture on page 5 is one of the forms of F, which seems to stand here not merely for human sacrifice, but also for war and the chase, and especially for the act of killing in general. Of the hieroglyphs, unfortunately only the fourth can be read in full (the sign *c*), the upper part of the second is the cross *b* and the lower part the sign Ahau; the number 11, which is peculiar to the god F, probably stood before the second sign. Did this god rule the eleventh of the 13 months of 28 days, as Moan ruled the thirteenth?

5. Day 8 = Chuen; Aztec Ozomatli, ape, then probably the constellation of Ursa

Minor, and hence belonging to the god C. The figure is unquestionably his, and the first hieroglyph is surely his sign. The other three are the familiar *a, o* and *r*.

6. Day 10 = Ben; Aztec Acatl, the fundamental significance of which is reed, rush, etc. The connection between this day and the god B pictured here must be left undecided. Of the hieroglyphs, the first points rather to the sun-god G, the second, with the numeral 7 as a prefix, is entirely destroyed, the third is the sign *u*, and the fourth, which is half obliterated, was *q*.

7. Day 12 = Men; Aztec Quauhtli, eagle. The figure to which the first hieroglyph with the numeral 11 belongs, is a form of the god F, but has the nose-ornament of the sun-god G. Hieroglyph 2, which we shall find again on 22c, may refer especially to the eagle; the third is the sign of the day Caban with a prefixed 3, and the fourth is the sign *o*.

8. Day 16 = Cauac; Aztec Quiahuitl. The meaning in the different languages points to rain, storm and summer, of which the tortoise and serpent are special symbols. I shall not venture to decide positively upon the deity pictured here; perhaps the object in his hand may be a tortoise; Seler, "Quetzalcouatl-Kukulcan" (1898), p. 403, calls him the young god. In the hieroglyphs we find the serpent sign Chicchan twice, just as in the first group on page 4; then follow *a* and Kan-Imix.

9. Day 18 = Imix; Aztec Cipactli. In my treatise on the day-gods, I have referred to the variations in the significance of this day. The Mayas connected with it the idea of the female breast, of drink, and, in particular, of the intoxicating beverage pulque. The deity pictured here, which is certainly a female deity, has a kind of vessel in her hand, from which the serpent resting on her head appears to be drinking. Hieroglyphs 2 and 4 are wholly obliterated, and 1 partly; there is a lock of hair, the sign of femininity, before 1 and 3. It is to be noted further that 3 is the sign of the death-god and that the deity pictured here has the death-sign on its cheek. Can this possibly suggest deathlike intoxication?

10. Day 20 = Akbal; Aztec Calli. The meaning is that of darkness, night, dark hole, then that of house as an artificial cave or as a place of shelter at night. The first picture on page 7, the black deity L with the beard fits admirably here. The black paint still visible proves that the first hieroglyph, which is almost effaced, was his sign, and the second may be a head more definitely identifying him. The third was the sign *q*, the fourth is an Ahau, perhaps intimating that Akbal belonged to the days beginning the Uinal sections of 20 days, and to the lords of the same. In addition to appearing with these 5th, 10th, 15th, and 20th days, an Ahau is found with the 1st, 6th, 11th and 16th as regent of the year, and lastly, but especially, with the 17th, which bears the name Ahau, and with the god D belonging to it.

11. Day 2 = Chicchan; Aztec Cohuatl, serpent. With this would agree also the third and fourth hieroglyphs (the latter *r*), which are the two we found in the first representation on page 4 belonging to the deity holding the serpent. But what is the meaning here of the dog-head of the figure, and of the first two hieroglyphs corresponding to it? And what does this creature hold in its hand? The lightning? The hieroglyphs seem to correspond to the seventh day, as if the scribe had recognized his mistake and referred here to the present and not to the past year.

12. Day 6 = Muluc; Aztec Atl, water, cloud. With this corresponds the image of the storm deity K and his two hieroglyphs 1 and 2, the first of which occurs frequently, and the second is found on pages 20 b and 47, while 3 (Ahau) designates the day as regent of the year and 4 is the hieroglyph *a*. The curious sign 2 is also given on Cort. 32 b.

13. Day 8 = Chuen; Aztec Ozomatli, ape. There is no agreement at all here, but everything points to the day 3 lying 5 days back, the picture of the Cimi as well as the hieroglyphs, even the third with the Akbal sign and the uplifted arm (as on page 36a), also the fourth (*c*) which is generally thought to be the death-bird. It even seems here as if the scribe had had the preceding year in mind; possibly he did not want to repeat the fifth group.

14. Day 11 = Ix; Aztec Ocelotl, jaguar. Here there is an admirable correspondence between the figure and the first hieroglyph, which on page 26, top, also refers to the jaguar represented there; the other three hieroglyphs are *r*, Kan-Imix and *q*.

15. Day 13 = Cib; Aztec Cozcaquauhtli, vulture. The bird is actually pictured here and its sign is the first hieroglyph; the third is *q*, the second and fourth are obliterated.

16. Day 16 = Cauac; Aztec Quiahuitl, meaning, as in the eighth group, rain, storm, summer. The figure, the first on page 9, seems, however, to indicate the day Ahau, as does also the second hieroglyph, which is Ahau; the first and third are effaced and the fourth is *r*. Perhaps the scribe did not wish to repeat the eighth group.

17. Day 18 = Imix; Aztec Cipactli, as in the ninth group. Here the allusion to pulque is still plainer than it is there. The picture is that of a woman with bound eyes and uncertain position of the hands, and here too with the death-sign, and on her head a bee from whose honey the beverage was prepared. I shall not venture to explain the first two hieroglyphs; the second with uplifted arm appears again on page 8c. The third is Cimi and the fourth *q*.

18. Day 1 = Kan; Aztec Cuetzpalin, denoting maize with the Mayas. The representation consists of the maize deity with the Kan sign on her head, the first hieroglyph is hers, then follows Kan-Imix, which I am inclined to interpret as meaning a meal, next the sign *a* and finally a head, which is uncommon and undetermined, with the leaf-shaped prefix as on pages 4c, 6c, 9c, 34b, 61a, 67b and 69a.

19. Day 3 = Cimi; Aztec Miquiztli, death. The first figure on page 10 is a deity with the head of the death-bird Moan and above the head is the death-sign. As has long been known, the first and third hieroglyphs unquestionably belong to this god, also the fourth with the Akbal sign agrees with it, and the second likewise recalls the Moan.

20. Day 5 = Lamat; Aztec Tochtli, meaning rabbit in the latter language. Neither the figure, which represents Cimi, death, nor the corresponding hieroglyphs, excepting the second one agree with this day. This second hieroglyph has both in front and above it the number 6. Two numbers added thus to the common Uinal

sign usually designate the Uinal period plus days, as is so very common on the inscriptions, so that the sign appearing here would denote 6 × 20 + 6 = 126 days. The hieroglyph here, however, is *not* the usual sign for 20 days. On the contrary, it has in the centre a straight line and on either side of it a parallel line ending in a little knob (or loop?). I propose to regard these lines as representing the ecliptic and the moon, which takes its course now to the north and now to the south of the ecliptic, and the sign as a whole as signifying the lunar month of 28 days. This is confirmed on pages 51, 55, 56 and 57. In that case this hieroglyph would denote 6 × 28 + 6 = 174 days.

Now bear in mind that in this passage the day X Lamat, which equals the Aztec Tochtli, is referred to.

In the year named after this day, and indeed on the 174th day of the same (1 Cipactli), in February 1502, the emperor Ahuitzotzin died; compare especially Brinton, "Essays of an Americanist" (1890), pp. 274-283.

Should this association in our manuscript of Cimi = death, X Tochtli and the numeral 174, be considered accidental? Or did the scribe, writing in the year after the event, actually record it in the year 1503 and, departing from his real subject, immortalize it in this place at the end of the greatest Tonalamatl? I will not refrain from expressing the conjecture I have long entertained, though I am quite prepared for differences of opinion.

Seler attempts to explain this series of 20 gods in another way; see his "Monumente von Copan und Quirigua" (1899), p. 729. (Cf. his collected papers p. 781.)

Pages 4b—5b.

It is my opinion that the Tonalamatl just now discussed connects with another, which is recorded directly below the beginning of the first, and which also differs from all the other ordinary Tonalamatls. It likewise divides the first 52 days into a large number of small parts (14) and has the following form, if we adopt Seler's correction in the last member:—

XII	4	III 4		VII 4	XI 3	I 4	V 3		VIII 4		XII 3
	II 6	VIII 3		XI 4	II 4	VI 4	X 2	XII			

Ix

Cimi

Ezanab

Ik

Oc.

The two days Ik and Oc should be read Oc and Ik. There is only one picture here:—a scaly green monster with the head of the principal god D. There are six hieroglyphs on its body, the first is that of Eb and the second that of Cimi, the fourth is the sign *c*. The others I shall not venture to determine.

According to a conjecture expressed verbally by Dieseldorff, this figure may represent the god who continually recreates himself. We are reminded here of the two-headed serpent (Seler, "Tonalamatl der Aubinschen Sammlung," 1900, pp. 65-66). There are two rows of hieroglyphs above the monster, the upper contains 8 and the second 6, but the second hieroglyph in the upper row belongs in the lower. Thus there are 14 hieroglyphs corresponding to the subdivisions noted above.

The upper seven signs are all alike and are also identical with the one, which, in the great Tonalamatl, recorded above, begins the heading of all the 20 groups; this likewise points to a close connection between the two Tonalamatls.

The remaining 7 hieroglyphs should be considered as only 6, for it is improbable that C occurs twice in this series. They are the gods D, C, H, N, A and B, to which perhaps an E or F or G is to be mentally added in place of the second C. They are all principal gods with the exception of N (as always, according to Schellhas's nomenclature). This N, an old man, denotes, as it seems, the five Uayeyab days at the end of the year, as he does also on page 21c. This sign with the number 4 has already been seen on page 4a. If in 4b this sign signifies the last day of the year, then this Tonalamatl falls in the year XIII Kan. The sign 5 Zac also appears in the Tro-Cort., *e.g.*, Cort. 29 c, Tro. 9*b and 28*b.

Now I shall proceed to examine all that has not yet been discussed to the end of page 12, taking up first the remainder of sections a and b and then all those of 4c-12c.

Pages 10a — 12a.

XI 12   X 8   V 12   IV 8   XII 12   XI

Lamat

Ahau

Eb

Kan

Cib.

The period of 52 days is thus divided into five sections of 12 and 8 days each, alternating regularly. A deity and four hieroglyphs belong to each of these sections, viz:—

1. D sitting, with his right hand pointing upward and his left downward; on his head is the Akbal sign as on page 15c. The hieroglyphs are destroyed with the exception of the third, which is the sign of D (Ahau). The fact that the 12 days happen to end with the day belonging to D (Ahau) is accidental.

2. R, a human figure with the head of the Moan (as on page 7c and 10a) and with the copal pouch around his neck. Of the hieroglyphs only the fourth, one of the common signs of Moan (c), is legible.

3. H, or, according to Seler, "the young god," as on 12b and 14b, with nosepeg and copal pouch. On his (her?) head sits a bird with an object, which I do not recognize, in its bill; compare page 12b. Of the hieroglyphs, the first is destroyed, the second is the unmistakable sign of H, the fourth is the common *a*, and the third I cannot as yet decipher.

4. A, with the usual design issuing from his mouth (the expiring breath of life?). Of the hieroglyphs, the first is a double Manik with prefixes, which probably denotes violent death; the other three are very common symbols of A.

5. E, holding a vessel containing plants (agave?) and with the cross *b* on his head-ornament. The first hieroglyph is an unexplained compound design apparently referring to the Moan, an Imix and two prefixes, the second is the monogram of E, whom the third hieroglyph, Imix-Kan, designates as dispensing nourishment, and the fourth, Ahau, as a leading deity.

Page 12a.

The scribe evidently wishing to carry out his material in some conclusive form in the top, middle and bottom sections of page 12, found insufficient space in the top section. He, therefore, condensed two independent unconnected Tonalamatls, by arranging them in such a manner, that the period of 52 days was divided, for the sake of brevity, into only two parts, viz:—

VIII	27 (IX)	25 (VIII)
Ahau	Oc	
Eb	Ik	
Kan	Ix	
Cib	Cimi	
Lamat	Ezanab.	

I have supplied the two numbers enclosed in parentheses; they are wanting in the Manuscript.

The hieroglyphs

1	2	5
3	4	6
		7
		8.

are sufficient for the two figures one expects to see here; but they are, in fact, intended for four figures—two for each of the two Tonalamatls. For the first of the two Tonalamatls we have only one figure, God K, who, however, from the dish held in his hand, probably containing honey (compare 10b), seems to stand here also in place of E. In agreement with this, Hieroglyph 2 and probably also 1 (*s*, which occurs again on page 13a, and also on page 10b) refers to K, while 3 clearly refers to E and 4 is the sign *a*. Hieroglyphs 5-8 belong to the second of the two Tonalamatls. The first two of these hieroglyphs, which are entirely erased, refer to an unknown deity, and the last two unquestionably relate to A.

Pages 5b—6b.

I   16   IV 9   XIII 25   XII 2   I

Manik

Cauac

Chuen

Akbal

Men.

Four hieroglyphs belong to each of the four subdivisions:—

1 2   5 6   9 10   13 14

3 4   7 8   11 12   15 16.

These four parts, however, form a whole, inasmuch as they all relate to making fire, as it is also represented in the Troano 6, 19 and 14*c. Hence the upper row of hieroglyphs contains signs which are repeated. 1, 5 and 9 are the same head, the last two cases have the sign for darkness (Akbal); this Akbal appears again in the parallel passages of the Tro. and in 13 it is somewhat enlarged simply owing to the absence of a head. The act of making fire seems to be denoted here rather by the second sign (2, 6, 10, 14), which I designate by *k* and which, originally, doubtless consisted of two hands (double Manik sign); the prefix is the same in 6 and 14, and different in 2 and 10.

The eight lower hieroglyphs are merely the monograms of the four gods making the fire. The first deity is F, the second either A or one of the black deities L or M, the third D and the fourth apparently F again, but conceived as feminine. In the third picture there is a second object, apparently a head (of D?), below the piece of wood in which the fire-stick is being whirled. Hieroglyph 11 belonging to this deity has an Akbal as a prefix.

Pages 6b—7b.

X   13   X 13   X 13   X 13   X

Kan

Cib

Lamat

Ahau

Eb.

This Tonalamatl is divided, by way of exception, into four equal parts, which all begin with the same week day X.

Here too, as in the preceding Tonalamatl, there are four subdivisions, and also 16 hieroglyphs arranged in the same way. And here too the upper line is a condensation of the whole, the same two signs being repeated four times. The first of these is *q,* which is still a problem and which occurs inverted also on Cort. 20d-21d (where there are figures with bird-heads); there too it is the characteristic hieroglyph. The second, however, is again the double Manik sign referring to activity of some kind, as in the preceding Tonalamatl. But the occupation of the four deities represented here is of very different kinds and altogether problematical. E, conceived as feminine, occupies the first place, with a Kan sign on her head and holding in her hand a vessel exactly like the one held by the figure just above on the same page. The third hieroglyph is hers and the fourth is the sign *a*.

The second figure is A with a hook-shaped object hanging around his neck. His hands also seem to be deformed, as are those of the third and fifth figures of the great Tonalamatl (on pages 4 and 5). His two hieroglyphs are among those usually belonging to him.

The third god is D sitting, by way of exception, on some object (stone?). Something resembling the pestle of an ordinary mortar is hanging down in front of his headdress, and he is holding a very similar object to his mouth. His two hieroglyphs are also those which usually refer to him.

The most striking figure is that of the fourth god, whom I do not recognize. He seems to be attracting to himself a bird flying down from above, whose bill almost touches his mouth. His hieroglyph has the sign Yax (strength) for a prefix and the fourth hieroglyph is *c*.

Page 8b.

VIII   26   VIII 26   VIII

Manik

Cauac

Chuen

Akbal

Men.

Again we have a Tonalamatl divided into equal parts, this time, however, into but two, and it seems thus to be closely connected with the preceding.

While hitherto four hieroglyphs have usually belonged to each figure, we find here ten in all and in the following order: —

$$
\begin{array}{cccc}
1 & 2 & 5 & 6 \\
3 & 4 & 7 & 8 \\
 & & & 9 \\
 & & 10. &
\end{array}
$$

There are two figures here, which stand in some relation to one another, — two persons sitting facing each other. The one at the left is certainly D, the one at the right can hardly be the old woman, whom Schellhas designates with O, but rather N, the old god of the Uayeyab days. The former seems to be about to take something from the hand of the latter. I surmise that it is one of the prophetic weaving implements. which we found on page 2. The two hieroglyphs *e* and *h* must refer to this; they are repeated, as usual, in the two groups, *e* in places 2 and 8, and *h* in

1 and 6.

Signs 3 and 4 refer unquestionably to D and hence 5 and 7 (the first q with Ben-Ik, and the latter unknown) must be the designation of the person sitting on the right. We shall meet the latter sign again on pages 15b and 18a, with the same person, and on pages 27a and 39b with entirely different persons. Sign 7 is an object, which also appears on 15b and 18a, held in the hands of women and may denote some special sacrificial offering; on 9b Kan-Imix appears in place of this sign, and on 39b beside it. It should be noted that sign 7 stands here in exactly the same proximity to 1 and 6 as on page 27a.

The hieroglyphs 9 and 10 stand outside the two groups, and since, as we know, they belong to the god A, this prophecy must concern death, as is more clearly indicated by the corresponding hieroglyphs on page 9b.

Page 9b.

Here, for the first time in this manuscript, we have a Tonalamatl in which the 260 days are not divided into five fifths of 52 days each, but into four quarters of 65 days. This may be represented as follows, if we supply the III, which is wanting at the beginning:—

III   33 X 32 III

Muluc

Ix

Cauac

Kan.

In the first place, the close connection of this Tonalamatl with that recorded on page 8b, just now discussed, is striking, for

> 1. Here too we find a division into two equal parts is intended, but which, of course, as the number is 65, cannot be mathematically exact.

> 2. Here too we not only find 10 hieroglyphs, but we find them in the same order as on page 8b, and here too the sign e stands in places 2 and 8, and h in 1 and 6; again 3, 4 and 9 are exactly the same hieroglyphs here as there, so that only 5, 7 and 10 are different.

> 3. The picture is again that of two persons sitting facing each other. Here D sits on the right and facing him is the grain deity E. D is speaking to E as is indicated by the sign before his face and by the position of his right hand. The signs belonging to E are Hieroglyphs 5 and 7, while those of D are 3 and 4. It seems, therefore, that D is announcing to E the prophecy contained in the preceding Tonalamatl.

> 4. Two hieroglyphs, 9 and 10, are again added, both relating to death—9 to god A and 10 to F.

Now what especially distinguishes this passage from the preceding one, is the fact that the four days are the so-called regents of the year, Muluc, Ix, Cauac and Kan, above which, perhaps to emphasize this circumstance, there is a particularly elaborate Ahau. Seler ("Einiges mehr über die Monumente von Copan und Quiriguá," p. 210), however, thinks that this sign is the hieroglyph for the numeral three, which should stand here.

The fact that the tenth sign, which is the last, is 13 Moan in the preceding Tonalamatl, while here it is 11 F, will be of special significance in deciding the interpretation.

Page 10b.

The manuscript gives the following:—

XIII   22   III   22

Oc

Ik

Ix

Cimi

Ezanab.

This cannot be correct, for 22 + 22 is not 52, and from XIII to III is not 22 days, while the last Roman numeral is wanting. I, therefore, propose to make a 6 of the numeral 2, which occurs twice, by changing the lower dot into a line, and to change the III into a XIII by the addition of two lines. This gives the series the form XIII 26 XIII 26 XIII. Then by its division into three equal parts, this Tonalamatl accords with the three preceding ones, which it also resembles in other respects. For here too we find two persons pictured; this time, however, they do not face each other, but are placed one behind the other. The first is B, the god of life strictly speaking, the second is F, who is represented by his hieroglyph in the preceding Tonalamatl, and who is the god of the chase and probably of death by violence. Both hold offerings in their hands, which have been presented to them, and this also seems to be suggested by the two pendent copal pouches. The dish in B's hand probably contains honey, while F holds a plant (agave?)—the very same articles, which we find on page 12a in the hands of other gods. It looks as if the gods had been propitiated and as if this were the conclusion of a drama running through four Tonalamatls. Again the two death-hieroglyphs, which were added on pages 8 and 9, are wanting here, and we find only the usual eight signs:—

1   2   5   6

3   4   7   8.

Of these, 1, 2 and 5, 6 are the usual comprehensive heading; 1 and 5 are the Manik sign, which must denote the offering, while 2 and 6 are the characters, which perhaps, not incorrectly, has been thought to denote a repetition, a kind of plural; we have already seen it on pages 12a-13a. 3 is the monogram of B, yet it looks more like a fist with the thumb prominent—a figure I have frequently found in the inscriptions of Palenque. It must also refer to the sacrifice offered to B, which is confirmed by the *a* added to it in 4 and probably denoting a good day. 7 is the hieroglyph of F to which the sign in 8 corresponds, while the prefixed arm in 8 seems to refer to the presentation of the sacrifice.

Pages 10b—11b.

VIII   8   III 9   XII 9   VIII 10   V 16   VIII

Chuen

Akbal

Men

Manik

Cauac.

I have corrected the 15 in the manuscript by making it 16.

20 hieroglyphs correspond regularly to the five sections in the following order:—

1	5	6	9	10	13	17
2	7	8	11	12	14	18
3					15	19
4					16	20.

This section seems to refer chiefly to the harvest. First the Muluc sign with suffix and affix, which is repeated in 1, 5, 9, 13 and 17 at regular intervals, suggests rain as a preliminary condition of the harvest. Next in 2 the hieroglyph of K, the wind-god, is added to this Muluc sign, and K is the patron of the day Muluc. Then the signs *a* and *o* follow in 3 and 4. There is no picture belonging to this group; it ought to be the god K. The second group adds to the Muluc in 6 the glyph of the sun, which is the second preliminary condition of the harvest. This is followed in 7 by the sign *u* apparently denoting wind and cloud and having the prefix of the storm-god, and in 8 is the sign, which, strange to say, stands also in the last Tonalamatl in the eighth place. I am not very clear in regard to this sign. The sun-god G with copal pouch and a vessel containing grains of maize is appropriately represented with this group. With equal fitness the third group contains E, the harvest-god proper, with copal pouch and grains of maize, and, as usual, a Kan sign on his head, but also with a parrot, probably as an enemy of the harvest. Sign 10 is E's hieroglyph, to which, as is so often the case, sign 11 (Imix-Kan) is added and in 12 the double Manik (*i*). The last two groups are without figures of deities; the double Manik (14 and 18), possibly a repeated summons to sacrifice, is common to both groups. There seems here to be a further reference to the *enemies* of the harvest, for 15 is the hieroglyph of the vulture, 16 that of the death-bird and 19 that of the night-god, after which this section closes with the quite universal sign *a*. If space had permitted, the vulture and the night-god would have been represented here.

Page 12b.

I		13	I	26	I	13	I

Ix

Cimi

Ezanab

Oc

Ik.

This is again a regular arrangement, half of the 52 days being in the middle and a quarter each at the beginning and end.

The first four days refer to the purport of the prediction, Ix, the tiger, Cimi, death, Ezanab, the wounding lance point, and Oc, the lightning dog. The 12 hieroglyphs indicate the connection with the foregoing Tonalamatl, for 1, 5 and 9 contain the same Muluc sign which we found there in the same places.

The three figures, it seems to me, signify the approach of death, the wound occasioning death, and the arrival of death.

The first picture represents the god probably as feminine, with which the illustration on page 9c should be compared. The lock of hair before sign 3, the death hieroglyph, agrees with this as do also the familiar signs 2 and 4. The god is making sounds, which is indicated by the figure issuing from his mouth. Is the snail in his head-ornament to be understood as the sign for retarded motion?

The second figure is the wounding serpent deity H, likewise represented here as feminine, with a lock of hair; the copal pouch hangs from her neck, her nose-peg resembles a flower as on page 19a. A bird is sitting on her head and is devouring a piece of an animal's body; we have already met this representation in the preceding Tonalamatl. Hieroglyph 6 designates the deity H, 7 (Imix-Kan) probably denotes the devouring of the flesh and sign 8, which is an Ahau with a prefixed knife, may also refer to this.

Finally, the third picture is again the death-god, who is clad in a gala cloak and, in contrast to the first picture, where the deity is sitting on some object, is squatting on the ground. The three hieroglyphs 10, 11 and 12 fit here admirably.

We will now turn back to page 4 and consider the lowest section (c) of pages 4 to 12, which like pages 5b-12b (I omit 4b here because its contents are of an entirely different nature) contain 7 Tonalamatls, that is, five ritual years of 364 days. If, however, we add 4b to these and bear in mind that 10c-11c contain a double Tonalamatl, we will have 9 Tonalamatls. We find a group of 7 Tonalamatls also on pages 51a-52a.

Pages 4c-5c.

XII		10	IX	22	V	11	III	9	XII

Cauac

Chuen

Akbal

Men

Manik.

The incorrect 10 of the manuscript has been changed to 9. The hieroglyphs are as follows: —

1   2   5   6   9   10   13   14
3   4   7   8   11   12   15   16.

and there are four figures of gods.

The sign of the rising Moan with its usual prefix and superfix (*d*) forms the principal part of this section, the meaning of which, however, is not yet very intelligible. This sign appears not merely as the 1st, 5th, 9th and 13th hieroglyphs, but all the four gods hold it in their hands. Placed after each of these signs are hieroglyphs 2, 6, 10 and 14, which are the double Manik or hand sign denoting a sacrifice (*i*).

The first god portrayed here is G, the sun-god, and the third hieroglyph is his sign, which is rendered yet more unmistakable here by the laterally elongated head *q*, the meaning of which is not yet wholly determined.

The second god is D with his two signs in 7 and 8. 7 designates him rather as night and moon-god and 8 more as the old god and lord of the gods.

The third god is the serpent deity H or Seler's "young god." His sign is hieroglyph 11, with which, to be sure, the unusual sign 12 (*v*) appears as a not very intelligible determinative.

The fourth god is A and his usual signs are given in 15 and 16.

Pages 5c—6c.

This is the second example in our manuscript of a Tonalamatl divided into four parts: —

XII   29   II   11   XIII   18   V   7   XII
Ezanab
Akbal
Lamat
Ben
Ezanab.

The repetition of the 15th day at the end is superfluous.

Here, then, we have the four days with which the 18 Uinals can begin; in the Tonalamatl on page 9b, the four regents of the year were given instead. Now, whether the beginning of these periods of 20 days was celebrated by a banquet or not, at all events, a feast is suggested by the sign Imix-Kan, which is repeated in hieroglyphs 1, 5, 9 and 13. The four vessels in the hands of the four deities, two of whom are sitting and two standing, would agree with the idea of a feast. The first vessel is a cup filled apparently with foaming pulque, and the other three are larger vessels meant to be hung up. The first deity is D with a snail on his head. Compare page 12b. His hieroglyphs are 2 and 3, and sign *a* is added as fourth. The next deity is A with his usual signs in 6, 7 and 8. C follows with his hieroglyph in 10 and lastly F with the sign 14 which belongs to him.

There still remain as the 11th and 15th signs, the elongated head *q* with the Ben-Ik superfix belonging to C and with another superfix belonging to F (with which he likewise appeared as sign 4 in the preceding Tonalamatl). The 12th sign (*v*), which occurs in exactly the same place in the preceding Tonalamatl, is no more intelligible to me here than there.

Pages 6c—7c.

I   17   V 19   XI 6   IV 10   I

Chuen

Akbal

Men

Manik

Cauac.

Four sitting gods with the regular 16 hieroglyphs. There is no collective sign, however, among these. It seems exactly as if the intention had been to represent the *different* offerings usually presented to the various deities. At all events the sacrifices are designated by hieroglyphs 1, 5, 9 and 13, and the same objects are also held in the hands of the four gods respectively, although they are clearly recognizable only in the case of the second and third gods.

Now what are these four different sacrificial gifts?

The principal part of the first looks like the sign of the month Mol. In excellent agreement with its appearance is the fact, that this word signifies egg in the Quecchi language. The god receiving the sacrifice here is A. Hieroglyph 2 is his monogram and 3 is that of his companion F and 4 fits both deities.

The second figure is D and his signs are hieroglyphs 6 and 7 to which 8 is added quite superfluously. The sacrifice proper is denoted by 5, which, I think, is a sign of multiplicity and which was originally the fin of a fish. In the manuscripts and inscriptions, when this sign is added to the sign for 360 days, it enhances the value to 20 × 360 = 7200 days.

The third picture represents the god with the bird-head of the Moan and his signs are hieroglyphs 10, 11 and 12. One of these, signifying rising birds, is also the offering in 9.

Lastly, the fourth picture is, according to Schellhas, the serpent deity H, and, according to Seler, the "young god," with the snail on his head. His sign is hieroglyph 14. Added to this is the sign *a* in 15, and in 16 it is *q* again with the same superfix as in sign 15 of the preceding Tonalamatl. The sacrifice in 13 is represented by a Kan sign, which is equivalent to maize, maize bread or tortilla.

Repeatedly, as on page 23b or 29b-31b of our manuscript, we see a portion of game (deer), a bird, a lizard and a fish represented as sacrifices. With this the fish and bird in our second and third pictures agree very well. I shall not venture to explain the other two in the first and fourth pictures. Perhaps future explanations of the curious head-ornament of the four gods will shed further light on the subject.

Page 8c.

III		9 XII	9 VIII	9 IV	9 XIII	9 IX	7 III
Cib							
Lamat							
Ahau							
Eb							
Kan.							

The horizontal line should be read in this order; in the manuscript the numbers are in a somewhat unusual order.

An attempt has been made to divide the 52 days into sections of 9 days each, and in doing this the sixth subdivision has fallen short of two days. Since this passage has but two pictures, six of the 12 hieroglyphs must belong to each of the figures. I read the hieroglyphs in the following order:—

$$1 \quad 2 \quad 5 \qquad 7 \quad 8 \quad 11$$
$$3 \quad 4 \quad 6 \qquad 9 \quad 10 \quad 12.$$

Each of the two pictures contains a building and a deity in front of it, each of whom seems to have placed another deity in the building. In the first picture D is putting C inside and in the second F is doing the same to A or the Moan. I will add also, that the day belonging to C (Chuen) is actually 9 days distant from that of D (Ahau). I am uncertain in regard to the other two. In the back of each building we see a cross.

A similar association of two gods appears again elsewhere, as on page 35a, where D lies on a building in which C is sitting, thus showing an association of the same two gods as in our first group.

In both groups the first two hieroglyphs form the common heading, since 1 corresponds in general to 7 and 2 to 8. In the first group 3 and 4 are the hieroglyphs of D and 5 and 6 are the signs q and v; does one of these last signs refer to the god C? In the second group 9 is the sign of F, who stands in front of the house and 10 that of the god in the house, as perhaps is also 11, when we consider the closed eye; this is one of the many hieroglyphs having an uplifted arm as a prefix. On page 9a we find exactly the same sign. The last sign is the hieroglyph q, which sometimes seems to be used merely to fill space; it corresponds, but with a different superfix, to the fifth hieroglyph of the first group.

The last three parts of this section of the manuscript all differ appreciably from the usual form (5 × 52 = 260 days).

Page 9c.

Here for the first time the manuscript contains a Tonalamatl, which is divided into 10 × 26 days. It is true the position of both the days and numbers is quite irregular. The manuscript presents the following order:—

III	III	VI	VIII
		3	2
Cauac	Ben	XI	II
Chuen	Chicchan	3	4
Akbal	Caban	VI	VII
Men	Muluc	4	1
Manik	Imix.	I	III
		7	2

I read it thus:—

III   3 VI 2 VIII 3 XI 4 II 4 VI 1 VII 7 I 2 III

Cauac

Chicchan

Chuen

Caban

Akbal

Muluc

Men

Imix

Manik

Ben.

Two figures and eight hieroglyphs are given here. I do not venture to decide whether each of the two figures with its hieroglyphs relates only to a period of 26 days or to the half of the whole, 130 days. I think the latter is more likely to be the case. The sign Imix-Kan, which I am inclined to refer to a sacrificial meal, is common to both groups and connects them. The two gods seem also to have a sign pertaining to a meal in their hands; this may be a cup.

The first deity is D or I, but with a female breast and with a serpent on his head. His signs are 2 and 3. The second god is A with a snail on his head and his signs are 6 and 7.

In addition to these, sign 4 of the first group is *v* and sign 8 of the second group is *c*.

Pages 10c—11c.

I   XIII   1   I 5   VI 10   III 13   III 15   V 8   (in error 9)   XIII
Imix   Cimi
Ben   Ezanab
Chicchan Oc
Caban   Ik
Muluc   Ix.

Here we have two independent Tonalamatls as on page 12a. There are subdivisions only for the second; the first should be regarded either as entirely invalid or else its division has merely been omitted.

6 gods with 4 hieroglyphs each are represented on these pages: —

    1   2   5   6   9   10   13   14   17   18   21   22
    3   4   7   8   11   12   15   16   19   20   23   24.

Here too Hieroglyphs 1, 5, 9, 13, 17 and 21 are the common factor; they have the form of the month Mol, but here, as on page 6c, they probably designate the particular object constituting the sacrifice. The following details are to be noted regarding the six divisions: —

1. The god A with his two signs in 2 and 3.

2. D with the signs 6 and 7.

3. F with the signs 10 and 11 (the latter *c*).

4. E with the signs 14 and 15, having on his head a structure, which is compounded apparently of a Kan sign, a snail and the suggestion of the maize plant.

5. G, clad in the gala cloak and the copal bag. His sign is 18, while 19 suggests rather the Moan or K.

6. B, his headdress displays the little circles, which often occur in connection with him, *e.g.*, pages 30c, 40a and 41a, and which may suggest the starry sky. His sign is 22; the hieroglyph *m* is added to it in 23 as a determinative.

As usual, the fourth sign of each group is the most puzzling. 4 and 12 are Imix with the uplifted arm as a prefix, as on page 13a, 8 is the hieroglyph *o*, 16 is *a*, 20 is *c* and the principal part of 24 is *r*. This sign *r* seems to me to suggest the week of 13 days (see above the explanation of page 4a); four weeks of this kind end here.

It is to be noted further that all the six gods are holding one hand outstretched: — A downward, B upward and the four in the centre forward.

Page 12c.

        XIII   26   XIII 26   XIII 13   XIII
        Chuen
        Cib

Imix

Cimi

Chuen.

This is another Tonalamatl divided into 4 × 65, the subdivisions being transferred to the end of the second, fourth and fifth weeks. The Chuen at the bottom is superfluous.

The twelve hieroglyphs standing here according to rule are grouped together in fours by the three pairs of the first row. Of these 1, 5 and 9 are the fist, familiar from the inscriptions, and which we also see on page 10b of this manuscript, where, to be sure, it occurs with the sign of B, as often happens, but here it has the closed eye of the death-god A. On the other hand, 2, 6 and 10 are the sign Kin = sun, with merely a dotted outline, and the three gods pictured below all hold the same Kin sign in their hands. This passage, may refer to the dying sun, the winter solstice.

The first god is D, who, however, has B's head on top of his own. An object like a spyglass projects from the eye of B, which one could hardly venture to pronounce a nose-peg. The sign 4 (Ahau) refers to D; but what is the meaning of 3, the hieroglyph of the serpent deity H? Is the sun wounded?

The second god is the baldheaded old deity, whom Schellhas designates as N. The hieroglyph 7, apparently referring to the five Uayeyab days, is his sign; we found it on page 4b and shall again find it on page 21c, and this time likewise with the old man. What is the meaning of the grain-goddess E denoted by sign 8? As N is connected with the close of the year, so E seems to be in various ways connected with the beginning of the new year.

The third picture is unmistakably the sun-god G with the copal pouch hanging from his neck. His sign is 11, while sign 12, which suggests the wind-god K and balled-up clouds, is as difficult to explain here as it was on page 11c. The signs 8 and 12 seem, therefore, to refer to one another, and, if I do not see too much, look like a promise of rain and harvest.

On page 12 the Tonalamatls of the three sections of the page come to an end and a new part of the manuscript begins.

Page 13a.

I shall here group together pages 13 and 14, the top third of 14 encroaches a little upon page 15. 13a has the following Tonalamatl: —

Imix

Ben

Chicchan

Caban

Muluc.

I have supplied the first day, which is effaced. The week days are wanting. The

52 days are divided into halves of 26 days each.

Of the 8 hieroglyphs the fifth seems to be the same as the destroyed first; aside from the prefix, it is the sign *s*.

The two halves of the period have two gods, the first is B with a very singular head-ornament, and the second A, perhaps with the symbol of a snail on his head. Both hold a plant (agave) in their hands, as on pages 10b and 12a. Hieroglyph 2, which is mostly destroyed, must have been B's monogram, 4 has the Ahau as its determinative, and 3 is the elongated head *q* with Ben-Ik.

In the second group 6 and 8 are the signs of A, and 7 is an Imix with the uplifted arm prefixed, as on page 10c.

Pages 14a—15a.

VIII	13	VIII 13	VIII 13	VIII 13
Ahau				
Eb				
Kan				
Cib				
Lamat.				

The month days 13 and 5 have changed places in the manuscript. The initial day VIII Ahau will prove to be of especial importance in the second part of the manuscript (compare page 70). Here, as in the preceding Tonalamatl, the period is divided into equal parts.

Little can be said of the hieroglyphs, 16 in number, since 6, 9, 10, 12, 13, 14, 15 and 16 are wholly or mostly destroyed. 3, 7 and 11 seem here to be a comprehensive element, as is also probably 15, but I am unable to refer this head to a particular god; 2, 6, 10 and 14 may also be alike, but this is very uncertain. 1, 5, 9 and 13 may have denoted the four cardinal points, at least 1 suggests the south and 5 the north.

Thus we have left for the four deities E, H, A and G, only the signs 4, 8, 12 and 16; 4 surely belongs to E, and 8 to H, but the other two are erased.

Pages 13b—14b.

VI	13	VI 9	II 7	IX 7	III 7	X 9	VI
Ahau							
Eb							
Kan							
Cib							
Lamat.							

There are 24 hieroglyphs for the 6 divisions:—

1	2	5	6	9	10	13	14	17	18	21	22
3	4	7	8	11	12	15	16	19	20	23	24.

Of these the upper row again contains the comprehensive signs, and the lower the discriminating characters. The closed eye in 1, 5, 9, 13, 17 and 21 suggests A, who also appears below as the first of the six gods, and the superfix of these signs suggests the south. 2, 6, 10, 14, 18 and 22 are the Kan sign, and we also find this sign in the hand of each of the six gods. Thus the subject of this passage seems strictly speaking to be harvest or food.

The six gods are A, E, C, L, F and D; the second, third fourth and fifth have a bird on their heads. The first and fourth birds are eating, as on pages 11a and 12b, and thus probably represent enemies of the harvest. The first is of a different species from the other two. The four gods in the centre have the copal pouch about their necks. Signs 3 and 4 are the common hieroglyphs for A; 7 that for E, to which *o* is added as a determinative; 11 is C's hieroglyph with an *a* added to it, and L is undoubtedly denoted by sign 15; 16 is *r* (equal to 13 days; it is meant here for the day III Cib). F appears quite according to rule in 19, which is appropriately followed by the sign *c* in 20. Finally the hieroglyphs for D in 23 and 24 are the usual ones.

We come now to the large section extending to page 23, which, owing to the numerous pictures of women, forms a section quite by itself. It is not likely that this contains anything else than oracles relating to pregnancy; in fact, the period of 260 days represented here with great frequency is in excellent accord with this subject. In the Codex Tro-Cort. there is also a section devoted to women, which corresponds to this chapter and particularly page 19* of the Troano affords remarkable parallels to the Dresdensis, even in details.

Pages 13c—14c.

II	II		7	IX 3	XII 3	II 13	II
Men	Chicchan						
Imix	Chuen						
Manik	Caban						
Ben	Akbal						
Cauac	Muluc.						

The second of the two vertical rows on the left should be considered as immediately joined to the first. Thus we have here the second example in this manuscript of a Tonalamatl of ten parts; the first was on page 9c.

The entire representation on 13c and 14c looks like an introduction to the following section, as though treating in general of the relation to one another of pairs of animals, of human beings and of deities. Corresponding with the Tonalamatl, there are four pairs of this kind represented.

The hieroglyphs belonging to these pictures are distributed among the four sections as follows: —

1   2   5   6   9   10   11   15   16   17
3   4   7   8   12   13   14   18   19   20.

Apparently, the first two pictures have only 4 signs each, and the other two 6, but this is equalized by the fact, that hieroglyphs 1, 3, 5, and 7 are clearly each composed of two signs. The comprehensive sign appearing in 2, 6, 9 and 16, is, properly speaking, the sign *t*, which may denote coition, and, not unsuitably, contains in its centre two black figures side by side.

Passing now to the separate four groups, I think the male figure is always on the right and the female on the left. In the first and second groups the two face each other, and in the other two groups the male is behind the female.

1. The female figure is an animal, perhaps a deer, the male is a black and white spotted deity having a human form and his head appropriately embellished with horns. The hieroglyphs belonging to these are:—1, a combination of Manik and Chuen with a prefixed 4, just as on page 21b; 3, likewise a compound sign, with a prefixed 7, which occurs also on page 46c on the left, and which I do not venture to explain, but which seems to denote horns, and lastly the hieroglyph *c*.

2. The female figure is an animal (on page 19a the female is represented more in resemblance to the human form) with a bird-head, to which belongs the compound sign *s*, still unexplained; the male figure is a barking (or howling?) dog, as on page 21b. Hieroglyph 7 is composite and contains first the sign generally belonging to the dog and suggesting a skeleton, which also represents the 14th month, and secondly, a Cimi closely related to it, precisely the same as in the parallel passage 21b. The well-known *q* follows in the 8th place.

3. The god D holds in front of himself an animal, which may be a rabbit. His signs are hieroglyphs 11 and 12, while 13, the principal part of which is a grasping hand, clutching a Moan sign, seems to refer to the animal in the picture. 10 is *b* and 14 is *a*.

4. Lastly, two beings in human guise, showing thus a closer connection with what follows. They are the black god L with his hieroglyph in 18 enlarged by an Imix, and a woman holding a Kan sign in her hand, hieroglyph 20 likewise showing the ordinary combination of Imix-Kan. Sign 15, however, refers to the woman, and lastly 17 and 19 are the signs *m* and *r*; I note that *r* ends a period of 13 days.

The contents of the following seem to suggest that we should first read page 15 (including the middle section of 16) from top to bottom, then pages 16-23, partly from left to right and partly from top to bottom, according to the subject.

Page 15a.

V   34   XIII 18   V
Ahau
Eb
Kan

Cib

Lamat.

There are two pictures with 4 hieroglyphs each.

The two pictures represent D and A, the latter probably as feminine. Both are falling headfirst, and both have leaves about them as if they were falling from a tree and a cry is issuing from A's mouth. The common element is given in hieroglyphs 2, 3 and 7, which are all signs of D. Further, 4 is the Chuen sign, the ape (as the animal living on trees?), its prefix is hieroglyph *r*, which I regard as denoting the week of 13 days and which falls here exactly on the day XIII. And the same Chuen sign is repeated in the second group as the first part of sign 6, the second part of which is illegible. 8 is the sign of A and 1 is effaced.

Pages 15b — 16b.

I   13   I 31   VI 8   I 13   I

Ik

Manik

Eb

Caban

Ik.

That is 4 × 65 = 260 days. Hence the sign of Ik repeated at the bottom, as is usual in such cases, is superfluous.

The Tonalamatl contains 4 figures, of which 1 and 2 form one pair and 3 and 4 another.

As on page 15a, the pair at the left are falling down and also have leaves about them. They are god B, who holds a Kan sign in his hand, and a woman, whose eyes are closed and who holds the sign of death before her breast. B is falling down in a similar fashion in Cort. 17. Hieroglyphs 1-8 belong to this pair. Of these, 1, 5 and 8 and also 7 refer to death, 3 with the determinative sign, 4, added (which is the sign *q* with a Ben-Ik), refers to B, while signs 2 and 6 belonging to god D, who occurred in the preceding Tonalamatl, should be noted.

The pair at the right on the other hand is *seated*, the woman apparently on the curved handle of a vessel. The head-ornament and hieroglyph of the female figure prove that she is the serpent deity H, while the male figure is the rare black deity M, whom we find again with his sign on page 43a for example; he holds a bone in his hand. Hieroglyphs 9 and 13 agree. The lower part of these hieroglyphs is the fist with the thumb unfolded, the sign at the top seeming to be merely an empty outline (Muluc?) and thus, like 1 and 5 of the preceding group, they seem to refer to a sacrifice offered to the death-god. 10 and 14 are again, strange to say, like 2 and 6 of the preceding group, the sign of D. 11 is the hieroglyph of H, who is represented below as feminine, and that 12 is a complement of 11 is proved by the upper part of this uncommon hieroglyph, which corresponds to the object in H's hand, and which is repeated on page 18a with the same figure; compare also page

8b. 15 is surely the hieroglyph of M, who is pictured below, as in the Tro. 2a and 22*a where the same M appears with the same hieroglyph, and to him belongs in 16 the sign *r*, which I am inclined to consider the week of 13 days, and which here, as on 14c, ends a section of 13 days.

Page 15c.

III	III	12	II 14	III
Lamat	Ix			
Ahau	Cimi			
Eb	Ezanab			
Kan	Oc			
Cib	Ik.			

This is a Tonalamatl of ten parts, the days are to be read in the following order:—Lamat, Ix, Ahau, Cimi, etc.

There are two figures, A probably conceived as feminine and D with the same head-ornament as on page 10; both hold in their hands a Kin = sun. Hieroglyphs 2 and 6 are also the Kin sign, while 1 and 5 have the closed eye of A, but differ in their secondary parts, the sign suggesting the south being a suffix in 1 and a superfix in 5; 1, however, has an affix, while 5 has as a prefix a sign differing from the affix in 1. 3 and 4 are the signs of A, 7 that of D, next to which in 8 one would expect to see an Ahau, but instead of this there is again the sign of H (borrowed from page 15b?).

This seems to end the subject of coition; now, in natural course, follows the subject of pregnancy, to which I believe the following Tonalamatl is exclusively devoted.

Page 16a.

Kan	21	31
Cib		
Lamat		
Ahau		
Eb.		

There are no red numerals, hence the Tonalamatl seems to apply to any one of the initial week days.

Two women are portrayed, both of whom are stretching a hand forward and upward. There are 8 hieroglyphs of which, however, the top row is almost entirely obliterated; 3 and 7 in the lower row are just alike, being the usual sign for woman.

There is a decided contrast between the two figures, which might suggest barrenness and fruitfulness. Observation of their physical differences would give us that idea. Furthermore, the first carries on her back an unfamiliar head, perhaps A's, while the second has the Ahau, Imix and Kan signs, from which plants seem to be sprouting. The first is represented in the fourth hieroglyph by the sign *c*, which is closely allied to the death deities, while the second woman is denoted by hieroglyph 8 which is the sign of the deity E, the grain-god.

Pages 16a—17a.

In the following I will group together all the pages from page 16-23 as follows:—First, I shall discuss the top thirds, then the middle and lastly the lower thirds. The sense, however, often seems to require that the first third should connect with the second, and the second with the third; but I find it impossible to determine exactly the intended order.

On pages 16a-17a, we find for the first time in this manuscript not a Tonalamatl, but in its stead all the twenty days arranged in four columns, each of which ends with one of the regents of the year:—

Men	Ahau	Chicchan	Oc
Cib	Imix	Cimi	Chuen
Caban	Ik	Manik	Eb
Ezanab	Akbal	Lamat	Ben
Cauac	Kan	Muluc	Ix.

This seems to establish the fact that the day of its birth was of importance to a new-born child.

Between each column and the next there is a picture and above each picture four hieroglyphs, which, however, are mostly destroyed, so that much of the meaning of this passage is lost to us.

The first is an old man walking, who beyond doubt is N, the Uayeyab god, with a staff in his hand and the signs Imix and Kan on his back. He is looking upward and is also pointing upward with his right hand. Of his hieroglyphs only enough of the fourth is visible to enable us to recognize in it the regular sign of N, 5 Zac. The second picture is again an old man walking with a stick, he is baldheaded and hence is probably also N, as on page 12c. His hieroglyph might be the fourth of those written above him, the other three are entirely unrecognizable. He has a carrying-frame on his back, but it is uncertain whether he is carrying anything upon it.

The third figure is a woman who is pointing upward with one hand and with the other holding the bundle on her back, which I am unable to explain (does it refer to the 14th Uinal—the end of pregnancy?) and from which rises an object resembling a flame. Her sign is in the fourth place and *q* is in the third. 1 and 2 are not legible and perhaps may be supplemented by the third picture on page 19c. Finally, the fourth figure is F, who is sitting and has a Cimi sign on his back. His monogram is the second of the hieroglyphs above him, the third is very appropriately *b* and the other two are not very clear to me.

The first two pictures might designate a male birth, the first indicating wealth and the second poverty, the third might denote a female birth and the fourth a still birth. But who can positively assert this!

Pages 18a—19a.

VIII   12   VII 12   VI 9   II 10   XII 9   VIII

Ik

Ix

Cimi

Ezanab

Oc.

This is a Tonalamatl of five parts with 20 hieroglyphs, which unfortunately are so much injured that no signs comprehending the whole can be distinguished.

There are five women in a sitting attitude.

The first woman corresponds exactly to the third figure on page 15b. She is sitting on a bench, the same implement is in her hand and there is also a serpent on her head, for which reason she likewise reminds us of H. The third hieroglyph is hers, and the 4th sign is an Ahau.

The second woman holds in her hand the Kin sign; above it is the Yax sign and above this a little cross between two dots (the numeral 18?). Compare pages 18c, 19c and 27b, and in the second part, 46b and 50c. I shall venture no opinion regarding the hieroglyphs.

The third woman with the copal pouch hanging from her neck has nothing in her hand. She is pointing upward with her right hand. Her hair seems to be wound in the shape of an 8 in horizontal position and above her is a sign denoting the union of two parts. The hieroglyphs are entirely destroyed. Does this represent the birth of twins?

The eyes of the fourth woman are closed, she is pointing forward with her hand and there is a bird on her head. Nothing is left of the hieroglyphs.

Finally, the fifth is distinguished by a large nose-peg, which, as on 12b, resembles a flower. Her hand is extended forward. The fourth of the hieroglyphs above her is her sign. There is nothing to be said regarding the three others. Are these five women engaged here in presenting their thankofferings and prayers of thanksgiving for the birth which has taken place?

Pages 19a—21a.

XI   13   XI 13   XI 13   XI 13   XI 13   XI

Ahau

Chicchan

Oc

Men

Ahau.

Instead of Men the Manuscript has incorrectly Eb. Ahau in the fifth place is superfluous, since we have here a Tonalamatl divided into four equal parts.

The hieroglyphs are so nearly obliterated that we can no longer distinguish a common sign. There were in all six signs for the first picture, of which the first two are above the day-signs, while the figures from the second to the fifth have only four signs each, as follows: —

1	2	5	7	8	11	12	15	16	19	20
3	4	6	9	10	13	14	17	18	21	22.

All that can be distinguished here is that the 4th and 13th have the same cross *b* and that 6 and 10 probably contain the same head.

Each of the five pictures contains a woman sitting. In the first representation she sits opposite a male figure, who bends down to her with his bird-head, which we have already seen on page 13c. In the other four pictures the woman is holding the figure of a god on her lap. I do not recognize the god in the first picture on page 20. In the second and third pictures he is related to A or the Moan and the first figure on page 21 may represent the god D. These can only be new-born children represented by the gods under whose signs they were born. It should also be noted that the second woman on page 20 has a serpent on her head and the third a bird. The bird's head resembles that on page 16c.

Pages 21a—22a.

The Cimi and Eb of the second column have changed places in the Manuscript. Instead of the X there is an erroneous 2 and there is no initial VII.

VII	VII	3 X 2	XII 7	VI 9	II 3	V 2	VII
Oc	Ahau						
Cib	Cimi						
Ik	Eb						
Lamat	Ezanab						
Ix	Kan.						

We have here a Tonalamatl consisting of 10 × 26 days, and the 26 days are subdivided into six parts. I have just assumed that the 2 is wrong and the initial VII is wanting over the first column, yet the 2 followed by the laterally elongated head *q* might here, perhaps, be explained in some manner as the sign of the day VII Oc.

Apart from this sign which occupies an entirely exceptional position, we have here 24 hieroglyphs, *i.e.*, 4 for each of the six groups.

The fourth sign in the first five groups is in each case a Chuen combined with the cross *b* and the suffix, which seems to be a knife, and also with a numeral, which, however, is not recognizable in the first group; in the second it is a 3, in the third a 7, in the fourth a 5 and in the fifth a 3. What can these numbers mean? 3 + 7 + 5 + 3 = 18, and Chuen with the meaning of 20 (especially in the inscriptions) would be 18 × 20 = 360.

In the fourth place of the sixth group there is a compound character, the main part of which (top, right) seems to be the sign for the thirteenth month, Mac, and which may also, as we shall see on page 24, denote the entire Tonalamatl. It is again compounded with a Chuen, an uplifted arm and a kind of suffix, and hence might denote the end of a Tonalamatl.

The remaining 18 signs are in the main destroyed. In the second of the fourth group we recognize the lock of hair denoting a woman, in the third of the second group the superfix suggesting the south, which we find above the Cimi sign, for example on page 13b. Lastly, the other third signs are in the third group Imix-Kan, in the fourth group the head q, in the fifth the bird c and in the sixth a Manik sign with prefix and superfix resembling the sign i; in a few places (24, 39a, 53a, 56b, 58b, 61a, 61c, 68c) the prefix might have the meaning of 20.

Since the intention was to close this section on the next page, the space had to be used as economically as possible, and instead of the six pictures to be expected, there is only one and that is the first. It is a woman in whom I observe nothing characteristic except that she has a kind of cloak, which has fallen down over the lower part of her body, and who therefore remains unexplained.

Pages 22a—23a.

			II 2 IV 8 XII 7 VI 10 III 12 II
II	II	II	
Men	Cib	Caban	Ezanab
Chuen	Eb	Ben	Ix
Manik	Lamat	Muluc	Oc
Akbal	Kan	Chicchan	Cimi
Cauac	Ahau	Imix	Ik.

The Tonalamatl is no doubt to be read in this way after the correction of a few inaccuracies in the Manuscript.

The 20 days, all of which occur again here as on pages 16a-17a, should be read from the right top to the left bottom, since they form but one series.

As a matter of fact Ezanab is distant 19 days from the future Caban, but 39 days distant from the desired weekday of the same name (see my "Erläuterungen," p. 24). Thus we have here a period of 20 × 39 days = 780, *i.e.*, a three-fold Tonalamatl. The three Tonalamatls represented on the pages between the preceding passage (pages 16a-17a), where all the 20 days appear, and this, are of three *different* kinds (5 × 52, 4 × 65, and 10 × 26). This in itself is very remarkable. Furthermore a fourth kind of Tonalamatl seems to be introduced here, which embraces, as it were, these three Tonalamatls.

The hieroglyphs, which are mostly destroyed, were arranged in groups of four for each subdivision, in the following order:—

			II	II	II	II
1	2	5	9	13	17	

$$
\begin{array}{ccccccc}
3 & 4 & 6 & 10 & 14 & 18 \\
 & & 7 & 11 & 15 & 19 \\
 & & 8 & 12 & 16 & 20.
\end{array}
$$

Of the above the third hieroglyph of each group, *i.e.*, 7, 11, 15, 19 (probably also 3) is always the same and is the sign of D, the moon and night-god. In detail we should expect to find five pictures here, but owing to lack of space only the first of these is given. It represents a deity with a Kan sign in its hand and a serpent on its head, who is probably E, and he is falling down here in exactly the same manner as the four deities on page 15 at the beginning of this section.

Now, which were the other four deities? Signs 8, 12, 20 refer to A, H and C. 16 is the laterally elongated head *q*, to which Seler is inclined to refer the day Men, and Schellhas an undetermined deity I. On account of its frequency this sign must have besides a more general significance. In addition, however, we have in 14 and 18 the signs of F and B. 6 is uncertain, 10 is probably C, and the top row is entirely illegible. If to these deities is added the D repeated five times in the third row, it will be seen that all the important gods are grouped together here on the last page of this section.

Pages 16b — 17b.

I will now attempt (for it cannot be more than an attempt) to separate into three parts, according to their contents, the middle and lowest thirds of pages 16 to 23. The first part, 16b to 18b and 16c to 20c, contains six Tonalamatls with pictures of women, each of whom carries on her back the figure or symbol of a deity. This deity can hardly be any other than the one to which the horoscope of the child especially refers.

The first of these Tonalamatls, on pages 16b-17b, runs as follows: —

> Muluc   13 4 35 (or 20 15)
> Imix
> Ben
> Chicchan
> Caban.

The red numerals are wanting and were probably forgotten.

The hieroglyphs stand thus: —

$$
\begin{array}{cccccc}
1 & 2 & 5 & 6 & 9 & 13 \\
3 & 4 & 7 & 8 & 10 & 14 \\
 & & & & 11 & 15 \\
 & & & & 12 & 16.
\end{array}
$$

Of these 3, 7, 11 and 15 are the sign for women, 2, 6, 10 and 14 are likewise all the same sign, which is repeated in the same places on pages 17c to 18c. I do not understand its meaning; it may have reference merely to the carrying-frame.

Instead of the four women, whom we should expect to find here, only the first two are portrayed. The first carries B, whose sign is the first hieroglyph, while the fourth hieroglyph is the sign *q*.

The second woman carries A to whom hieroglyphs 5 and 8 refer. The third woman would have carried D, which is plainly proved by hieroglyphs 9 and 12, and the fourth, F, as follows from sign 13 and probably also from 16 (*q*).

Pages 17b—18b.

Eb 11 7 6 16 8 4.

Kan

Cib

Lamat

Ahau.

Here again there are no red numerals.

The 24 hieroglyphs of the six divisions stand thus:—

1	2	5	9	13	14	17	18	21	22
3	4	6	10	15	16	19	20	23	24.
		7	11						
		8	12						

Again, six women should be portrayed here, but there are only four; the second and third are wanting. The signs for the women are given in 3, 7, 11, 15, 19 and 23, but in 15 and 19 the prefix is different from that of the rest. As from here on the women repeatedly carry a bird, the signs for this are 2, 6, 10, 14, 18 and 22, which are the symbol of a rising bird, as in the sign of the 15th Uinal (Moan), which in my opinion generally coincides with the 13th month of 28 days.

The women pictured here have nothing in their hands, which they hold stretched forward, as is usually the case in this section. The first woman carries a vulture on her head. Compare 8a. In regard to it see also Schellhas, "Göttergestalten," p. 31. The hieroglyph of the vulture, which we find repeated on page 17c, 24, 37b, 46, 50, 65, is here hieroglyph 1, usually regarded as the sign of the bat deity, and near it in 4 is *q*.

The second woman would have carried the black deity L (hieroglyph 5), to which *q* is added in 8.

The third would have had the dog, *i.e.*, the lightning dog, which we find in hieroglyph 9 and in the month sign Kankin; an *a* is added to them in 12.

The fourth woman carries A, as is proved by his signs in 13 and 16.

The fifth carries nothing; according to the hieroglyphs 17 and 20 she ought to carry D.

Lastly the sixth carries the Moan as is proved by signs 21 and 24.

Pages 16c—17c.

Muluc 8   13   13   13   8   10

Ix

Cauac

Kan

Muluc.

This is a Tonalamatl of 4 × 65 days. The Muluc at the bottom is, therefore, superfluous. I have been obliged to correct the 12 in the last column of the Manuscript by changing it into a 10. The red numerals are again wanting.

This passage admirably continues the one in the preceding Tonalamatl containing the women carrying birds, and is also divided into six parts.

The hieroglyphs stand thus:—

1	2		5	6		9	10		13	17	21
3	4		7	8		11	12		14	18	22
									15	19	23
									16	20	24.

Signs 3, 7, 11, 14, 19 and 23 (14 and 15 have changed places) denote women. Of the six women only the first three are here portrayed.

The first carries the Moan with which signs 1, 2 and 4 agree perfectly. The second and third carry two birds, which may be parrots of a different species. They are very seldom represented elsewhere and hence their hieroglyphs, 5 and 9, with the added determinative 10 are unfamiliar. In 8 and 12 the well-known determinatives *a* and *c* are added.

Judging by sign 13 the fourth woman would have carried the same vulture, which we see in the middle section of this page; 15 and 16 are again signs *c* and *q*.

The fifth woman would have carried an unknown bird of prey, the signs of which are 17 and 18, and 18=10; 20 is again *q*, but with a superfix different from that in 16.

Finally the sixth woman, like the third in 17b, seems to have carried the dog, as is proved by sign 21, but in 22 the symbol of a bird is again added. This passage ends in 24 with the well-known Imix-Kan.

Pages 17c—18c.

IV   15   VI 33   XIII 4   IV

Ahau

Eb

Kan

Cib

Lamat.

Here we again find the regular red numerals (Roman in my transcription of the text), which were wanting in the last three Tonalamatls. That they were not added until after the black script and drawings were completed, is evident in several passages of our Manuscript and also in this one, where they have been faintly indicated in black by the scribe (or corrector). The absence of red numbers in the passages 17b-18b and 16c-17c is an evidence that I was right in proceeding directly from the former to the latter.

Of the 12 hieroglyphs, 2, 6 and 10 have again the form which we found on pages 16b-17b, and which seems to refer to a carrying-frame; compare, however, the explanation of pages 25-28 below. The women themselves are designated by hieroglyphs 3, 8 and 12. The first woman carries the god A and hieroglyphs 1 and 4 are his regular signs. The second woman has on her back a Kin sign, above that a Yax, and this combination overtopped by a cross between two dots also forms hieroglyph 5; compare the upper section of the same page. That this hieroglyph is nothing else than a designation of god D follows from hieroglyph 7. Finally the fourth woman carries a figure, which has a Moan sign for a head and to which hieroglyphs 9 and 11 certainly refer.

Pages 18c—19c.

XIII   32   VI 20   XIII

Ahau

Eb

Kan

Cib

Lamat.

The first woman carries the god A, who is denoted by hieroglyphs 4 and 1, though somewhat irregularly by the latter. 2 is the carrying-frame and 3 the woman herself.

The second woman has again the Yax-Kin sign on her back as in the preceding Tonalamatl, and hieroglyph 5 is also a combination of these signs, but here in 7 we find, not the sign of D, but that of E, to which also the Imix-Kan in 8 corresponds. 6 is again the carrying-frame, though, as is also the case in 2, more indistinctly drawn than in the earlier Tonalamatls.

Pages 19c—20c.

XIII   11   XI 11   IX 11   VII 10   IV 9   XIII

Ahau

Eb

Kan

Cib

Lamat.

This is a Tonalamatl divided into five parts, to which 20 hieroglyphs belong. The hieroglyphs are in the following order:—

1	2		5	6		9	10		13	14		17	18
3	4		7	8		11	12		15	16		19	20.

At places 2, 7 (6 and 7 have changed places), 10, 14 and 18 we find again the sign which we think means a carrying-frame, while signs 3, 6, 11, 15 and 19 are those of the five women.

The first carries a figure with a Moan head and agreeing with this is the second death-god F in hieroglyph 1 and his determinative in 4.

The second woman, who is seated, carries the same object regarding which I am still uncertain, which is carried by the standing woman on page 17a. This object is denoted by hieroglyph 5 (*w*). Its determinative is probably 8. It may perhaps be a step in the right direction to point out that this sign suggests the god K.

The third, like the first, has a figure with a Moan head, with which a female form of A in 12 and hieroglyph 9 accord.

The fourth woman carries the maize deity E. 13 is his sign and the food hieroglyphs, Imix-Kan in 16, agree with it.

The fifth woman seems to carry the somewhat indistinct form of D, if this may be inferred from the Ahau of the 17th sign. 20 is the universal sign *a*.

This ends the six Tonalamatls, which are represented in what I have called the section of the burden-bearing women. Five other Tonalamatls follow, which again suggest the idea of conception, which we met once before on pages 13c-14c.

Page 19b.

X		29	XIII	23	X
Ik					
Ix					
Cimi					
Ezanab					
Oc					

The most frequent sign in the five Tonalamatls, which I have grouped together, is the cross *b*, which plays the most important part in all the Tonalamatls, excepting the third, which differs from the rest also in other respects. It is essentially the sign for union, referring in the case of the stars to their conjunction and here to sexual union.

In this Tonalamatl we see the cross in hieroglyphs 1 and 5, the sign for woman in 2 and 6, and their determinatives in 3 and 7.

The first woman has a deity facing her who is devoid of all characteristic marks, and sign 4 is also nothing but the universal *a*.

The second woman whose eyes are closed, sits facing A, whose hieroglyph is in 8.

Pages 19b—20b.

VI   28 VIII 24 VI
Cib
Lamat
Ahau
Eb
Kan.

The arrangement of this Tonalamatl is very similar to that of the preceding.

Hieroglyphs 1 and 5 are again the cross, and 2 and 6 the signs for woman.

The first picture is wanting; hieroglyph 3 with the number 7 as a prefix denotes a deity with whom I am not familiar. The same sign is found on page 50, left, middle; in 4 the usual head *q* is added.

Beside the woman in the second group—not facing her—is the serpent deity H, again, as on pages 11c and 12b, with the nose-peg resembling a flower. His sign is 7 to which in 8 the familiar Ahau is again added.

Page 20b.

II   20 IX 19 II 13 II
Cauac
Chuen
Akbal
Men
Manik.

The hieroglyphs stand thus:—

```
1  2   5    9
3  4   6    10
       7    11
       8    12.
```

The subject now passes into the province of astronomy. This is already proved by sign 1, which represents the clouds, between which the sun or moon is usually pictured; the sun is probably omitted here merely owing to limited space. Sign 3 suggests the storm-god K (compare pages 7a and 47 left) to which in 2 the Ahau might be appropriately added, inasmuch as it rules the year here under consideration as on pages 25b to 26c. On account of the Ben-Ik sign I see in 4 one of the months of 28 days as a more exact determination of time. Below the Ben-Ik a head is represented with eyes apparently closed, and this head is repeated in 6 and 10, though, probably for lack of space, without the Ben-Ik. In each of the three places a sign is used as an affix which might readily be the year sign, contracted laterally.

The two similar hieroglyphs 5 and 9, which have the following form, are especially worthy of consideration:—

The part on the right recalls by its trisection the sign *r*, which I regard as the week of 13 days and, in fact, the interval between the two hieroglyphs is 13 days. On the left is the inverted figure of a person in a squatting attitude, the head surrounded by stars as on pages 57b and 58b and a sign on the back which may be a suggestion of the sun-glyph. In this figure, which occurs also in the Tro-Cort. and in the inscriptions, I see the planet Mercury and I believe that that planet's retrogression (which lasts 17-18 days) or disappearance into the light of the sun during this week, is the subject of this passage. 7 and 8 are the sign for D with the usual Ahau, and 11 and 12 are the hieroglyphs of the death-god A.

Instead of three pictures there is only one here, viz:—a woman with nose-peg, sitting on a mat and apparently waiting for something. We also find figures sitting on mats elsewhere, for example on pages 7b and 68b.

Page 21b.

VII	VII	7 I 7 VIII 7 II 5 VII
Oc	Ahau	
Cib	Cimi	
Ik	Eb	
Lamat	Ezanab	
Ix	Kan.	

This is also a Tonalamatl of 10 parts (10 × 26). The first column should be read first from top to bottom and then the second. The days are exactly the same as on page 21a, and here too Cimi and Eb have changed places.

The hieroglyphs run thus:—

1	5	6	9	13
2	7	8	10	14
3			11	15
4			12	16.

The signs forming the hieroglyphs into groups are, in addition to the cross in 2, 6, 10 and 14, the heads in 1, 5, 9 and 13 with an Akbal sign (indistinct in 9) which, by the lock of hair in 5, 9 and 13, refer to a woman. This lock of hair is replaced by a hand in 1.

Sign 3, with which *m* in 4 is associated as a determinative, shows that the first group ought to have a picture of the black god L grouped with a female figure.

The second group is the only one with a picture. On the right there is a female figure, which, judging by the headdress, we have already met on page 19a. Opposite her sits the dog which we saw on page 13c. Here (in sign 7), as on page 13c, the hieroglyph of the dog is combined with a Cimi sign, and this hieroglyph is repeated in 8 with the sign *c*, which is so closely allied to Cimi.

For the third group the god A should have been represented with the woman, as is proved by sign 11 so peculiarly combined with *r* as a superfix. To this hieroglyph *a* is added, doubtless referring to the good days, as if merely to fill space.

The hieroglyphs of the fourth group do not, I think, convey a clear idea as to which deity belongs here. His sign is 15, which is compounded of Manik and Chuen with a superfix, nor does the Cimi added in 16 shed light on the subject. As for 15 we have already found it on page 13c with the prefixed 4, which I find prefixed in this way in at least 12 different signs.

Pages 21c—22c.

Caban   5   21   16   10

Muluc

Imix

Ben

Chicchan.

This is a Tonalamatl of five parts in which the red numerals are wanting.

The hieroglyphs are in the following order:—

1	2	5	6	9	11	13
3	4	7	8	10	12	14
						15
						16.

Among these are hieroglyphs which are common to all the groups:—the cross in 1, 5 and 9 and the woman in 3, 7 and 15. In 13 this cross is replaced by another sign, perhaps that for the year of 360 days, and in 12 the sign for woman is replaced by the universal *a*.

Each of the three pictures contains a woman facing a deity. I will consider first the second picture in which H is the deity, as is proved by hieroglyph 6 to which an Imix is added in 8, with the uplifted arm prefixed as in 10c and 13a.

Between the first and third pictures there is some confusion. The first is D, for while his type inclines more to that of N, the other old god of the Maya Olympus, comparison with 23c clearly shows that D is intended here. But the year-sign on his head also suggests in some measure the Uayeyab god N and moreover this sign does not belong to D and only occurs again with him on page 23c. Further, there is no hieroglyph at all for D and instead we find in 2, 5 Zac, the regular sign of N. Also sign 4 fits N better than it does D. Furthermore this passage relates to the day Ik, which might very well be the last day of the year.

On the other hand the third picture contains, unquestionably, the figure of N. I look for his sign in the 11th hieroglyph, which is the head of an old man with a prefixed 4, referring to the four different forms of N in the Kan, Muluc, Ix and Cauac years. The Ahau in 12, however, does not fit N, but D.

This confusion can only be adjusted by transferring D from the first group to the third and also, perhaps, the sign of the woman in 3, which applies to all the three groups, and by transferring to the first group N and the 11th sign of the third group.

The fourth group has no picture. It should have, as hieroglyph 14 shows, the god F, who represents death by violence in human sacrifice and the chase. The hieroglyph Cimi in the 16th place is a suitable sign for this deity.

Pages 22c — 23c.

II   10 XII 12 XI 9 VII 6 XIII 7 VII 8 II
Oc
Ik
Ix
Cimi
Ezanab.

The hieroglyphs are arranged in the following order: —

1	2	5	6	9	13	14	17	18	21	22
3	4	7	8	10	15	16	19	20	23	24
				11						
				12						

This Tonalamatl, the fifth and last of this section, presents much that is irregular and puzzling.

It can hardly be said that there are comprehensive hieroglyphs here, forming the heading of the six groups. The sign for woman occurs only in 2, 8 and 24, and the cross *b* only in 14 and 18, but it is sufficient to make it clear that here, too, connection with a woman is the principal theme. Let us pass, therefore, directly to the single groups.

The first group contains A and a woman. The god, however, is not facing the woman but sits beside her. The Cimi sign in 1, the familiar *c* in 3 and the unknown sign in 4 (=6) hardly explain this particular proceeding.

The second group contains two persons who sit facing each other, but the representation is so obscure and peculiar that it is difficult to determine which is the male figure and which the female. The hair of the person sitting on the right stands up in a manner not found elsewhere. It forms a figure similar to that which is issuing from the mouth of the dog on pages 13c and 21b. The Cimi sign in 5 and the sign *c* in 7 are familiar, but the infrequent 6=4 remains a puzzle.

Uncertainty regarding the third group is increased by the fact that there is no picture belonging to it. The well-known signs, 10 (Cimi) and 12 (*q*) afford no explanation, nor does the head with the uplifted arm in 11, which we find with the same hieroglyph on pages 8a and 36a. The most puzzling is the 9th sign, which is composed of two crouching persons leaning back to back, and who also appear in the astronomical sections of the Manuscript on page 68a, not merely in the form of a hieroglyph, but also carried out in a picture. In my article on the Maya chronology published in the Zeitschrift für Ethnologie of the year 1891, I attempted to explain this Janus picture as meaning the change of the year, but that interpretation would make no sense here.

The fourth group contains the woman opposite D, who is clad in the gala mantle and has on his head a bird and apparently the sign for a year, and is designated by the Ahau in 16, while Imix-Kan in 13, *b* in 14 and *a* in 15 are rather meaningless.

The fifth group represents the woman united with A, who is designated by the Cimi sign in 17. 18 with its *b* and 19 with its *q* display little that is characteristic, *r* in 20, which I think is the sign for the week of 13 days, invites further study. The sixth picture, which is the last, is very peculiar; it represents three women sitting side by side denoting perhaps the virgins who still remain. Sign 21 as Imix-Kan, 23 as *a* and 24 as sign of femininity supply nothing in the way of explanation. As 6, 9 and 20 are the characteristic signs in the preceding groups, so here the characteristic sign is 22—an open hand holding the day Ben—which perhaps designates these virgins by referring to the house in which they are held fast by the hand. Cf. Tro. 23* d.

Now of the entire woman section closing with page 23 only the two Tonalamatls on pages 22b-23b remain. These Tonalamatls again display very many peculiarities and seem to be but loosely connected with the five Tonalamatls last discussed.

Page 22b.

III		13	III 13	III 13	III 13	III
Akbal						
Men						
Manik						
Cauac						
Chuen.						

This is a regular Tonalamatl, in which the 52 days are divided into four equal parts.

The hieroglyphs are in the following order: —

1	2	5	6	9	10	13
3	4	7	8	11	12	14
						15
						16.

An Ahau is added here as the 17th sign, which is very unusual.

We find elements here forming the hieroglyphs into groups in three different ways.

1. The signs 1, 5, 9 and 13 designate the four cardinal points as they so often stand together in this Manuscript in the order of East, North, West and South, *i.e.*, in the sequence of the annual and not of the diurnal course of the sun.

2. The hieroglyphs 2, 6, 10 and 14 are all alike and are the head with the Akbal eye, which in 6 is closed.

3. The three persons pictured here all carry a Kan sign in their hands, probably as the offering they have received. Similarly we found the Kan sign held in the hand twice on page 16b.

The first picture is B; his sign is the third with the *q* in 4 as a determinative, which has above it a Ben-Ik sign.

The second figure is a goddess with a serpent as head-ornament, though we find in the 7th sign, not her hieroglyph, but merely the one generally used to denote a woman. 8 is the usual *a*, which in my opinion is the sign for the *good* days, to which also the Kan sign refers in the hands of the three personages.

The third picture is that of the sun-god G; his hieroglyph is the 11th, to which in 12 is added the sign *q*, the sign for the bad days, with a superfix.

The fourth picture is wanting. According to the 15th hieroglyph it should be the maize deity E. My theory that 16 is the sign for the week of 13 days is supported by the fact that the division into 4 × 13 days is the prevailing one.

Page 23b.

VIII	12	VII	12	VI	12	V	12	IV	12	III	5	VIII
Kan
Muluc
Ix
Cauac
Lamat.

This is a Tonalamatl of 4 × 65 days divided as evenly as possible into 5 × 12 + 5. The 5th day added after the 16th must be a mistake (suggested by the 5th day of the last section) for it is usually the first of the days, which is repeated superfluously.

The hieroglyphs are:—

1	2	7	11	15	19	23
3	4	8	12	16	20	24
5	6	9	13	17	21	25
		10	14	18	22	26.

Contrary to practice the first section has six hieroglyphs, and the other five but four each.

As the characteristic hieroglyph we find in 1, 7, 11, 15, 19 and 23 a sign, the meaning of which is still undetermined and which we shall meet again on page 60, where it may refer to darkness.

The groups have in common, furthermore, the head without an underjaw and the hair gathered up in a tuft in 4, 10, 14, 22 and 25 (in 18 perhaps represented by q, the evil days). We shall find this sign on pages 25, 28, 30-35, 42-44 and 65-69, repeated a number of times in many instances. I consider it the sign for fast-days. It appears also in the Tro-Cort. Associated with this sign here as in other passages are the four sacrifices derived from the animal kingdom:—a haunch of venison, a bird, an iguana and a fish. The fish is beyond doubt denoted by 3, the mammal by 21 and the bird by 13, and I believe, therefore, that the iguana with its spiny back is denoted by 9. We find the four animals, though in a different order, also on pages 29b-30b, 30b-31b and 40c-41c, as well as in Cort. 3-6 and 8, for example. They seem to have a certain reference also to the four cardinal points.

Only the first of the six groups has a picture (I?). This represents a woman with a serpent in her hair, holding in her hand a dish containing a fish. The woman is denoted by the fifth hieroglyph and the fish by the third. The 6th sign is an Ahau, which is not quite intelligible here. Sign 2=5 Zac is very remarkable; it is the hieroglyph of the Uayeyab days and of their god N. If this Ahau refers, as it often does, to the god D, it suggests the relation between D and N, which follows from page 21c.

According to the 8th sign, the second group might refer to the serpent deity H, and the 9th sign would not improperly denote the iguana.

In the same way sign 12 in the third group probably denotes the storm-god K, with whom the bird in 13 accords very well.

In the fourth group both the animal and the sign of fasting, belonging to it, are wanting, while 16 and 17 as well as the unlucky day in 18 clearly refer to the death-deity A.

The fifth passage belongs, as sign 20 shows, to the maize deity E and to this is added the haunch of venison in 21.

In the sixth group we recognize Imix-Kan, the sign for food derived from the vegetable kingdom. It stands beside the grain-deity E of the fifth group. I do not understand the vulture-head in 26.

The five deities specified here may be compared with those on page 24, which are denoted by hieroglyphs 21-25 of the second column, though the agreement is not perfect.

This ends the first great section of the Manuscript, in which Tonalamatls are represented in uninterrupted succession. We come now to a page which stands quite alone, being the first which treats of astronomy and which ends the front of the first part of the Manuscript.

Page 24.

In my article "Zur Entzifferung IV" I discussed this remarkable page in detail and in what follows I shall conform to that treatise, though omitting many things which since then have become the established possession of science, and shall endeavor to shed a still clearer light upon other points.

This page presents in brief the subject which is more fully treated of on the front of the second part of the Manuscript (pages 46-60).

The first problem it presents is to find periods in which the solar year (365 days) is brought into accord with the apparent Venus year (584 days). This takes place in a term of 2920 days = 8 × 365 = 5 × 584. Sequent to this is the still higher aim of bringing the Tonalamatl (260) into harmony with this period, which is accomplished in 37,960 days (= 146 × 260 = 104 × 365 = 65 × 584).

The revolution of the moon (28), the ritual year (364 = 28 × 13) and the apparent revolution of Mercury (115) come in question as secondary matters.

I will now give an approximate reproduction of the page:—

HIEROGLYPHS.

1	17	29	151,840	113,880	75,920	37,960
2	18	30	(4 × 37,960)	(3 × 37,960)	(2 × 37,960)	(13 × 2920)
3	19	31	I Ahau	I Ahau	I Ahau	I Ahau
4	20	32	185,120	68,900	33,280	9100
5	21	33	I Ahau	I Ahau	I Ahau	I Ahau
6	22	34	35,040	32,120	29,200	26,280
7	23	35	(12 × 2920)	(11 × 2920)	(10 × 2920)	(9 × 2920)
8	24	36	VI Ahau	XI Ahau	III Ahau	VIII Ahau
9	25	37	23,360	20,440	17,520	14,600
10	26	38	(8 × 2920)	(7 × 2920)	(6 × 2920)	(5 × 2920)
11	27	39	XIII Ahau	V Ahau	X Ahau	II Ahau
12	28	40				
13			11,680	8,760	5,840	2920

14	(4 × 2920)	(3 × 2920)	(2 × 2920)	
	VII Ahau	XII Ahau	IV Ahau	IX Ahau
15				
16	2,200	1,366,560	1,364,360	
	IV Ahau	I Ahau	I Ahau	
	8 Cumhu	18 Kayab	18 Zip.	

First let me observe that I have restored the four large numbers at the top, which are almost entirely effaced, as follows:—

$$
\begin{array}{cccc}
1 & 15 & 10 & 5 \\
1 & 16 & 10 & 5 \\
1 & 6 & 16 & 8 \\
14 & 0 & 0 & 0. \\
& 0 & &
\end{array}
$$

And furthermore, at the right, bottom, I have substituted the third month for the second of the Manuscript, which proceeding will be justified later on.

The least difficult portion of the contents of this page is the first series consisting of 16 members, each being a multiple of 2920. It begins with the date I Ahau (which is always concealed in these series), regularly stops at the month day Ahau (since 2920 = 146 × 20), but necessarily advances in the week days by 8 days each (since 2920 = 224 × 13 + 8), until 37,960 is reached, when the day I Ahau again appears (since 37,960 = 146 × 260).

According to my method of filling in the numbers, the top row of the page consists only of multiples of 37,960.

On the other hand, the four numbers of the second row from the top are more difficult. They are, it is true, all divisible without remainder by 260, but otherwise they seem to be without rule, and they give one somewhat the impression of a subsidiary computation such as one might jot down on a slip of paper in the course of some important mathematical work.

Nevertheless, the following remarkable results are obtained when the first and third and the second and fourth numbers are combined by addition or subtraction:—

1) 185,120 + 33,280 = 218,400, which is just 600 years of 13 × 28 = 364 days, 280 Mars years of 780 days, 840 Tonalamatls of 260 days or 7800 months of 28 days.

2) 185,120 - 33,280 = 151,840, *i.e.*, precisely the highest number of the top row, = 416 solar years of 365 days each or 260 Venus years of 584 days each, *i.e.*, the product of the days of the Tonalamatl multiplied by the Venus years. We shall again find the 151,840 on page 51, and Seler ("Quetzalcoatl and Kukulcan," p. 400) finds this same period on a relief of Chichen Itza.

3) 68,900 + 9100 = 78,000, *i.e.*, 100 Mars years or 300 Tonalamatls. The half of

this number, or 39,000, we shall find again on pages 69-73 by computation; also the whole 78,000.

4) 68,900 - 9100 = 59,800, *i.e.*, 520 Mercury years of 115 days, or 230 Tonalamatls, or five times the period of 11,960 days, in which these two periods are united. By computation again we find the 59,800 on page 58. This period of 11,960 days is, however, to the period of 37,960 in the proportion of 23:73, *i.e.*, 23 × 520:73 × 520. 23 is the fifth part of the apparent Mercury year, as 73 is of the solar year.

Let us now turn to the numbers, which form the bottom of my transcription, but only the left hand lower corner in the Manuscript. Here, in the latter, we find the following (with the correction already mentioned of the second to the third month):—

2200	1,366,560	1,364,360
IV Ahau	I Ahau	I Ahau
8 Cumhu	18 Kayab	18 Zip.

The first thing to be done is to arrange and fill out these numbers to suit our purpose.

The 2200 is clearly nothing more than the difference between the two high numbers. We can therefore dispense with it.

Further, we find by the usual computation, that the second number belongs to the first date and the third to the second. Hence the number corresponding to the third date is wanting from lack of space. This number can be calculated from that date; it is 1,352,400. It would suit this date equally well if the number were higher or lower by 18,980 or a multiple of 18,980; but it will be seen directly that it agrees with the other two numbers only at the value given above.

Now, if we add to this passage the years in which the dates must lie, they are in the case of the date on the left, the year 9 Ix, in the case of the middle date, the year 3 Kan, and of that on the right hand, the year 10 Kan.

Then if we arrange the three numbers with the dates and years belonging to them, according to the value of the first, this part of the page will run as follows:—

1,352,400	1,364,360	1,366,560
I Ahau	I Ahau	IV Ahau
18 Zip	18 Kayab	8 Cumhu
10 Kan	3 Kan	9 Ix.

Let us now consider the properties of the three numbers individually.

1) 1,352,400 = 28 × 48,300 and = 115 × 11,760, hence it is divisible by the month days of the year of 364 days and by the Mercury year. At all events this is the least important of the three numbers.

2) 1,364,360. This looks as if it referred particularly to the moon and to Mercury; to the latter since it is equal to 115 × 11,864, and to the former if we assume that the lunar revolution has been fixed at 29⅔ days, in which case this number

is exactly equal to 46,000 such lunations. If this last number be again divided by 115, the number of days required for a revolution of Mercury, the quotient is 400, which is a round number in the vigesimal system and which was therefore denoted by a single word, by Bák in the Maya (according to Stoll) and by Huna in the Cakchiquel (according to Seler). 1,364,360, therefore, is a Huna of lunar revolutions multiplied by the number of days in the Mercury period. Later on we shall find the lunar revolution fixed at 29⅔ days.

3) 1,366,560. This is the most comprehensive number of the entire Manuscript, for it is divisible into each of the following periods:—Those of the Señores de la noche or Lords of the Cycle (9 × 151,840; this is, however, the first number of the top row), the Tonalamatls (260 × 5256), the old official years (360 × 3796), the solar years (365 × 3744), the Venus years (584 × 2340), the Mars years (780 × 1752), the Venus-solar periods (2920 × 468), the solar year-Tonalamatls (18,980 × 72), the Venus, solar, Tonalamatl periods (37,960 × 36), and the periods which are generally designated Ahau-Katuns (113,880 × 12).

We have next to consider the intervals which elapse between the three dates.

1) From 1,352,400 to 1,364,360 is 11,960 days, which period we have already found once on this page by computation. 11,960, however, is equal to 104 × 115 and 46 × 260, *i.e.*, the Mercury revolution and the Tonalamatl combined. 11,960 is again equal to 32 × 365 + 280, and from the year 10 Kan to 3 Kan it is actually 32 years, and from the date 18 Zip to 18 Kayab it is, in fact, 280 days. The day I Ahau must be common to both dates.

2) From 1,364,360 to 1,366,560 is 2200 days, as the Manuscript expressly states. 2200, however, is equal to 8 × 260+120, and the distance from the day I Ahau to IV Ahau is in fact exactly 120 days. Further 2200=6 × 365+10; from the year 3 Kan to 9 Ix it is 6 years and from the date 18 Kayab to 8 Cumhu it is 10 days.

3) From these two statements the third follows. The distance from 1,352,400 to 1,366,560 is 14,160. This contains first the 14040, in which both the Tonalamatl and the old official year of 360 days meet, and second 120, which is again the interval between I Ahau and IV Ahau. But 14,160 is also equal to 38 × 365 + 290, and the interval between 10 Kan and 9 Ix is of course 38 years, and from 18 Zip to 8 Cumhu it is 290 days.

The numbers with which we have had to do here will again occupy our attention further on, especially the 2920 and the 37,960 on pages 46-50, the 11,960 and 115 on pages 51-58, and the 14,040 on page 73.

That these computations are not confined to the Dresden Manuscript is proved by the cross of Palenque, where we find in signs A B 16 precisely the date I Ahau 18 Zotz, a Tonalamatl before 18 Kayab, in D 1 C 2 exactly the difference 2200 and in D 3 C 4 the date IV Ahau 8 Cumhu. This is in favor of the theory that our Manuscript did not originate far from Palenque.

Now, the question finally arises as to what may, strictly speaking, be considered the significance of these numbers, dates and differences.

In the first place, I would recall the fact that the dates of the monuments of

Copan and Quirigua, which doubtless refer to present time, are in the neighborhood of 1,400,000. The high numbers of our Manuscript, so far as they are in question here, form first a group, which extends from about 1,200,000 to 1,280,000, and then there is a blank, and next a large group extending from about 1,350,000 to 1,480,000, then another blank and lastly a group extending from about 1,520,000 to 1,580,000. If we assume that our Manuscript belonged to about the same date as these inscriptions, then the three numbers discussed here would extend over a past period lying about 160-170 years back, when a new period of importance had begun probably dating from the immigration of the Aztecs into Mexico, which they placed in the first half of the 14th century (see "Weltall," Vol. 5. pp. 374-377). Now, however, the number 1,366,560 contains the statement that 3744 years ago (each year having 365 days) an event must have occurred, which can hardly be anything other (according to the belief of the Mayas) than the creation of mankind. Hence all the *historical* dates of the Mayas were computed from this starting-point. But how did this event come to have the date IV Ahau 8 Cumhu?

In my opinion this date is to be regarded only as the result of the far more important date I Ahau 18 Kayab, lying 2200 days earlier. Day 17, Ahau, belongs, without doubt, to the chief of the gods, and as the first week day it must have been especially sacred. The prophecies of the Tonalamatl preferably begin with the Ahau and with the I. The series on the page under discussion, constructed with the difference 2920 as a basis, begins with I Ahau, and the three series on pages 46-50 also have the same day as the zero point of departure. I Ahau is therefore the starting-point of the astronomical computations as IV Ahau is of the historical.

Now, however, all the periods of 260 days end each time with I Ahau. Why is precisely this day chosen here, which is the 18th day of the month Kayab, therefore in the year 3 Kan, and lying 2200 days earlier than the historical date?

Day 18 Kayab is our June 18th. In my treatise "Schildkröte und Schnecke in der Mayaliteratur" (1892), I have sought to prove that the tortoise served as symbol of the summer solstice, that the sign of Kayab was the head of a tortoise, and that probably the 18th of June was regarded as the longest day. The middle one of the three series on pages 46-50 begins with exactly this date, I Ahau 18 Kayab.

But whence come the 2200 days? I will offer a suggestion which may serve until a better theory is propounded. Let us assume that each of the five principal planets had in succession regulated its time of revolution by this astronomical starting-point, thus:—sun 365, moon 356, Mercury 115, Venus 584, and Mars 780 days, these numbers added together give exactly 2200. It will scarcely excite surprise that I should set down the lunar year at 356 days (and not at the usual 354 days) for there are 12 × 29⅔ lunations in a year and we thought we had already found this period on this page, while discussing the number 1,364,360; also on pages 51-58, in addition to the half lunar year of 177 days, we shall find one of 178 days. Were the planets therefore created 2200 days before the appearance of mankind? Jupiter and Saturn, of course, with their 397 and 380 days are probably not considered here, because their periods of revolution so nearly correspond to that of the sun, and on pages 51-60 they are also treated as of secondary importance.

I confess I am quite unable to discover what may have happened 11,960 days before the creation of the stars—possibly the birth of one of the principal deities. Perhaps one of my fellow-students may succeed in finding an answer in one of the creation myths.

We come now to the 40 hieroglyphs on the left half of the page. These are intended simply to familiarize the reader with those signs which are of importance in the calendrical-astronomical portions of the Manuscript. Since no phonetic system of writing existed, we cannot, of course, expect that the scribe should have explained these signs.

Signs 1-4, which are mostly destroyed, can hardly denote anything other than the four quarters of the globe, at least we can still recognize in 4 the sign for the east, which has also the fourth place in pages 46-50. They stand thus together five times in the middle of the left side of pages 46-50, which pertain to this subject. 5 to 9 are the sign for Venus repeated 5 times, probably denoting the four parts of its revolution as on pages 46-50 and also the revolution as a whole. In connection with this first appearance of the Venus sign, I would mention that the same hieroglyph also occurs in the Tro-Cort., *e.g.*, Cort. 25c, though this Manuscript contains little else that is astronomical, yet it also has the rectangular heavenly shields.

10. This is a well-known form of the Moan sign. In the Globus, Volume LXV, 1894, I sought to make it appear probable that the Moan also denoted the Pleiades, with whose disappearance and reappearance the beginning of the years seems to be connected. Likewise on page 50, where the 2920-period ends, the Venus and Moan signs appear at the top on the right-hand side.

11 and 12 are the same sign, being that of the 13th Uinal (Mac), with which 260 days of the year end, and hence this sign is also used as the sign of the Tonalamatl. The repetition seems to show, that not until the 73 Tonalamatls of the period of 18,980 days are doubled—thus obtaining the number 37,960 of such importance here—are the sun and Venus periods brought into unison (with the whole system).

13. The Kin sign (sun, day) with the superfix, which in all probability expresses conjunction, union, and which, in my opinion, we also see on page 51, combined with Kin and Imix, as the sign for 18,980 days, is used here after the two Tonalamatls to denote the doubling of this period.

14-18. If the preceding signs led us to the Venus-solar period and to the continuation of this subject on pages 46-50, these five hieroglyphs bring us to the Mercury-lunar period and later, on pages 51-58, which are devoted to the same period, we shall find a parallel especially on the last page. First comes 14, which, as has been acknowledged, is the sign for 20 × 360 = 7200 days. 15, a hand holding a rectangle divided by a cross into four parts, is, I believe, the sign for the period of 20 days augmented to 21 by the 1 in front of it. The much more distinct form of sign 16 on the middle of page 58 and also at the top of page 53, should be compared with the sign as given here. The top part is the familiar Ben-Ik sign denoting the 10th and 19th days, and the bottom is the sign of the 14th division of 20 days, which make up the year. Now, however, the 10th day, when it becomes the 19th of the next 20 days, is distant from the first 29 days. The prefix consists of two parts:—

First two small circles joined by a zigzag line, which I think denotes the division of a day into halves; the sign would then equal 29½ days, *i.e.*, very nearly the true lunar month. Second, of two vertical lines, which might denote a doubling. The whole would then be equal to 2 × 29½ = 59. I admit that this interpretation is very artificial and I should be very glad if a better explanation could be found. On the other hand the 17th hieroglyph becomes quite clear when it is compared with the parallel passage on page 58; it is 13 × 360 = 4680 days, a third of the remarkable period of 14,040 days.

Thus we have

$$
\begin{array}{lll}
\text{Hieroglyph} & 14 = & 7200 \\
\text{Hieroglyph} & 15 = & 21 \\
\text{Hieroglyph} & 16 = & 59 \\
\text{Hieroglyph} & 17 = & \underline{4680} \\
& & 11960,
\end{array}
$$

which is exactly the lunar-Mercury period.

The sign Xul = conclusion, end, is fittingly added in 18 to the end of this period, as also on page 58. This sign is very common on pages 61 and 62 at the end of the long periods.

From signs 19 and 20 we see that the four parts of the Venus year are also about to be treated of here, that is, the periods of 236, 90, 250 and 8 days respectively, which are discussed on pages 46-50. For 19 is the sign for Venus, and 20 is a hand with a knife as a superfix, which divides the Venus revolution. This hand appears 20 times in like manner on the pages mentioned above.

Signs 21-25 represent five gods, who in all probability are N, F, H, the bat-god and A. These are the same signs which are repeated twice on the left-hand side of pages 46-50, both times at the beginning and end of the period of 236 days, that is, the period during which Venus is the morning star and which is under the dominion of the east. The fact that there is a 4 with N has reference to the four forms which this Uayeyab god assumes. Now we ought to expect a similar treatment of the periods of the planet, which are under the rule of the south, west and north, but there is no room for this. Instead, we find in 26, 27 and 28 three different signs plainly belonging together, the first of which is the day Caban, *i.e.*, the earth; the second may be Muluc denoting rain and water; the third is Chuen (the ape) which fittingly denotes the north, for Chuen denotes the little bear, as I have proved in my treatise on the day-signs of the Mayas. The Chuen sign in 28 also has a prefix, which probably refers to the night-god D. I find exactly the same combination in signs 8 A and 8 B of the inscription on the Cross of Palenque, but I must leave to others the task of connecting 26 and 27 likewise with the north, which is very evident in 27 (Muluc).

Sign 29 is entirely effaced. Nevertheless, I am positive that it represented the day IV Ahau, the beginning of Maya chronology, for 30 may still be identified as 8 Cumhu belonging to IV Ahau, and sign 31 is the same sign as 18, *i.e.*, the sign Xul

= the end, and denoting here the end of the long period.

The comprehensive hieroglyphs, 29-31, stand here in the wrong place. A more suitable position for them would be before 19 or just after 35. For they are intended to specify the periods during which Venus is in the west and south, *i.e.*, the time during which it is the evening star and the period of its inferior conjunction.

Sign 32 is the black deity, L according to Schellhas, here denoting the west, and 33 is the Venus sign with the prefix denoting division. In the same way we find these two signs together on page 46 at the right in the middle series, where presumably the four Venus periods are specified in close succession. The black deity is also found on page 50 in the middle of the page in the beginning, at the end of a period of 250 days. On page 24 it has as a prefix the sign Imix with three rows of dots proceeding from it. Imix, however, among the Mayas and Aztecs (as Cipactli), under some circumstances often, and under others always, denotes the first of the 20 days. Hence this sign may mean:—here begins the Venus period of 250 days.

34-35. The sign for the south still remains to be found. Sign 35 is again the Venus hieroglyph. In 34 we should expect to find one of the five gods of the south, which are found on pages 46-50, *e.g.*, the Moan, who is represented on page 47 as the regent of this cardinal point. But there is no figure of a god here, and in place of it we find set down here, as on page 47, middle, right-hand, an actual date as the beginning of this short southern period of only eight days. It is the date 10 Zip (third month), the month sign of which does indeed suggest a hieroglyph of the Moan. Now, if we recall that in hieroglyph 21 the god N is designated in exactly the same way by an actual date, viz:—4 Zac (11th month), then we see that the interval between 4 Zac and 10 Zip of the second year following, is exactly 236 + 90 + 250 = 576 days, and this corresponds exactly to the interval of time from the beginning of the period when Venus is in the east to the beginning of the period when she is in the south. If we knew in what years the morning star made its first appearance on February 4th and disappeared as the evening star on the 3d of September, we should make some progress in the comprehension of this subject, but not much, since these events fall approximately on the same dates after each period of 8 years.

36-40. The last five of the 40 signs appear in the same order again on pages 46-50, *one* sign on each page, in the middle group of the right-hand half of the page at the beginning of the third line, but with this difference, that on page 24 each sign has the same prefix, which is wanting on pages 46-50, where a similar hieroglyph always *follows*. From their position on pages 46-50 it follows that these are hieroglyphs of five gods, each of whom belongs to a whole Venus year of 584 days. I am not very sure in regard to these gods. I prefer to call 36 K, 37 F, 38 E and 40 A. Sign 39 with the person crouching, I am obliged to leave entirely unsettled. We shall find this hieroglyph again, *e.g.*, on pages 47 and 49 right, middle. Let it suffice that in these five signs we have a repetition of the Venus-solar period of 2920 days, with which we will end the discussion of this page. Only F and A have already been met with among the five gods denoted by hieroglyphs 21-25.

Pages 25—28.

As these four pages, which are the beginning of the back of the first part of the Manuscript, not only belong together, but also display a parallel arrangement of their separate parts, the corresponding parts will be considered together as a whole.

There are seven of these parts on each page, viz:—the column of day-signs on the left hand; the top, middle and bottom pictures, and lastly the top, middle and bottom groups of hieroglyphs; but I will consider the pictures and hieroglyphs of the same section as belonging together.

1. The Columns of Day-Signs.

On the left-hand side of each page two days are repeated 13 times. They are as follows:—On page 25 Eb and Ben, on page 26 Caban and Ezanab, on page 27 Ik and Akbal, and on page 28 Manik and Lamat. Cyrus Thomas first made the important discovery that these pages represent the transition from one year into the next, but held the erroneous opinion that the last two days of each of the four kinds of years were treated of on each page. While Seler, on the other hand, found that we have here to do with the last day of one year and the first of the following year, and that, therefore, Ben, Ezanab, Akbal and Lamat are the beginnings of the years and thus of the 20-day periods. The years, however, were always named after their second day (*i.e.*, Kan, Muluc, Ix and Cauac years), since the New Year's Day was considered unlucky and it was the practice of the Mayas to conceal the real starting-point.

These four pages, therefore, extend over 13 × 52 years, that is, over a period of 18,980 days, after which period all the calendar dates are repeated. A list of all these dates is given in "The Maya and Tzental Calendars" by William E. Gates (Cleveland, 1900).

The transition from the Muluc to the Ix years is represented on page 25; from the Ix to the Cauac years on page 26; from the Cauac to the Kan years on page 27, and from the Kan to the Muluc years on page 28. The Ix years are represented first, because the beginning of the historical chronology lies in an Ix year (IV Ahau; 8 Cumhu). This section treats of ceremonies, especially of the setting up of the idols at the changing of the year, which I can pass over here since they have already been described by Diego de Landa and in our own day by Cyrus Thomas in his "Study of the Manuscript Troano," and elsewhere.

2. The Top Pictures.

The principal representation on all the four pages is a priest, but disguised as an animal with the head of a beast of prey as a mask (always the same one) and also with a tail. He is pictured with the same three articles in each of the four representations, viz:—First, in his right hand, the staff of office with the hand at the top, which, according to Seler, "Mittel-Amerik. Musikinstrum.," p. 112, is the rattle-stick, second the incense-pouch, *i.e.*, for copal, and third in his left hand a rattle, or, according to Schellhas, "Vergleichende Studien" (1880), a fan. There is one point, however, in which the first two pages differ from the other two; on the first two the priest is walking on dry land and on the second two through a stream of water. Was the city, to which this calendar especially refers, bordered in two directions by water, so that the road led across it?

On all the four pages, however, the priest carries on his back a different deity, and I cannot find out by what rule these gods are connected with one another, or with the one which is represented below them, or with the years. On page 25 the god is B, on 26 he has the form of a jaguar (Ix), on 27 he is undoubtedly E, and on page 28 he is the god A, Cimi.

Now to the left of the priest on each page there is one of the familiar Chuen bundles, such as are also frequently found in the the Tro-Cortesianus. Here, on pages 25-28, there are always three of these Chuen signs in a bunch. If Chuen really denotes the eighth day (which, of course, is only possible when Kan = 1), and at the same time the period of 8 days, then in this passage these three Chuen signs would properly designate the 24 days which elapse *before* the last day of the year, which is the last day of the 18th month. In the same way we shall find the Chuen bundle appropriately given this meaning on pages 42c-45c. Likewise the simple Chuen sign at the top of page 52 seems to denote 8 days. But what do the Chuen bundles in the Tro-Cortesianus mean, some of which are much larger?

In close proximity to these Chuen bundles we find numbers as follows:—on page 25 numbers 8 and 9, on 26 number 13, on 27 number 2 and on 28 number 13. I can offer no opinion, which would be even approximately acceptable in regard to the meaning of these numerals, but we shall discuss them later.

3. The Top Hieroglyphs.

I shall discuss these glyphs in this place, although each group seems to relate not merely to the top picture, but to the whole page. There are 16 on each page, and arranged as follows:—

$$1 \quad 2 \qquad 9 \quad 10$$
$$3 \quad 4 \qquad 11 \quad 12$$
$$5 \quad 6 \qquad 13 \quad 14$$
$$7 \quad 8 \qquad 15 \quad 16.$$

Unfortunately, the writing at the top is obliterated, which makes it impossible to understand not merely this passage, but also those on all the rest of these pages. Of the 16 signs in the top line only one is legible, and that is the first on page 28. This is the usual cross *b*; as a comprehensive heading it perhaps occupied places 1 and 9 on each page, alternating with another sign in 2 and 10.

In spite of this obliteration there are a few points which can be profitably discussed here.

I would call attention first to signs 7 and 8 on page 25. The first seems to contain twice repeated the figure, which is thought to represent eagle feathers, and which we found on pages 10b and 13a, for example. As this double character is also used to change the 360-sign into a 7200-sign, so it may also combine the 52 years of this passage. The 8th sign on page 25 is the head with the tuft of hair and no underjaw, which I think refers to fast-days, such as might properly occur at the transition point of one long period to another.

The sign for the year stands five times on the other three pages, which is in keeping with their contents. On page 26 it appears three times. This page treats of the transition of the Ix to the Cauac years. In the 6th place the Ix sign seems actually to be used as a prefix, in 7 the prefix is plainly the Kin-Cauac sign, just as on page 37a, and in 5 the prefix is probably Ezanab, the beginning-day of the Cauac years. At this last place the suffix is the same as that which we often see with the year sign on pages 13c-14c. On page 27, in the 7th place, the year sign has a prefix and a suffix, which seem to indicate that here it was intended to represent 365 as separated into 5 × 73 or 360 + 5. Lastly, on page 28 the 8th sign can be explained as meaning that the ritual year of 364 days is separated into 4 Bacab periods of 91 days each.

Resembling the year sign in form, and placed near it on these pages, is the following sign:—

This sign frequently appears on pages 8b-9b, 16b-17b, 17c-20c. We find it with slight variations once on each of the four pages 25-28. It is the 6th on page 25; the 8th on 26; the 6th on 27; the 6th on 28. Its lower part, especially the (phallic?) sign added at the left, suggests the hieroglyphs of the Bacabs, as we find them on pages 52, 55, 56, etc.; they might refer to the separation of the ritual year of 364 days into 4 × 91 days. On the other hand it has been considered simply as the reproduction of the carrying-frame pictured below it (compare above under page 17c.)

While the hieroglyphs, hitherto discussed, demonstrate the connection between the parts on the left of the four pages, two other signs prove the connection of the portions on the right.

One of these looks like the Ik sign surrounded by a dotted circle; it occurs on page 25 as the 13th sign, on page 26 as the 15th, on page 27 as the 14th and on page 28 as the 15th. To this sign are prefixed successively the numbers 9, 7, 11 and 6.

The second is unquestionably the hieroglyph for the numeral 20 or for the moon. It is effaced on page 25 and on pages 27 and 28 has a prefix, which on page 26 is used as a superfix. This sign is the 14th on page 25, the 16th on page 26, the 15th on page 27 and the 16th on page 28. The prefixed numbers are 7, 16, 5 and 6.

The meaning of these two signs and that of the apparently irregular numbers is still a mystery. The latter will be discussed presently.

The 4th sign on all the four pages seems to refer to a period like the one hitherto discussed. On page 26 the sign resembles that for the 13th Uinal (Mac) and hence appears to refer to the Tonalamatl, as in the first column on page 24. Above it is the sign for the south. The corresponding hieroglyphs of the other pages are obliterated, but strange to say the vestiges suggest that they too had *below* them the sign for the south. Now the south and the Bacab of the south preside over the fourth quarter of the year from which ensues the transition to the new year in question here.

Among the signs on the left side we should expect to find those of the gods to whom the expiring year belonged. On page 25 it ought to be B. Sign 5, however, though it can with difficulty be identified, points rather to god K. Sign 3 on page 26 corresponds better; this is the hieroglyph of the tiger already known to us, which is carried by the priest in the upper section of page 8a; here its prefix is the sign for the west. On page 27 we ought to see the grain-god E carried by the priest; his hieroglyph may be destroyed, but sign 5, which is Kan-Imix (food and drink) is his determinative. Finally the 5th sign on page 28 is, just as we should expect, the hieroglyph of A and, in addition, we find his determinative in 7.

But what is to be said of the fact that the tiger appears again on page 28 in sign 3, and this time with the sign for the east?

The Ahau on page 27, sign 16, refers to the god D of the middle section.

There maybe some reference here to sacrifice, thus:—the 11th sign on page 25 is Kan-Imix, the 12th on page 27 is Kan, which is followed in the 13th sign on page 27 by another one with a Yax and a suggestion of a second Kan-Imix. Also the curious sign in the 8th place on page 27, which we have already discussed under page 8b, is used to denote the sacrifice on pages 18a and 15b. Here its position with reference to sign 6 is the same as on page 8b. On page 26 the prefix of sign 13, which is half destroyed, may be recognized as a serpent. Signs 12 and 15 on page 25 are unintelligible. Unfortunately the following signs are entirely effaced:—Sign 1 on pages 25, 26 and 27, as well as 2 on all the four pages, 3 on page 25, 9 and 10 on all the four pages, 11 on pages 26, 27 and 28, 12 on pages 26 and 28, 13 on page 28, 14 on pages 26 and 28, and 16 on page 27.

4. The Middle Pictures.

On each page at the right there is a house, the back wall of which is always marked with the cross often met with. In front of the house with his back turned towards it, sits a deity. Each of the four deities has the front of his body covered with a gala mantle. Now we know that the god of the new year was set up before the house of the chieftain. On page 25 the god is K with his eyes apparently destroyed, and on page 26 it is B with a Kin sign on his head covering, hence designated here as a sun or day-god. On page 27 the god is D, and on page 28, A with the cross-bones on his robe, his own hieroglyph on his cheek, and the Akbal sign on his forehead. Only on the last page, therefore, and apparently by mistake, the god in the top picture is the same as in the middle picture.

At the left of each page, *i.e.*, opposite the house and the god, is a flaming altar, bearing the sign Ix equivalent to fire.

The centre, between the gods and the altars, is occupied by vessels of which there are two on each of the first three pages and but one on the fourth; they contain food, without doubt intended for the sacrificial feast. On page 25 the lower vessel contains Kan (maize) and the upper probably a food prepared from Kan. Or are the spines on the back of the iguana indicated on this vessel? (Compare 40c and Cort. 8 and 12c). The contents of the lower vessel on page 26 are still unknown (birds?). The upper vessel contains a Kan, but the sign has a superfix, which corresponds to the sign for the west. On page 27 the lower vessel contains a fish and the upper the sign for the south. Lastly, the single vessel on page 28 contains the cross-bones (mammal?) and above them the Kan sign repeated three times.

Finally here on the last three pages, we find some numbers, which are still undetermined; on page 26 there is a 7 with the lower vessel, and on page 27 with the upper vessel two dots with a cross between them (perhaps this may mean 20 - 2 = 18, which is used in place of the usual clumsy numeral?). On page 28 we see above the vessel a 6, and below it, in place of a second vessel, a double Chuen sign, as in the upper section of the page, therefore it can hardly be the Akbal sign resembling Chuen.

5. The Middle Hieroglyphs.

On each page these signs consist of but *one* line containing 5, 6, 3 and 3 glyphs respectively. The first of these signs in all of the four places is the same (*o*), which very suitably refers to the change in the year. The second sign is always the hieroglyph of the god represented in the middle section:—K on page 25, B as the sun-god on page 26, and D on page 27. The second sign on page 28, which is the head without an underjaw and with the prefixed four, probably referring to four fast-days, must, therefore, be an uncommon sign for A, who was similarly designated on page 25 in sign 8 of the upper section.

If the gods in the top thirds are those of the past year and those in the middle the gods of the year just beginning, we should expect to find in each top third the deity who is represented in the middle of the preceding page. But this does not hold good. For then we should expect to find K on page 26 and not the tiger, on page 27 B or G and not E, on page 28 D and not A, and on page 25 A and not B.

Hence there is some confusion here. Yet it seems to be in the nature of a correction, that on page 26 the third sign, next to that of the sun-god, is actually the sign for E who is in the top section on page 27, and that the sixth sign is Kan-Imix belonging to this god.

On pages 25 and 26 this line also refers to the past year, *i.e.*, to the year set down in the top third. The fourth sign on page 25 is a Manik, *i.e.*, originally a grasping hand denoting taking away, disappearance, and the fifth sign on this page is a Muluc, which seems to denote the ending of the Muluc years. The fifth sign on page 26, is, in fact, the tiger pictured above.

The lunar hieroglyph as the third sign on page 25 and the *a* as the fourth on page 26 are strange and unaccountable. Both appear to be almost without significance here and seem almost like mere points between the names of gods in groups of two each.

The Ahau as the third sign on page 27 is the usual determinative of D, whose hieroglyph stands beside it.

On page 28 the main part of the third sign corresponds to the sixth of the upper section. I do not know, however, how to explain either the upper part suggesting a mat or the familiar leaf-shaped prefix.

6. The Bottom Pictures.

In the left-hand lower corner of each page we see the sign for the year of 360 days, which at the same time designates the heap of stones, on which the stelae were erected, the two thick black lines indicating the two columns of hieroglyphs usually found on them. A tree is growing out of this sign, having on its trunk an abbreviated Cauac sign, at least, on pages 26, 27 and 28, which probably refers to rain as the most desired event of the year. The tree on page 25 has no leaves, but the top is carved into the shape of the head of the god B. In the other three cases it has leaves, but instead of ending in the god's head the tree is draped with a mantle and a breech-clout, and a serpent is coiled about it denoting a period of time (here, the year). Furthermore there are foot-prints on the trunk or the drapery of the tree, which represent it as the goal of a pilgrimage.

If the top and middle thirds refer to the mere transportation of the idols, the bottom thirds refer to the feasts connected with this act, or, at any rate, to those dedicated to the *new* god. For we see here on page 25 the god B, on 26 the god K, on 27 A and on 28 D, *i.e.*, the same deities as in the middle sections, yet so placed that the first two and the last two have changed places.

Each of the four deities hold in one hand a hen with its head cut off; "degollavan una gallina" is the statement made by Landa concerning these feasts. Perhaps all four gods, at any rate the last three, are scattering grain; this was one form of divination; we found the other on page 2. There are besides, on every page, several small objects between the two pictures, just as in the middle section. On page 25 the object is probably an altar, but instead of the flame it has the number 19. Above this is the sign for the west (the Ix days) with that for the sun, and on top of them the sign which we found in the middle section of page 26 as the contents of the lower vessel. On page 26 we see a vessel containing a bird, then another whose contents are indicated by Yax and a double Kan sign. Above it is the sign for the moon or for 20 with a prefix, and above this a 9. At the bottom of page 27 there is a vessel containing two Kan signs and a fish; above this another vessel the contents of which are the same as we found in the vessel in the middle section of page 26 and in that of the lower section of page 25. Above these is again the sign for the moon or 20 with a superfix, which is the same as the prefix on page 26, and beside it is a 16. Page 28 has the usual haunch of venison (Landa:—"una pierna de venado"), above this is a vessel with a bird and Kan and above this again the sign for the moon or for 20 with the same superfix and the numeral 15. I shall discuss below the numbers scattered over these four pages.

7. The Bottom Hieroglyphs.

These hieroglyphs also form but *one* line on each page and each line contains six hieroglyphs. The *first* of each line is always the same (*p*). It consists of a surface divided into four quadrants thus suggesting the four cardinal points, the four Bacabs presiding over them and the four kinds of years. The superfix seems to be the abbreviated hieroglyph of the north; the sign for the north, however, is Muluc and these four pages begin with the Muluc years.

The *second* sign is the head of D as the supreme god; to this a Yax is joined on pages 26-28 as the symbol of strength, and on page 25, but probably by mistake, the abbreviated sign for the west.

The *third* sign always represents one of the four cardinal points:—on page 25 the east, on page 26 the south, on page 27 the west and on page 28 the north; here then the usual order is reversed and the signs are set down according to the diurnal instead of the annual course of the sun, probably occasioned merely by exchanging the sign for the west (Ix), which belongs on page 25, with that for the east (Kan), which belongs on page 27.

The other three signs do not stand in the same order on every page.

The *fifth* sign on pages 26 and 28 and the *fourth* on page 27 show correspondence most clearly. This sign is always a head, undoubtedly that of the god pictured in the bottom third. But on page 25 it is the hieroglyph of E, who is pictured on the top of page 27, instead of that of B.

In the same way the 6th sign on page 25, the 4th on page 26, the 5th on page 27 and the 4th on page 28 have something in common. One element of the hieroglyph is always the sign for the year of 360 days, combined on page 25 with cross-bones and the Cauac sign, on 26 with Yax and Kan, and on 27 and 28 simply with Yax.

The most puzzling and divergent of these hieroglyphs are the remaining ones. The 4th on page 25 has an oblique cross (or bones?) and the abbreviated glyph for the west, the 6th on page 26 is the head of E, the 6th on page 27 is the 360-day sign combined with Kin and Cauac, and the 6th on page 28 is the usual Kan-Imix sign. Here, too, there seems to have been a displacement.

Before I leave the four pages 25-28, I will glance at the numerals, which are scattered over them and which apparently have no connection with one another. I have discussed these numerals in my article "Die Mayahieroglyphen" in Volume LXXI, No. 5, of the Globus, and the following is borrowed therefrom.

First of all, I believe that I proved there, that the sign composed of two dots with a cross between them is an abbreviation for the usual clumsy representation of the numeral 18 and designates it like a duodeviginti by 20 - 2. Next, that in this passage as on pages 18a, 18c, 19c, 46b and 50c, the sign is combined with the hieroglyphs Yax-Kin. Third, that it is closely related to the god D, inasmuch as it stands on page 27b close beside the picture of that god.

Assuming this as a known fact, we find scattered over these four pages the following numbers:—

25:	9,	7,	8,	9,	19,
26:	7,	16,	13,	7,	9,
27:	11,	5,	2,	18,	16,
28:	6,	6,	13,	6,	15.

It is very remarkable that the sum of the numbers on each of the first three pages is equal to 52, and as an accidental freak it would be most surprising; somewhere on the fourth page six units may have been omitted; but perhaps the 6, which stands above the *two* Chuen signs in the centre, is to be counted twice. The 52, however, designates the very 52 years, which are treated of on these four pages.

As yet I know no reason to account for the fact that the 52 is here separated into these apparently very irregular numbers. The discovery of this reason would be an important step in advance. Or does it means 52 *days*, perhaps those which follow a Tonalamatl coming in the middle of the year?

Page 28 is followed in the Manuscript by three empty pages. The scribe's object in reserving them is beyond our ken; possibly they were intended to represent the period of 8 years.

Pages 29-45 (*i.e.*, to the end of the first part of the Manuscript) all belong together. After the Maya manner there is very little system displayed in their arrangement, and though here and there there may be occasion to consider the three parts of each page consecutively, I will discuss them here as follows:—First, the top thirds, which are most difficult owing to the destruction of a large portion of them; then the middle, and last the bottom thirds. They all consist in great part, with a few interruptions, of representations of the regular Tonalamatl, such as we find represented from the beginning of the Manuscript to page 23.

The element which these pages have in common is the fact that the god B, who can hardly be Kukulcan or Quetzalcoatl, occurs on almost all of them. He is the god of wind, fire, breath, *i.e.*, the true god of life and is here represented in his relation to the most varied manifestations and activities of a human being, so that this section bears a certain resemblance to the Tro-Cortesianus. With this is closely connected his relation to all four cardinal points, which so often occur. He may have been the local god of the region from whence this Manuscript came; in the Tro-Cort. It seems rather to be C who lays claim to this office.

Pages 29a—30a.

XI		13	XI	13	XI	13	XI	13	XI	13	XI
Lamat											
Ben											
Ezanab											
Akbal.											

This is a Tonalamatl of 4 × 65 days, each part subdivided into 5 × 13 days. The four days written on the left are those which may begin the year.

In each of the five sections B is pictured in a sitting posture, the first four times on a tree (the tree of life rather than the sacrificial tree).

In the first picture he holds in one hand the haunch of venison, so often occurring as an offering, the last time on page 28; the object above it is probably the Kan sign. There is a vessel at the god's feet, probably a receptacle for the venison, bearing the hieroglyph of the 13th day Cib, which, however, refers rather to a bird.

In the second picture an animal with a protruding tongue lies on its back at the feet of the god, who kneels upon its stomach. This probably represents the lightning-dog as vanquished. The same animal is pictured on the next page and also on page 40b and perhaps on page 60. There are a number of small dots around B's head, which on page 11c we attempted to interpret as the starry sky.

I can find nothing of special importance in the third and fourth pictures, but in the fifth, B is sitting in a house, which is marked repeatedly with the sign Caban (ground). Here the god is holding the hatchet (machete) in his hand, as if prepared for some terrestrial activity. Four hieroglyphs in the usual order belong to each of the five pictures. They are almost entirely destroyed, but the vestiges show that the fourth sign was always that of B, while the third sign with the first picture had the abbreviated hieroglyph of the west as a prefix; with the second picture it had that of the south, and therefore with the third and fourth it must certainly have had the signs of the east and north. We should expect the signs with these prefixes to contain references to Ix, Cauac, Kan and Muluc, but they are not distinguishable.

Thus B is represented in pictures 1-4 as ruler of the four cardinal points and in 5 as the ruler of the earth in general.

Pages 30a—31a.

This passage looks like an amplification of the middle picture on page 29a. Here B is represented with the hatchet in his left hand and holding aloft by the tail with his right hand the animal, which is spitting out something upon a stepped pyramidal structure, probably the pyramid of a teocalli. That this is probably meant to represent lightning is rendered almost a certainty by the picture on page 40b. In this passage there are several red and black numerals scattered around the animal in an irregular manner, which we find nowhere else in our Manuscript, but with which the Tro-Cortesianus has made us familiar. The sum of the black numbers still legible is 23, probably a 3 is effaced and the sum should be 26, the sum which so often occurs in the Cod. Troano 8-13 with the animal represented there. The red numbers likewise do not admit of exact determination. This passage also contained hieroglyphs, four standing side by side on each of the two pages. The legible portion is limited to the Cimi sign in the third place, perhaps an Imix in the second, and possibly an Ahau in the first.

Pages 31a—32a.

In my article "Zur Entzifferung, etc., VI," published in the year 1897, I discussed this passage more in detail, and the following will be in continuation of what I stated there.

The real aim of the computation on these pages is to find a number in which the following periods of time are united with the Tonalamatl of 260 days:—1. The ritual year of 364 days, and consequently also a quarter of it, the Bacab period of 91 days. 2. The period of 104 days, being the number of days which remain after a Tonalamatl has been deducted from a ritual year. The hypothesis advanced by Mrs. Zelia Nuttall ("Note on the Ancient Mexican Calendar System," Stockholm, 1894) and also the entirely different opinion held by Mr. Charles P. Bowditch ("The Lords of the Night and the Tonalamatl of the Codex Borbonicus" in the American Anthropologist, N. S., Vol. II, New York, 1900) prove the existence not only of merely arbitrary Tonalamatls for the purpose of prediction, as those in our Manuscript, but also of Tonalamatls having a fixed position in certain years. But after the manner peculiar to priestcraft, the number sought is found only by an indirect and mysterious process.

In the first place we find on page 32a all the days set down in the following manner:—

XIII	XIII	XIII	XIII
Manik	Cib	Chicchan	Ix
Chuen	Ahau	Muluc	Ezanab
Men	Kan	Ben	Ik
Cauac	Lamat	Caban	Cimi
Akbal	Eb	Imix	Oc.

That is to say, a series counting from the day XIII Akbal, the New Year's day of the year I Kan, recurring every 52 years, furthermore a series which shows the same difference of 91 from the day XIII Akbal to XIII Ix, XIII Chicchan, etc., and finally ends with XIII Akbal again, after it has run through a period of 20 × 91, *i.e.,* 1820 days = 7 Tonalamatls, like a similar representation of 7 Tonalamatls on page 51. Above these 20 days, and to the left of them, numbers are set down rather irregularly, which begin with 91 and are multiples of that number. The signs of the days corresponding to these numbers are joined to them; but they are omitted with the numbers of lowest value. Hence we have:—91, 182, 273, 364 (4), 455 (5), 546 (6), 637 (7), 728 (8), 819 (9), 910 (10). Then with a bound follow 1456 and 1820; with the last number Akbal is reached in the natural way, which day the scribe had erroneously set down again with 1456 in place of Cauac.

The number 728 already united the numbers 91, 104 and 364, but did not include the number 260. This inclusion is accomplished by the number 3640 on page 32, quite on the left where we find the numbers 10 and 2, under which only a 0 has been omitted. With the usual hiatuses this series seems to end on page 31, where I think the numbers 4, 0, 16 and 0 ought to stand, but they are almost wholly effaced; this would then be 320 × 91, 280 × 104, 112 × 260, 80 × 364 = 29,120.

We have thus gone far in advance of the first problem, but a second always presents itself in these series, it is that of using these periods for larger numbers, which refer to a not too remote past or to a future not too distant. The first numbers are, as a rule, in the neighborhood of 1,252,680, the close of the eleventh Ahau-Katun, and the latter in the neighborhood of 1,480,440, the close of the thirteenth Ahau-Katun. The Manuscript presents the following: —

1,272,544	1,268,540	1,538,342.
XIII Akbal	XIII Akbal	XIII Akbal
121	17	51,419
IV Ahau	IV Ahau	
8 Cumhu	8 Cumhu	IV Ahau.

In connection with this it should be noted first that I have restored the 8 in the statement of the months, and second that the two numbers on the right were found with the aid of page 63 only by an easy conjecture. For with the reading of the Manuscript 10, 13, 3, 13, 2, I do not agree, but read instead 10, 13, 13, 3, 2; the number below, however, is given in the Manuscript as 7, 2 and then a black 14 joined to a red 5; I read this 7, 2, 14, 19.

The three numbers nearest the bottom have red circles around them, indicating subtraction, or, according to my present point of view, addition.

Now let us see how the computer arrived at the large numbers.

Day XIII Akbal, the New Year's day of the 1 Kan years, is given; also the differences of the series 91 and 104, therefore also in the proportion of 7 to 8. If we combine these last two numbers by addition and then by multiplication with 260, the result is $(7 + 8) \times 260 = 3900$. If, however, 7, 8 and 3900 be combined by multiplication the product is $7 \times 8 \times 3900 = 218{,}400 = 2400 \times 91 = 2100 \times 104 = 840 \times 260 = 600 \times 364 = 1120 \times (91 + 104)$. We have already met with the 218,400 on page 24, which was obtained by the addition of $33{,}280 + 185{,}120$.

My opinion is as follows: — First 11 Ahau-Katuns = 1,252,680, were taken as a point of departure, and to this sum was added $15{,}600 = 4 \times 3900$, and 243 as the interval between the normal date IV Ahau and XIII Akbal. The result was 1,268,523. The position of this day, however, is XIII Akbal 11 Xul (1 Ix).

Then the 3900 mentioned above was added to this number and the result was 1,272,423 = XIII Akbal 16 Pop (12 Muluc).

Then to the 1,268,523 was added the 218,400 and the sum was 1,486,923 = XIII Akbal 1 Kankin (1 Kan), the very place in that year where a Tonalamatl ends.

The following numbers were thus obtained: —

1,272,423   1,268,523   1,486,923.

These numbers are suppressed in the Manuscript. But if the encircled numbers are added to them, viz: — 121 (interval between XIII Akbal and IV Kan), 17 (interval between XIII Akbal and IV Ahau), and 51,419 (= $197 \times 260 + 199$; 199, however, is the interval between XIII Akbal and IV Ik), the result is the three large numbers set down in the Manuscript, which have the following properties: —

1) 1,272,544 = IV Kan 17 Xul (12 Muluc). This number = $13{,}984 \times 91 = 12{,}236 \times 104 = 3496 \times 364$. It also = $4894 \times 260 + 104$, the interval between IV Ahau and IV

Kan.

2) 1,268,540 = IV Ahau 8 Mol (1 Ix) = 4879 × 260 = 3485 × 364 = 74,620 × 17. 17 is the interval between XIII Akbal and IV Ahau.

3) 1,538,342 = IV Ik 15 Zac (12 Muluc). It also = 5916 × 260 + 182. The 182, however, the half of the ritual year of 364 days, is the interval between IV Ahau and IV Ik and between IV Ik and IV Kan. The fact that the interval is the same in each case is clearly the reason for the choice of the days IV Kan and IV Ik, which are otherwise not at all prominent.

It is remarkable that the third number is obtained by the addition of 51,419, *i.e.*, of 197 × 260 + 199 (there are 199 days between XIII Akbal and IV Ik). But it was evidently desirable to obtain as large a number as this. On page 63 a number of nearly similar value is associated with it, viz:—1,535,004. It is set down almost in the middle between the 13th and 14th Ahau-Katuns, for it is 57,902 days greater than 1,480,440, and 55,978 days less than 1,594,320.

Now, however, the Manuscript presents in the last column but one of page 31 a number, 2,804,100, which occupies a very unique position, since it is nearly twice as great as all the other large numbers, with the exception of those in the serpents. It must refer to the year 9 Muluc, and to the date IV Ahau 13 Mol. It has many remarkable properties, for it is:—

1) = 10,785 × 260

2) = 17,975 × 156 (156 = IV Kan - IV Ahau).

3) = 35,950 × 78 (78 = IV Ik - IV Ahau and IV Kan - IV Ik).

4) = 719 × 3900. We have already met with this 3900 above. Now, however, the 2,804,100 by virtue of its magnitude creates the suspicion that it may be composed of two ordinary large numbers. It might be

5) 1,308,580 + 1,495,520, therefore 14,380 (91 + 104).

6) 1,380,600 + 1,423,500, therefore 3,900 (354 + 365).

That is to say, the important 3900 multiplied by the days of the lunar year and also by those of the solar year, hence the 719, referred to under 4, separates into these two parts. The lunar year of 354 = 6 × 29 + 6 × 30 days was not unknown to the Mayas. We shall find its half, 177 days, several times on pages 51-58.

We might also use the two important numbers 14,040 and 18,980, the first of which is divisible by 260 and 360, and the second by 260 and 365, without remainder.

Then we have the large number desired:—

7) 147 × 18,980 + 14,040.

8) 200 × 14,040 - 3900.

What future student will penetrate more deeply into the meaning and purpose of these numbers?

We might now expect to interpret also the upper right-hand corner of page

31, but here almost everything is in a deplorable state of obliteration. In the first three of the five columns over each of the three large numbers there was a date consisting of a numeral and a hieroglyph, but these admit of no certain nor even probable determination.

Four hieroglyphs still remain in the fourth column, respecting which compare my treatise "Zur Maya-Chronologie" in the Berliner Zeitschrift für Ethnologie XXIII, pp. 141-155.

In the top sign I recognize an Imix with a prefix and probably also a superfix. I think this denotes the period of 18,980 days.

I am forced to pass over the second entirely, inasmuch as a red 6 inserted in it remains a mystery (6 × 18,980 = 113,880?).

As I stated in the above-named work, I think the third is three times the sacred period of 2920, *i.e.*, 8760 days.

Finally, the fourth sign certainly denotes the period of 7200 days.

Whether or not there was a fifth sign above the one now at the top is as uncertain as the meaning of the whole.

The most remarkable thing about it is that in three other passages of this Manuscript these three signs appear in close proximity to another. On page 61 we find the third in the 11th place in the second column, the first in the 12th place in the same column, and the fourth in the 14th place in the first column. Page 70 has the first sign in the middle of the 4th column; the second somewhat lower down in the 3d column and the 4th two places below. Finally all three signs appear in succession on the top of page 73 in the same order as on page 31.

The fifth column on page 31 may have contained another numeral belonging to the series, the loss of which is not so serious a matter, but there may have been one or two hieroglyphs above it, the obliteration of which is greatly to be deplored.

Pages 32a — 39a.

This is a large section extending over eight pages, which is difficult of interpretation owing to the prevailing disorder and because a large part of the hieroglyphs are effaced. Here, too, the principal subject is the god B, who is represented in manifold activity. A series of numbers extends through the entire representation. I read them as follows: —

I 11   XII 28   I 12   XIII 26   XIII 12   XII 19   V 5   X 1   XI 20   V 12

IV 6   X 8   V 5   X 7   IV 12   III 5   VIII 8   III 11   I.

There are thus 18 divisions, the different lengths of which reveal no rule. They embrace 208 days, *i.e.*, 2 × 104, which may well be considered as a continuation of the computation in the preceding section, of which the 104 was so important a number. The red numbers are entirely lacking in the beginning, then they are very slightly indicated, and finally they are distinctly written out on pages 36-39. I assume that the scribe has set down the 4th, 3d and 2nd numbers from the end, one too little. The last number has been entirely omitted. I have supplied these omissions though in a manner somewhat different from that adopted by Cyrus Thomas, "Aids," p. 28. I would note in addition that a period such as this, consisting of 208 days = 16 weeks, might be explained in an entirely different way, if there were a column of five days at the left having a difference of 8 days; then the whole would signify four Tonalamatls. But there is no such series of days.

Another point of view presents itself, however. If we take cognizance of the fact that a group of four hieroglyphs usually belongs to a picture, then it is evident that here there are such groups not for 18, but for about 22 subdivisions. It may, therefore, be assumed that about four subdivisions averaging 13 days are not specified, in which case this passage would extend not over 208, but over 260 days. The very irregularity in the arrangement of these numbers is an argument in favor of this hypothesis; it may be occasioned by the fact, that the pictures do not correspond exactly to the subdivisions. For the present, however, we shall discuss the single pictures assuming that there are 18 subdivisions.

1. Pages 32a-33a. Here at the very beginning it is uncertain whether the signs at the end of page 32 and at the beginning of page 33 are to be regarded as a single group of 8 hieroglyphs, as seems to follow from the numbers, or as two groups of 4 hieroglyphs each. At the end of page 32 we see two persons facing one another, one of whom, to be sure, is barely visible. The other wears a head-covering like a man's silk hat, similar to that worn by the priests on the inscriptions of Palenque. It is a remarkable fact that of the four hieroglyphs above these figures, 1, 2 and 4 (the last probably the god C) seem to have the sign for the west as a prefix, while the prefix of 3 (Imix) suggests the usual representation of the tortoise head. Below the persons there is a Kan sign, the prefix of which is also the sign for the west.

On page 33, B is represented walking and carrying the Caban sign in his hand. The first of the four hieroglyphs is the sign for B, the second is Imix, probably again with the sign for the west as.a prefix, the third is an Akbal sign with Kin, and the fourth is the cross-hatched sign with Kan.

2. The rest of 33a is occupied by two persons, one of whom is clad in a gala mantle, but neither admit of further identification. They are occupied in fishing, inasmuch as they are sitting on the shore of a body of water and are either casting a net or drawing it in. There is a fish between them and above it is a vessel with something apparently cooking in it. Of the 8 hieroglyphs belonging to this picture, only the following are distinguishable:—the 1st containing an Akbal, the 3d, which is the common cross *b* with a 9, the 4th, an Imix also with 9, and of the 7th only the prefix Yax. The 3d and 4th appear again on page 35a, 28 days later.

3. Page 34, like page 3, represents a human sacrifice. The victim, very vaguely drawn, lies on a step-shaped sacrificial stone, or on the pyramid of a teocalli. There is a Caban (earth) sign between the sacrifice and the pyramid, and also on the walls of the buildings; the shrieking of the victim is plainly indicated. As on page 3, there are four persons in the form of gods surrounding the sacrifice, but here they are different ones. The one at the left above is the black god (L?), holding the rattle-stick (Seler, "Mittelamer. Musikinstrumente," p. 111), and at the right, above, F, the companion of the death-god, is sitting with a rattle in his hand. Below, the

two have changed places, F is on the left and L on the right. The former is beating the drum and the latter blowing a wind-instrument. The sounds emitted by the two instruments are represented by drawings. This may, therefore, be regarded as an instrumental quartette. The following objects are also in this picture:—at the left above is a vessel the contents of which are cooking; at the left below, another vessel with three Kan signs, and at the right above, a Kan sign with a bird's head and below the food known to us from pages 27b and 29b. These four objects refer to the sacrificial feast. Lastly, at the bottom on the right there is a ladder, probably intended for scaling the pyramid. Ten hieroglyphs in the upper line belong to this picture:—the first, which is effaced, is followed by a Cauac, then comes the cross *b*, then a Cimi appropriate to the sacrifice, and lastly a head with an Akbal eye, probably D's. The first sign in the lower row is likewise destroyed, the second sign is a Kan, the next is the cross *b*, both having a different prefix, then here too is the hieroglyph of B with Yax as a prefix, and the last is an unknown sign.

4 and 5. Page 35a. According to the numbers there are two sections here, but neither the pictures nor the hieroglyphs can with certainty be assigned to either. On the left is a house in which C sits holding a Kan sign in his hand; on the roof, as if guarding him, and also holding a Kan sign, lies the god B. In the Cort. 24b-25b, there are six gods lying on houses, within which other gods are also represented in a recumbent position. Then follow two vessels, again denoting the sacrificial feast, the contents of which are probably cooking, and which, from the sign on the second, are probably liquid. Above these are three others, one with the Cimi sign (human flesh?), one with a bird and the third with the haunch of venison. At the right of these is an implement, which is unfamiliar to me and is similar to that held in the god's hand on pages 5c and 6c. And quite on the right sits B with foot-prints pictured below him and on his clothing.

The hieroglyphs on page 35, when they were all legible, numbered 14 and were arranged in two rows. 4 of the upper row are preserved, the lower part of the first is a year-sign (?), similar to that which often appears on pages 25-28, the upper element is the cross, and the prefix is the one resembling a leaf, which occurs so frequently. The second sign is an Imix with a prefixed 9, the third a cross and the fourth a head (probably D's) with Akbal. In the second row there is a cross with a prefixed 9 (sign of the second or third month?). These two signs with the prefixed 9 are perhaps to be read as a calendar date IX Imix 9 Zip (1 Ix), as on page 33a. Ix, however, belongs to the west, which is the predominant cardinal point from 32a onward. The second sign is a compound of Kin and Akbal (day and night) which often occurs here, the third is the compound of the Moan and Caban signs with the number 1 above each, and the fourth is the hieroglyph of B. The fifth sign is unfamiliar to me. The sixth contains an Imix with the sign for the west as a prefix, and the seventh is effaced.

At this point the representations begin to display a more orderly arrangement.

6. Page 36a. Here the head of B forms the head of a serpent (cf. pages 61 and 62) represented in pouring rain, while on page 35b it is emerging from the water. Of the four hieroglyphs 1 and 2 are entirely and 3 for the most part destroyed, and 4 is the usual Kan-Imix.

7. The lightning-beast with flames pouring forth from his forepaws and tail, is plunging down from the rectangle, which primarily designates stars and then the sky in general. This rectangle occurs for the first time here, but will often be met with later. Here it may be a combination of Mars and Venus. Of the four hieroglyphs, 1 is effaced, 2 is a compound of Kan and Kin, 3 a head with Akbal and Kin (D?) with the uplifted arm as a prefix, and 4, corresponding with the picture, is the compound of the rain sign Cauac with the prefix of the storm-god K.

8. Here B himself is the bringer of lightning. In one hand he holds a burning torch and flames are bursting from his carrying-frame. The third hieroglyph is his sign. It is doubtful whether the fourth is the hatchet (machete) or is not rather intended for an ear pierced for the purpose of ritual blood-letting, as on pages 44b and 45b; the first and second signs are rather indistinct.

9. Page 37a. Unless I am entirely mistaken, B is here represented with his arms bound behind his back. Cf. the pictures on page 2, top, and 60, bottom. Are the ends of the rope fluttering in front of the god intended to render this still more plain? Hieroglyph 1 contains the sign *t*, which resembles, but is not the same as, the year sign. This sign has already occurred frequently, especially on pages 25a-28a, and the last time on page 35 in the first hieroglyph. As on page 35, hieroglyph 4 is the compound Kin-Cauac, but here it is joined to the year-sign, *i.e.*, it denotes the Kin-Cauac year, just as it does on page 26a. 3 is again Cauac and 2 is the hieroglyph for B.

10. Rain is falling from the heavenly shield, already seen on page 36, here however designating different planets (Mars and Mercury?) and the figure represented in the rain is the one which we have already seen on pages 12c, 17a and 21c. It is that of the old Uayeyab god N with a hatchet in one hand and an unfamiliar object in the other like the one on page 39a, and with another unknown object on his back shaped like a shield marked with a Kin. That this figure is really meant to represent N follows from the fourth hieroglyph (which, however, is not his regular sign 5 Zac), which is repeated on the head of the figure. The lower part of the hieroglyph is replaced by the year-sign just as it is in the hieroglyph on page 47, left, middle. The third hieroglyph contains 2 Caban signs, the first and second cannot be clearly identified.

11. This is a deity which I hardly think appears elsewhere. It has an animal's head resembling that of a bear, thus recalling page 7a, and it also has the paws of a bear. Of the hieroglyphs only a Kin-Akbal is recognizable.

12. Page 38a. Here we have another heavenly shield (Mars and Venus?) and under this shield B is represented seated and strangely enough facing himself, the figures not being back to back as on page 68a. Hieroglyphs 1 to 3 are wholly and 4, which is a head, is for the most part destroyed.

13. B is here represented in very close connection with a female figure. Cf. pages 21c-23c. The representation on page 68b is a still closer parallel to this passage. The first hieroglyph is destroyed for the most part, the second is B, the third is probably only a determinative of the latter, but has the sign for the west, and the fourth is Kan-Imix.

14. B holding a Kan sign is sitting on an object, which may be meant for the stone on which the idols were set up at the change of the year. Of the hieroglyphs the third is again B, and the fourth is probably the frequent sign *a*. The first sign is the most remarkable. In the Zeitschrift für Ethnologie, Vol. XXIII, p. 147, I stated that this was the sign for the change of the year, which is its meaning on pages 41b, 52b and 68a. The Kan year follows here after the Cauac year of page 37. The prefix of the sign is the hieroglyph for the east to which the Kan years belong. The Kan sign in B's hand also corresponds to this. The second hieroglyph is destroyed.

15. Page 39. The picture represents the lightning-beast with two flaming torches walking under the heavenly shield (Mercury and Jupiter?). Of the hieroglyphs the third belongs to B, the fourth has as a prefix the sign of the storm-god K, but otherwise admits as little of determination as do the first and second.

16. Here we see B in the rain holding in one hand a machete, and in the other a strange implement similar to that on page 37a. Of the hieroglyphs the second was the god's sign, the third is *a*, and the fourth may be an Akbal sign with Kin. The first sign somewhat suggests the sign for the Moan; its prefix is curious.

17. Here in place of the picture and the superscription, owing perhaps to lack of space and in order not to omit the last picture, we have a vertical row of seven hieroglyphs interrupted between the sixth and seventh by the red and black numeral belonging here. The top sign is effaced and the second is B's. I will not venture to determine the third, which contains a Yax. Could it belong to the serpent deity H? The fourth is probably Kan-Imix and the fifth is indistinct. And the same is true of the sixth, the prefix of which we have already met with as the sixteenth hieroglyph on page 24, and shall meet with again on pages 53, 56, 58, 61, etc. The seventh sign, which is quite at the bottom, consists of a vessel with a foot-print beneath it; it seems to be in the place of the picture.

18. The entire section ends with a picture of B, who carries the hatchet and probably the copal pouch. The hieroglyphs are wholly obliterated.

Pages 40a—41a.

The following Tonalamatl, one of the form of 10 × 26, has suffered much from the carelessness of the scribe and from injury. I have attempted to restore it as follows:—

X	X 7	IV 4	VIII 4	XII 2	I 1	II 8	X
Ahau	Oc						
Cimi	Cib						
Eb	Ik						
Ezanab	Lamat						
Kan	Ix.						

The first row should be read from top to bottom, and then the second in the same order.

The six subdivisions all refer to some activity of B. Among the 6 × 4 hieroglyphs his sign occurs five times as the fourth and only in the last group as the third. Let us now examine the six groups individually.

1. B is traversing the water in a canoe, as on pages 29c and 40c, with the paddle in his hand. All the hieroglyphs belonging to him are obliterated.

2. B is sitting on the laterally elongated head q, which here, as on page 69, is enlarged and drawn with special care. Seler ("Charakter der aztekischen, etc. Handschrift" in the Zeitschrift für Ethnologie, 1888, p. 83) discusses this sign in connection with the day Men. It seems to me to denote unlucky days, the influence of which may here be checked by B. B holds in his hand a hatchet. The head (q) is repeated in the third sign, perhaps also in the second, and the superfix of these two signs is probably the same as that of the sign beneath the picture of B. The first sign is mostly destroyed.

3. As on pages 30a and 31c, and again just as on page 69a, B is sitting on the tree of life or sacrificial tree. A branch of this, which he grasps in one hand, ends in a serpent-head, and the root of the tree also represents B's head. Around the god's head are again the familiar dots, probably signifying stars. Of the hieroglyphs, the first is probably f, the second is destroyed, the third may be a variant of a, although it recalls the sign which, I believe, has the meaning of 73 days on pages 46-50; the prefix of 1 also suggests this meaning.

4. B's head is again surrounded by stars and he holds in one hand the outline of a hieroglyph. He is sitting on a peculiar ornamented structure resembling the crenelations of a wall. This wall displays the spiral which we found also on pages 33b-35b, and which in the treatise, "Zur Maya-Chronologie" (Zeitschrift für Ethnologie XXIII, p. 147), I regarded as an abbreviation for a serpent and hence as a symbol of time. It is further to be noted that B is wet with rain and with this the third hieroglyph is in keeping, if it is actually intended to denote the rainy season and not the week of 13 days ("Zur Entzifferung" V, 6); still the red numeral 13 below is more in keeping with the second meaning. The second sign is an Ahau with the leaf-shaped prefix, which also appears in the first sign of the third group. The first is effaced.

5. B, represented with a gala mantle hanging down in front and with the copal pouch, is sitting on a head, which looks like his own, especially as to the eyes, but which notwithstanding probably belongs to D and is marked with Ik (wind) and Cauac (cumulus clouds). Of the hieroglyphs the first and second do not admit of positive identification, and the third is Kan-Imix.

6. The god is sitting on a mat in a house. All the hieroglyphs except his own are obliterated.

Pages 42a—44a.

Another Tonalamatl of the form of 10 × 26; I have restored the effaced day-signs as follows: —

XIII	XIII 3	III 2	V 2	VII 6	XIII 2	II 2	IV 2	VI 7	XIII
Oc	Cib								

Ik   Lamat

Ix   Ahau

Cimi   Eb

Ezanab   Kan.

Thus the month days are the same as in the preceding Tonalamatl, but should be read in a different order:—Oc, Cib, Ik, Lamat, etc.

Here each of the 8 subdivisions has 6 hieroglyphs, and the order is as follows:—

1 2

3 4

5 6.

A few of these signs are common to all the groups. Thus the first sign (*v*), as far as what remains is distinguishable, seems to occur in all the groups. It has the leaf-shaped prefix, but I cannot understand the rest of it; we shall find it again several times on pages 29c-41c.

Again the sign in the sixth place, as far as we can see, is always the head without an underjaw and the tuft of hair tied up on top of it (O, according to Schellhas), which we found above on page 25 and which we shall meet again on pages 65-69 no less than 13 times, with regular intervals of 6 signs between them. Indeed that passage is a remarkable parallel to this one.

That the sign for B, who here too plays the most important part, occurs often, is self-evident. It appears in the fourth place, in the 1st, 3d, 4th, and 7th groups, and in the third of the 8th group; in the 6th group it is destroyed. In the 2nd and 5th groups B has neither picture nor sign.

The hieroglyphs of the cardinal points I shall mention in connection with the separate groups. They are especially conspicuous in this section, being sometimes represented in full and sometimes in an abbreviated form as mere prefixes.

1. B with arms crossed sits above a serpent denoting time, and holding in its coils the cross *b*, which so often refers to astronomical conditions. Above the head of the serpent is the vessel with the three Kan signs, which we have already found several times on pages 25-28. It is remarkable that the flourish, which usually appears as the nose-ornament of the sun-god G (*e.g.*, pages 11b and c), is added to these Kan signs. As the stars are again indicated on B's head, he plainly denotes a time-god here. The third hieroglyph, the sign of the east, corresponds with this meaning, and the Kan sign, which we see in the fifth hieroglyph probably combined with Ahau, also belongs to the east; the prefix of the fourth hieroglyph is the sign for the west.

2. A deity whom we shall probably have to call F, the god of human sacrifice, is sitting on a stepped pyramidal structure (a teocalli as a place of sacrifice?). He holds something in his hands, resembling a long and broad scroll, joined to which is the head of the god of the north, C, and in the third hieroglyph of this group the

sign for the north also appears, prefixed to the head of F, who seems to be repeated in the fourth hieroglyph. The fifth hieroglyph with an Imix is unintelligible to me.

3. Page 43. B is sitting in the water, the copal pouch hangs from his neck and the hatchet is raised as if ready to attack. The second hieroglyph clearly denotes water, while the third is the sign for the west and the fourth is the sign for B, its prefix being the sign for the east abbreviated; the order of the cardinal points is thus exactly the reverse of that in the first group. The fifth hieroglyph is not clear to me, but it appears to be repeated in the same place in the next group.

4. B is sitting here astride a sort of bench again holding the hatchet in his hand. Belonging to this picture in the third hieroglyph is the sign for the south, which is repeated in an abbreviated form in the fourth hieroglyph.

The fifth is Kan, joined to what appears to be the same sign as the one found in this place in the preceding group. The second sign is indistinct.

5. This is an aged deity, probably M according to Schellhas, seated on an indefinite object. In front of the deity is a Cauac sign, which contains exactly the same cumulus clouds as those in the sign 5 Zac, which belongs to N. Cauac, however, belongs to the south, and therefore corresponds with the north of the second group on page 42. Sign 5, a Kan, corresponds exactly with the same sign in the fifth place of the preceding group.

6. Page 44. B seems to be in a state of collapse. Behind him is a second person, who is either trying to support him or to pull him up by some kind of a sling. I think the second person is E, the grain-deity, if it is not Seler's young god. If the hieroglyphs were not completely effaced, they would probably shed some light on this interesting passage.

7. Here we see B, holding a fish in his hand, and sitting on a hieroglyph, which is compounded of Imix and a prefix, which resembles the tortoise head and which appeared once before in this combination on page 32a. This passage recalls page 40a, where B is seated on the laterally elongated head *q*. Nothing more can be said of the hieroglyphs, than that 6 is the head without an underjaw.

8. B is sitting here in a house; his sign in the third place has Yax as a prefix. Hieroglyph 5, with the number 4 prefixed, recalls the one which we found on page 21c belonging to the baldheaded old man. Hieroglyph 4 is the common Kan-Imix.

Page 45a.

The last page on the front of the first section of this Manuscript is used for a series, which presents itself as a second improved edition of the series which was found on pages 31a-32a. The very fact that the writing is so much better proclaims it an amendment. The chief aim of both series is the same, viz:—to bring into unison the numbers 91, 104, 260 and 364. But the two series gain this end by different means. On page 32 the series begins with 91, and at first has only 91 as a difference, until with 728 a multiple of 104 and 364 is obtained, then it returns to the simple difference 91, in 1456 it obtains again the 104 and 364, loses these two last numbers once more in 1820 and finally in 3640 obtains the desired multiple of all four numbers, which is retained in 7280, 14,560, 21,840 and 29,120. The series on page 45a proceeds much more briefly. It begins at once with 728 (91, 104, 364), loses the 104 in 1092, gains the 260 and loses the 104 in 1820, arrives at divisibility by all four numbers in the 3640, loses the 104 again in 5460, but then comes to a standstill after having obtained the same multiples (double at that) of 3640, which I mentioned just now in the preceding series. Indeed it can be seen from what is legible in the third column above, that the series went still further. But so much is obliterated that I have obtained the numbers 14,560 and 21,840 in both series only by conjecture.

In the earlier passage the starting-point of the series is the day XIII Akbal and in the one before us it is the day XIII Oc. In the former the days specified were 91 days apart from each other, and here they are separated by 104, *i.e.*, XIII Ezanab, XIII Ik, XIII Cimi, XIII Oc.

The initial days of the two series, XIII Oc-XIII Akbal, are separated by 13 days, and the reversed series, XIII Akbal-XIII Oc, by 247 days. Hence the subject of both passages is essentially the week of thirteen days, *i.e.*, the year of 364 (28 × 13) days.

Now this series is also accompanied by a number amounting to millions. It is in the second column of page 45; only, in order to understand it, we must add a zero as the bottom figure; then it becomes 1,278,420. XIII Oc stands below this number as the beginning of the series. The first column has 30 as an encircled number and below it the normal day IV Ahau.

The large number must have been formed as follows:—

The point of departure was 230, the interval between IV Ahau and XIII Oc, to this was added 98 × 260 = 25,480, the sum being 25,710. The result of this number added to 11 Ahau-Katuns = 1,252,680, was 1,278,390, which number is not revealed in the Manuscript. It is concealed in XIII Oc 3 Mol (2 Muluc). But 1,278,390 = 42,613 × 30, *i.e.*, it is divisible by the interval XIII Oc-IV Ahau.

Now if we add to this large number the 30 set down in the Manuscript, the result will be the above-mentioned 1,278,420. This number in the Manuscript has the date IV Ahau 13 Chen. (2 Muluc). It is, of course, divisible by 30 and by 260, hence = 42,614 × 30 and 4917 × 260. It corresponds not merely in this respect with the largest number on page 31a, viz:—2,804,100, but also with regard to its divisibility by 78, 156, 195, which are all multiples of 13.

On page 45a, top left, there were doubtless five hieroglyphs, of which the two topmost ones are effaced. First we see only the sign of the eleventh or twelfth month, Zac or Ceh, with an uncertain number prefixed, then the signs for beginning and end are distinctly legible. Ceh begins and Zac ends the year of 364 days; see page 4 of my treatise "Zur Entzifferung V."

Pages 29b—30b.

We come now to the middle section of pages 29-45, in which we shall not be so hampered by obliteration in our attempts at interpretation, as we were in the upper section.

We have here first a Tonalamatl of the usual kind, arranged as follows:—

III   13   III 13   III 13   III 13   III

Ix

Cimi

Ezanab

Oc

Ik.

That is to say, the 52 days divided into four equal parts.

To these four divisions, as on page 23b, belong the four usual forms of animal food, which are joined in three places to Kan (bread) and probably denote sacrifice. They are, first a mammal, which, however, is erroneously represented by a fish; second, a fish, third an iguana and lastly a bird. I would add, that in the hieroglyphs above, the east, north, west and south correspond in turn with these representations of food.

The hieroglyphs are arranged as follows: —

$$1 \quad 2 \qquad 5 \quad 6 \qquad 9 \quad 10 \qquad 13 \quad 14$$
$$3 \quad 4 \qquad 7 \quad 8 \qquad 11 \quad 12 \qquad 15 \quad 16.$$

Of these, 2, 6, 10 and 14 are the cardinal points just mentioned; 4, 8, 12 and 16 are the sign for B, and 1, 5, 9 and 13 are the head with the tuft of hair and the Akbal eye to which I attribute the meaning of *beginning*. Likewise the remaining four signs, 3, 7, 11 and 15, although they are not exactly alike, have something in common, the 15th being a distinct Imix; they are not yet wholly intelligible to me.

Four pictures of B belong to these hieroglyphs. In the first the god is seated with crossed arms on two of the ordinary astronomical signs (Jupiter and Mars?). In the second, where he is pointing forward with his hand, there are footprints on his seat, as, for example, on page 35a. In the third the seat contains the usual cumulus clouds in clusters. Finally, in the fourth, he is seated on the tree of life or of sacrifice, the hatchet is in his hand and he is clad in the gala mantle; cf. pages 31c, 40a, 69a.

Pages 30b—31b.

This passage is in some respects closely related to the preceding Tonalamatl, but in other respects it differs significantly from this and from what is usual, for the Tonalamatl is divided here into only four principal divisions of 65 days each, which begin very regularly with the days VIII Oc, VIII Men, VIII Ahau and VIII Chicchan. There are neither subdivisions nor the usual pictures belonging to them. But on the other hand each of the longer periods of time written down here have eight hieroglyphs for each section in the usual order.

B's sign occupies the places 6, 4, 4 and 4; from this it follows that here too he forms the principal subject.

Here, as in the preceding Tonalamatl, the first place in each group contains the sign denoting beginning, while the eighth sign is invariably the head without an underjaw, which seems to me to refer to *fasting*, as if a fast-day fell at the end of every 65 days.

In the fifth place we see in succession the four animals, which in the preceding Tonalamatl are not included in the groups of hieroglyphs. Here they stand in the order of mammal, bird, amphibian and fish, but the bird in the second group is replaced by the sign which usually occurs with the dog (lightning-beast).

The signs in the second place are those of the cardinal points, and they are given in the same order as in the preceding Tonalamatl, *i.e.*, east, north, west and south, so that they do not belong to the same animals as they do there.

The third signs are the cardinal points again, but in the abbreviated form discovered first by Schellhas, and in a different order:—west, north, east and south, and always joined to the head of C around which everything revolves as around the polar star. The Kan sign with different accompanying signs occupies the seventh place in the first group, and the sixth in the other three.

Four signs still remain:—the fourth of the first group I am inclined to consider the abbreviated sign for the sun; the seventh of the second, rain with the sign for the west as a prefix; the seventh of the third, Caban, ground, with the sign for the east as a prefix; the seventh of the fourth is Kan with the Yax sign above it, probably denoting the vegetable kingdom.

Pages 31b—35b.

This entire passage is devoted to a single Tonalamatl, which is divided and written out in an unusual manner. Like the preceding it is divided into four parts of 65 days each, but the remarkable thing about it is that these divisions of 65 days are each subdivided into two periods of 46 and 19 days, and the 46 days again into eight unequal parts, which are exactly the same each time, while the 19 days run their course without further subdivision. On pages 33, 34 and 35 this 19 is always on the left at the bottom, on page 32 it is wanting, probably because it was self-evident and there was no suitable place for it.

We shall next discuss the division of these four periods of 46 days each. This division is indicated with especial exactness on these pages, since not merely the length of the separate divisions and the week days are specified, but also the month days. This representation has the additional peculiarity, that the two columns on each page must be read from bottom to top, and of each group of two days standing side by side, the one on the right is to be read first and then the one on the left. If the Tonalamatl were written in the usual manner, it would have the following form:—

X   9 VI 9   II 9   XI 2   XIII 4   IV 9   XIII 4   IV 19   X

Ben

Ezanab

Akbal

Lamat.

Instead of this we read in greater detail as follows (the pages and the stated *length* of time are in parentheses): —

(31)	X Ben (9)	VI Ik (9)	II Chuen (9)	XI Ahau (2)
	XIII Ik (4)	IV Cimi (9)	XIII Men (4)	IV Cauac (19).
(32)	X Ezanab (9)	VI Manik (9)	II Cib (9)	XI Chicchan (2)
	XIII Manik (4)	IV Chuen (9)	XIII Ahau (4)	IV Kan (19).
(33)	X Akbal (9)	VI Eb (9)	II Imix (9)	XI Oc (2)
	XIII Eb (4)	IV Cib (9)	XIII Chicchan (4)	IV Muluc (19).
(34)	X Lamat (9)	VI Caban (9)	II Cimi (9)	XI Men (2)
	XIII Caban (4)	IV Imix (9)	XIII Oc (4)	IV Ix (19).

In spite of the seemingly wholly irregular division of time, the following relation, which is certainly not accidental, results from this arrangement: — the first of the eight members of each row is one of the days which may begin the year and the months, and the eighth, on the other hand, one of the four regents of the year. The remaining six members are the remaining 12 of the 20 days repeated twice and the second always corresponds with the fifth of its own series, and the third to the sixth and the fourth to the seventh of the following series.

Two pictures of god B belong to each of these periods of 65 days, the first of these pictures referring to the divided period of 46 days and the second to the undivided one of 19. It is also in agreement with this that on pages 61 and 62 the fourth, sixth and eighth pictures represent the god as rising from the jaws of a serpent — the serpent being represented each time as lying in water which invariably contains the number 19.

As the hieroglyphs belonging to the periods of 46 days are allied to one another, and as this is also true of those belonging to the periods of 19 days, I will first consider the hieroglyphs of the first period by themselves, then those of the second, and the pictures shall be treated in the same manner.

Therefore, let us first examine the four pictures (1, 3, 5 and 7) on the right side of the pages: —

1. The first page shows the god walking with the official staff in his right hand, in his left the hatchet raised for a blow and with the copal pouch hanging from his neck.

2. He is walking and holding a flaming torch reversed in his right hand, in his left the hatchet is raised aloft, the pouch hangs from his neck, the mantle is indicated and around his head are the little circles which are so frequently his adjuncts and probably signify stars.

3. He is walking and holding the reversed torch in his left hand and the hatchet in his right.

4. He is walking and holding a torch in each hand. He wears on his head the head of K. He seems to be bringing storm and fire.

Now let us examine the hieroglyphs, which I have numbered thus:—

1   3   5

2   4   6.

The first hieroglyph on each page certainly represents one of the cardinal points. They are in the usual order:—east, north, south and west.

2 is the same sign on each page. I take it to be the sign for Xul = end, denoting, it may be, the end of the period of each cardinal point.

In each group 3 is the head with tuft of hair and the Akbal eye; probably the sign denoting *beginning*. This beginning and end occur most distinctly repeated on page 63, and the end alone eight times at the bottom of pages 61-62.

On page 31, 4 is B's sign, on page 32 B's with the prefix of the north, on page 33 it is B's sign again and although quite indistinct its is plainly joined with the east. On page 34 there is another indistinct sign which may be that of the serpent deity H.

Owing to indistinctness I do not venture to determine the fifth sign on pages 31 and 33; on page 32 it is the laterally elongated head *q* with the Ben-Ik superfix, and on page 34 the ordinary Kan-Imix.

The sixth sign varies as much as the fifth; it seems here to denote four different gods, perhaps the four given on pages 25-28. On page 31 it is a Cauac, the prefix of which here, however, suggests K, on 32 it is certainly the hieroglyph of E and on 33 possibly of A, on 34 it most resembles Muluc of the day-signs, but also suggests the line crossing F's face from top to bottom.

We come now to the four pictures 2, 4, 6 and 8 and to the hieroglyphs belonging to them, which are on the left side of the pages and belong to the periods of 19 days.

1. B is pictured walking, raising the hatchet in his right hand, and holding an uncertain object in his left; the serpent with the 19 set down in its coils does not appear here. The 2nd, 3d and 4th pictures belong together. In each picture on these three pages there is a serpent with water in its coils and the number 19 in the water, denoting the number of days belonging here. As on pages 61 and 62 B is emerging from the open jaws of the serpent. In each case he is brandishing the uplifted axe in his left hand. The difference in the three pictures consists, first, in the fact that only in the 2nd and 3d B wears the copal pouch, second, that only in the 3d and 4th he has an implement in his right hand (the two implements differ somewhat but are both, apparently, adapted for hanging up) and third, that only in 3 the whole picture is painted blue, which means that the entire scene is enacted under water.

The hieroglyphs are as follows:—

The first in all four cases is a Manik, *i.e.*, originally a grasping hand, perhaps referring to the chase; on page 32 it has a prefix and on pages 33-35 a superfix corresponding to the first.

The second sign on each page is simply B's.

The Cauac sign in the third refers in all four cases to the water represented at the bottom of pages 33b-35b. On page 32 it has an Akbal as a superfix, on 33-35 a prefix, which is familiar and in keeping with the sign and probably also the same suffix, though it is indistinct on page 34.

The fourth sign shows, as do several other things, that the representation on page 32 differs from that on pages 33-35. On the first of these pages we see an Imix with a puzzling 1 prefixed. If the numbering of the days really begins with Kan, as is probable in this Manuscript, then Imix is the 18th day and 1 + 18 might denote the 19, which is not set down here. On pages 33-35 this sign contains the spiral, which refers to the serpent in the picture below (and probably therefore to time). A curious element, however, is the numeral 9 prefixed three times to the spiral. This number is rarely a prefix, but it occurs, for example, on pages 33a and 35a before the cross *b* and on page 60 right, middle, prefixed to Xul (= end). The interval 9 occurs in this Tonalamatl 16 times, including therefore 117 of the 260 days.

The fifth sign each time contains the head without the under jaw, just as it recurs regularly in the preceding passage, pages 30-31.

The sixth sign in each group is the not uncommon compound of Caban and the sign, which resembles Muluc and which we saw before in the sixth place among the hieroglyphs on the right side of page 34.

Pages 35b — 37b.

I		11	XII 6	V 9	I 4	V 7	XII 9	VIII 6	I

Caban

Muluc

Imix

Ben

Chicchan.

That is, a regular Tonalamatl of five parts, 5 × 52. That the 52 days are divided into two halves (11 + 6 + 9 = 4 + 7 + 9 + 6), may only be accidental.

I will designate the hieroglyphs of the seven divisions thus: —

1	2		5	6		9	10	13	14		17	18	21	22	25	26
3	4		7	8		11	12	15	16		19	20	23	24	27	28.

I will first consider those signs, which are repeated and by means of which the sections seem to be brought into connection with one another. But I shall attend in detail to those hieroglyphs which contain characteristic references to each picture, when I discuss the latter.

The first place both among the pictures and among the hieroglyphs again belongs unquestionably to B. He is plainly designated in the 10th, 17th, 21st and 26th hieroglyphs, but, for an unknown reason, C's sign is joined to B's in the 16th, probably also in the 6th and perhaps in the 9th, and in 20 and 28 C's sign forms an integral part of a hieroglyph. Now in discussing the great Tonalamatl, pages 4a-10a, I attempted to make it appear probable that C belongs to the eighth day (Chuen) and in that case the Chuen sign in the thirteenth hieroglyph may be probably set down here. Further, in discussing pages 25 to 28, I expressed the conjecture that this Chuen sign might simply mean eight days, if we begin with Kan as the first day, for which proceeding there is some warrant in the "Dresdensis." Now, in hieroglyphs 8 and 24 we find an 8 inscribed; in hieroglyph 8 it is joined to an Imix, exactly as on page 39c; on page 65a it is joined to Kin, and on 67a and 68a to a hand. Is it possible that here also the 8 is intended as a sign for Chuen = C?

Then the familiar Kin-Akbal sign (day and night) is in the fourth place as well as in the eleventh and nineteenth.

The other signs which appear but once, I will discuss in connection with each of the seven pictures:—

1. A serpent in the water, with B emerging from its head, exactly as on pages 36a, Tro. 26 and Cort. 10.

The third sign, that of the serpent-deity H, refers to the serpent. The first sign is the one which I think may be Caban-Muluc, while the second, owing to its indistinctness, eludes interpretation.

2. This also represents a deity sitting in the water, whom we are probably safe in calling H, for the top of his head changes into a serpent, ending, however, in a bird's bill holding a fish. The deity holds up both hands. The union of serpent and bird should be noted in connection with the fourth picture. The deity is represented in the fifth sign; the sixth, seventh and eighth signs have already been discussed.

3. B is traversing the water in a boat, exactly as on pages 29c, 40a and c, and 43c. Here, however, there is a person beside him (probably a woman) whom, from the ninth hieroglyph we recognize as the deity E, unless this sign is C's. In 12 we see with Kan a sign which may suggest the usual hieroglyph denoting a year.

4. A serpent is pictured here, with a bird sitting upon it. We met with the same bird on page 17b. Schellhas, "Maya-handschr.," p. 51, has already expressed the opinion that this is probably a rebus for the name Quetzalcoatl or Kukulcan, and this theory is certainly worthy of consideration. In this connection I would call to mind that it is probably also Kukulcan with serpent and bird who occupies the first place on page 4a. The bird appears again in the fourteenth sign, while the thirteenth is a Chuen, which, according to the statement made above, may be connected with the C in the sixteenth. The fifteenth sign is the cross *b*, which probably denotes the connection between the thirteenth and sixteenth or else between the bird and serpent. Or is Chuen intended here to represent the serpent and not the ape?

5. This picture represents B carrying a burning torch, with the copal pouch hanging from his neck. His left hand touches a strange object, a kind of frame, the top of which ends in the head of a bird of prey.

The eighteenth sign is obliterated and the twentieth is a curious combination of Caban, C and the front part of K.

6. B is walking, with the hatchet in his left hand and in his right an object which looks like the representation of sounds issuing from musical instruments, as on page 34a. Perhaps B is represented here as the air-god.

The twenty-second sign is the familiar Kan-Imix. The twenty-third sign (*w*) is not intelligible to me; it occurs on pages 19c, 40b, 58, on the right, with a superfix suggesting K.

7. Water, in which a small human being seems to be emerging from a snail (the symbol of birth). Above the water is B, grasping a serpent which is in the water, as if to protect the new-born being from the serpent. The twenty-fifth (with Kin) is the so-called bat-god, who on page 50 at the left ends the series of twenty gods. The twenty-seventh sign (with Yax) is still undetermined.

Pages 38b—41b.

VI	16	IX 8	IV 11	II 10	XII 1	XIII 12	XII 6	V 12	IV 11
		II 11	XIII 6	VI					

Cauac

Akbal

Manik

Chuen

Men.

The sum of the black numbers is 104, the whole is, therefore, a double Tonalamatl = 5 × 104 = 520. While the series on pages 31a-32a primarily brought the 91 and the 104 together, and the series on page 45a accomplished the same result with the 104 and the 364, here, though the process is a different one, the 104 is combined with the 260 in another number.

It is characteristic of this part of the Manuscript, that the astronomical rectangles, which are very rare in the preceding pages, appear here in no less than five of the eleven divisions and six of them represent showers of rain. One is very readily, therefore, led to infer that the 104 days have reference to the rainy season and to its dependence upon the position of the planets. I will now analyse the eleven sections separately.

1. Rain is streaming down from two astronomical signs (Mars and Jupiter? Day and night?) and in the rain stands a black human form, grasping an implement with the right hand held downward and pointing upward with the left. It has the vulture head which occurred on pages 8a and 13c.

Hieroglyphs 1 and 2 represent the sun and moon, both surrounded by half white and half black envelopes, which must denote clouds. The third sign is Imix, which just here might refer to the rainy season productive of nourishment. The fourth sign is the vulture head of the picture.

2. B is walking in the rain and holds in one hand a stick pointed at the lower

end. This is doubtless a farming implement, likewise occurring frequently in the Tro-Cort., which was used for making furrows or holes in the ground.

The second hieroglyph is B's, the first is Caban = earth, the fourth might be a compound of Caban and Muluc, referring to the rain, and the third is the familiar Kan-Imix, which, as the designation of food and drink, would be especially appropriate here.

3. B is apparently resting from tilling the soil, since he is sitting on a support consisting of the signs just spoken of, *i.e.*, Caban and Muluc (?).

The latter signs are repeated in the second hieroglyph, while the third is B's with the sun-glyph (?) prefixed; the first is the head apparently open on top with the Akbal eye, probably the sign for beginning, and the fourth is the familiar sign *a*, which I think signifies a good, auspicious day.

4. Page 39. This represents a violent shower of rain, which might be pronounced a cloud-burst. The old red goddess with tiger-claws and a serpent on her head is pouring water in a stream from a jug. The same goddess occurs on page 43b and on the last page, 74.

Her hieroglyph is the second; it is more distinct in the two other passages. The first part of the third hieroglyph is indistinct, and the second part is the hieroglyph denoting the year. The first hieroglyph is a head with the Akbal sign, and the fourth is the usual compound of Kin and Akbal.

5. The cloud-burst seems to have destroyed the cultivation of the field, for B walks forth again with the implement for tilling the soil, as in the second picture. The second hieroglyph is B's with the prefix of the west, therefore probably denoting sunshine, the first again contains Caban and Muluc and the fourth is Kan-Imix referring again to the produce of the field. I shall not venture to explain the third sign here any more than I did in the previous passages. Compare page 8b.

6. B is again sitting in the rain and under the same astronomical signs as before on page 38. He is pointing downward (to the sprouting seed?). He has the sun-glyph on his back. The first two hieroglyphs are unfamiliar to me (Yax); the third is Imix with the sign for the west, and the fourth is again Muluc.

7. Page 40. B is plunging down headfirst from the same astronomical signs and is brandishing the hatchet.

Hieroglyph 1 is the cross *b*, 2 is B's sign, 3 probably that of the grain-god E, and 4 being Kan-Imix refers to grain. Favorable weather seems to have set in.

8. The astronomical signs are not the same as those in the three preceding instances (Mercury and sun?). Below them is a deity with tortoise-head—in my opinion, the sign for the longest day—holding a torch in each hand and thus referring to the heat.

Hieroglyph 1 (*w*) with the superfix suggesting K still puzzles me. 2 is the cross *b*, 3 is the tortoise-head with the number 4, which probably refers to the Kan, Muluc, Ix and Cauac years, as the 4 sometimes appears prefixed to N's hieroglyph. In exactly the same way the tortoise-head with the tortoise itself occurs frequently in the Cortesianus. 4 is the sign of the year with prefixed Kin and Cauac, *i.e.*, day-Cauac-year.

9. A thunder-storm, which is very appropriate after the longest day. The lightning-beast, likewise holding a burning torch, is plunging down from the astronomical signs, which are different ones again (Venus and the moon?).

The second hieroglyph contains the sign of the dog together with the cross *b*, while the third is that of the north-god C, and the fourth is Muluc. I cannot explain the first sign; its prefix, which rarely occurs, appears also on pages 23b, 25a, 37b, 63a, and possibly on pages 53b, 62-63a, 69b.

10. Page 41. Another representation of rain. There is an old deity in the rain, who is N rather than F, denoting the end of the old year. He is emerging from a snail (cf. with this page 37b), and is pointing upward; a part of the first hieroglyph is on his head.

This first hieroglyph recalls the sign which, in the Zeitschrift für Ethnologie, XXIII, p. 145, I ventured to connect with the change of the year; but it also suggests the snail pictured below, hence the birth of the new year. The beginning of the year for the Mayas, although of course not for all parts of the country, is fixed, as a rule, to fall on the 16th of July. This would agree admirably with the eighth and ninth sections, which represent the time of the longest day and of thunder-storms.

The second hieroglyph is B's, the fourth the cross *b*, probably referring here to a union of two years, and the third with its Cauac to the duration of the rainy season or to the god N.

11. The rain seems to fall with less violence. B is seated, clad in the gala mantle with a Kan on his head, as the sign of grain. His headdress also strongly recalls that of the grain-deity E (which is also the case of the headdress on the preceding picture.)

Hieroglyph 1, the upper part of which is very like that of the first sign of the preceding group, looks like a plaited mat. Does it not suggest that the name of the first month of the new year is Pop and that this word is denoted by carpet, mat? Hieroglyph 2 is B's, 3 is the sun between a dark and a bright sky, and 4 is the common Kin-Akbal, day and night.

If the seventh picture really refers to the beginning of the year, then the entire period of 104 days extends from April 15th to August 2nd, which, with the addition of the five days not counted at the end of the year, does indeed make 109 days. All this, however, is only true on the supposition that I have not seen more in these representations than they contain.

Pages 41b—43b.

VI   12 V 7 XII 6 V 21 XIII 6 VI.

Caban

Muluc

Imix

Ben

Chicchan.

Another regular Tonalamatl, and like the preceding one apparently referring to the change of the year, the tilling of the soil and the rainy season. B's sign is regularly repeated in the second place of all five groups of hieroglyphs, and moreover each of these groups has six signs. The head with the missing under jaw is in the fourth place of groups 2 and 3, in the sixth of group 5 and might perhaps be intended also in the fourth of 1 and 4. The usual Kan-Imix is in the third sign of group 2, in the fifth of 4, and the fourth of 5; possibly also in the fifth of 1; the third hieroglyph in group 3, at any rate, contains Imix.

Let us now consider the five groups individually:—

1. The rainy season seems to have been delayed; the beginning of the year draws near. B is kneeling on a kind of footstool, the hatchet is in his right hand and his left hand holds a kind of chisel with which he is carving something out of the trunk of a tree. The purpose of the work is indicated by the god's own head directly below (probably placed in front of the tree as a model?). No doubt this is intended to represent the making of the statue of the god of the new year destined for the beginning of the year, as we know it from pages 25-28.

Corresponding with this is the first hieroglyph denoting the year with Yax as a superfix, and also the sixth being the sign to which in the article in the Zeitschrift für Ethnologie cited above, I attributed the meaning of change of the year. I cannot decide whether the third sign is intended for an Imix-Chuen with the sign of the south as a superfix, the fifth for a Kan-Imix and the fourth for the head without the under jaw.

2. Page 42. Prayer for rain. B (that is to say, his priest) is seated apparently on the same footstool. He is gazing upward and presenting a vessel containing an offering, the nature of which is uncertain. The vessel ends in a tube; cf. page 67b.

The first, fifth and sixth hieroglyphs are not finished, and the third is Kan-Imix.

3. The rain-goddess promises aid. B is seated opposite the old red goddess, who is holding intercourse with him. The god is seated on the Caban sign (earth) and the goddess on Muluc (rain?).

The first, fifth and sixth hieroglyphs are also unfinished; the third is Imix with its meaning intensified by the prefixed Yax (the luxuriantly growing grain?).

4. B is again tilling the ground in the manner already familiar to us. Under him lies his own head with the Imix-Kan sign, denoting food and drink, as a superfix. The first hieroglyph is the sign of the eighteenth month Cumhu, *i.e.,* of the end of the year. The third is a Kin-Akbal, the fifth a Kan-Imix, the sixth is not finished, and the fourth may be intended for the head without the lower jaw, but it is carelessly drawn.

5. Page 43. The solicited rain begins. The goddess with the serpent on her head is pouring streams of water from her vessel.

The first hieroglyph repeats the month Cumhu, denoting the beginning of rain, before the close of the year; the third is the sign of the goddess met with on page 39b, here also with the sign for the west as a prefix; the fifth is her determinative, the serpent, and the fourth is Kan-Imix.

If the first sign in the first group is not regarded as the sign of the year, but as that of the sixteenth month (Pax) resembling it, and the fact is taken into consideration that there is an interval of 34 days between the second and fourth groups and of 40 days between the second and fifth, this would be found to correspond with the interval between the months Pax and Cumhu.

Pages 43b—44b.

This is the fourth and last series of the first part of the Manuscript; the first is on page 24, the second on pages 31a to 32a, and the third on page 45a. The first series is quite by itself, but the second and third are similar in form to this fourth, though their initial days are different from those of the latter:—XIII Akbal, XIII Oc and III Lamat. All three begin with differences which are divisible by 13:—91, 104 and 78, equal to 7, 8, and 6 × 13. All three aim and arrive at numbers which are common factors of 260, 104 and 364, and therefore also of 3640, which last number is written out in the other two series, while in this series it can only appear later on and then, increased by multiplication.

Since this series has the difference 78, the week day numbers remain the same, while those of the month days must advance by 18 each, that is, from the hidden starting-point III Lamat they go on to III Cimi, III Kan, III Ik, III Ahau, etc., until the tenth member of the series is 10 × 78, *i.e.*, 3 × 260 and thus comes again to the day III Lamat.

From 780 onward this number is itself always the difference of the higher terms of the present series. At the same time 780 days are the duration of the apparent revolution of Mars, which is here supplementary, as it were, since page 24 treated of the revolutions of the sun and of Venus, and also of those of the moon and of Mercury. Hence in the present passage we find the numbers 1560, 2340, 3120 and 3900, always accompanied by the day III Lamat. The larger numbers require a few corrections; I read them 13,260 (17 × 780), 15,600 (20 × 780), 31,200 (40 × 780), 62,400 (80 × 780) and 72,540 (93 × 780). The very largest again are correctly set down; first 109,200 equal to 140 × 780, but here also equal to 1050 × 104 and 300 × 364, so that in this series the goal aimed at is not reached until later than it is in the two preceding series. Then follows 131,040 = 168 × 780, 1260 × 104, 360 × 364, but finally 151,320, which number = 1455 × 104 and 194 × 780, but is not divisible by 364.

Detached in the usual way from this series on the left of page 43 is the number 1,435,980. Above and below it is the day III Lamat, further down IV Ahau, and between them is 352 in a red circle. This number seems to have been obtained in the following way:—The writer began with the distance between III Lamat and IV Ahau, which is 92, added to it 172 × 260 = 44,720, and subtracted the result 44,812 from 13 Ahau-Katuns = 1,480,440. The remainder was 1,435,628, which number would correspond to the date III Lamat 6 Zotz (4 Kan), which, however, is suppressed in the Manuscript. The 352 = 260 + 92 was added to this sum, and the result was the 1,435,980 written out in the Manuscript, *i.e.*, a day IV Ahau 13 Zip (5 Muluc). Now this number is the one sought; it is 5523 × 260 = 1841 × 780 = 3945 × 364, and hence must also be equal to 263 × 5460, since the 780 and 364 are united in 5460. According to our present knowledge, it would seem to lie in the future, but not far from the present; the solar and Mars revolutions are united in it. There is but a single hieroglyph here, the hieroglyph of the animal which is the chief subject of the next section; from which it appears that the two sections are closely connected.

Pages 44b — 45b.

This section supplements the pictures and hieroglyphs belonging to the series just examined. Therefore it likewise extends over 78 days and divides them as follows: —

III 19   IX 19   II 19   VIII 21   III.

These five days are plainly intended to be the days III Lamat, IX Manik, II Cimi, VIII Chicchan, III Cimi.

With regard to the real purport of this section, it is my opinion that it has reference to the time of the shortest day and also to the four winds and that this section therefore forms, in a measure, a contrast to pages 38-41, where attention was called to the rainy season, the longest day and the thunderstorms.

We see here in the first place four of the ordinary heavenly shields, with two astronomical signs each. I cannot decide, at present, whether these are 1st, the moon and Saturn, 2nd, Mars and Mercury, 3d, the moon and Mars, and 4th, Jupiter and Venus.

From each of these shields hangs a figure not unlike an heraldic beast. It cannot be the canine lightning-beast; it has no flames, it is cloven-footed and with the upper lip bent upward and the lower lip curved downward suggesting the storm-god K, and therefore probably represents the four winds; this wind-beast repeated four times also occurs on Cort. 2.

Six hieroglyphs belong to each picture. Those in the first place are pierced ears and refer therefore to the ritual bloodletting, which may have been performed at this season. In Tro. 5*b we also find the pierced ear; a pierced *tongue* (Tro. 17*b), however, does not occur in the Dresdensis. The second place always contains the sign of the beast like the one instance on page 43.

The third place seems to be devoted to the four cardinal points, *i.e.*, to the four winds. First we see Akbal-Kin, *i.e.*, the transition from night to day, the east. The north-god, C, is here in the second group; in the third we see Kin and beside it in the fourth place Akbal, both enveloped by clouds denoting the transition from day to night, the west. The fourth group, it is true, has the year-sign here, but with the compound Kin-Cauac prefixed, and Cauac always belongs to the south. I believe I have found a distinct reference to the season of the year in two other places. The fourth hieroglyph of the second group and the sixth of the fourth both have the familiar prefix suggesting K, the storm-god. The first of the two contains the month

Mol (December 3d-22nd); the second might very well be the month Yax (January 12th-31st). This is quite in keeping with the distances 19 + 21 = 40 set down below.

In my "Tagegöttern der Mayas" (Globus LXXIII, 10) and above in my discussion of the great Tonalamatl under pages 4a-10a, I have assigned the day Chuen to C, and Muluc to K, *i.e.*, the first to the dark north and the latter to the wind, which are both under consideration here. In fact, we find the Chuen sign in the fifth place of the fourth group with the same prefix that C has in the second group. The Muluc sign, however, seems to occur three times:—1st, group 1, sign 6, where it may be joined to the month Mol belonging here; 2nd, group 3, sign 5, joined to the Akbal, which also belongs here; 3d, group 4, sign 4, with a usual prefix. In the second group it may be included in the very similar month sign of Mol. Four hieroglyphs remain:—1st, Akbal in group 1, sign 5, hence probably denoting the darker time of the year in general; 2nd, A in 2, sign 5; 3d, E in 2, sign 6; *i.e.*, probably referring to the death of the grain (I do not know to what extent this expression may be used in relation to the Maya country); 4th, Kan-Imix in 3, sign 6, perhaps expressing the hope of new harvests.

This finishes the middle sections of the pages of the first part of the Manuscript, and we must now turn back again to page 29 in order to examine the lower sections.

Pages 29c—30c.

III		16	VI 16	IX 16	XII 17	III
Ix						
Cauac						
Kan						
Muluc.						

Here is a Tonalamatl of four quarters, 4 × 65.

In the Manuscript 16 is again erroneously set down for 17 and the III following it is omitted. The initial day is exactly the same III Ix, as in section 29b above it, to which in other respects the passage now under consideration shows a great likeness, since the four familiar animals occur here as well as there. But in spite of beginning in the same way the days here are different ones, being the four regents of the year, as on page 9b.

The four parts are grouped together by the sign, which always occupies the first place in each part; I have denoted this sign by *f*, and I think it must have a very general significance, since from pages 29c to 40c it always begins the groups. The connection between the four parts is further shown by the four cardinal points in the second place:—the north in the first group, the west in the second, the south in the third and the east in the fourth. In the third place these cardinal points are again indicated by their usual abbreviations; the east is erroneously set down in the second group. These abbreviations are here invariably joined to the head of C as the representative of the north, the first of the cardinal points occurring in this passage; the others revolve about the north pole.

As B's sign always occurs in the fourth place, there is nothing further to be said concerning the hieroglyphs. We now come to the pictures:—

1. B is rowing a boat, as we have already seen him several times (36b, 40a, *c*, and 43c). To the left of his head there is a bird's head and in the left, bottom, corner, a pot in which apparently a soup of fowl is cooking, emitting bubbles. The Cib sign on the pot refers to the cooking or bubbling.

2. B, with his head surrounded by the familiar stars, is seated in water, in which are represented the iguana over a Kan sign, and the familiar spiral probably denoting a serpent. He is painted black (perhaps corresponding to the west?) and holds in his hand an implement not yet determined. Perhaps it may be intended for a tree, *past* which the water is flowing.

3. The god is seated, holding in one hand the spiral with a Kin sign over it and a Yax on top of that, and in the other hand something which looks like a bird's feather or a fish's fin. Above him is a fish with a Kan sign, as on page 27, where the fish and Kan are also combined.

4. Holding a hunting-spear, he is sitting on an animal slain in the chase, as on page 45c.

Finally, I have remarked that pages 42c-45c, the last part of the first division of the Manuscript, look like an enlargement or amendment of the section just considered.

Pages 30c—33c.

To begin with, the day signs are set down in the following order:—

XI	XI	XI	XI
Ahau	Chicchan	Oc	Men
Caban	Ik	Manik	Eb
Ix	Cauac	Kan	Muluc
Chuen	Cib	Imix	Cimi
Lamat	Ben	Ezanab	Akbal.

Here then, as is frequently the case in this Manuscript, all the twenty days are specified. But in order to obtain equal periods of time, the left column should first be read from top to bottom and the following ones should be treated in the same way. Then each succeeding day is 17 days distant from the preceding, but in reality the interval is 117 days, since the same week-day is always implied. The hieroglyphs seem to indicate that these 117 days are divided into three distinct parts, 52, 39 and 26.

117 days, however, are equal to 9×13 and hence in what follows we find a black 13 set down 9 times as the interval between the days, and a red XI being the number of the week-day an equal number of times. Now, since the whole series extends over 20 such sections of 117 days, the duration of this calendar is 2340 days or 9 Tonalamatl.

Consequently we find nine pictures of the same god B. In five of them (in Groups 1-4 and 9) he is sitting before or on a sacrificial tree or tree of life; cf. 30b. It is probably not accidental that in these five cases the hieroglyphs refer to the cardinal points. In the eighth group the god is surrounded by the suggestion of one or more trees; he is sitting in water as if in a forest; or in a cave bordered by trees? In the remaining groups, 5, 6 and 7 he is seated on various supports, in 5 on an object, which is not completed and which cannot, therefore, be explained, in 6 on astronomical figures (Mars and Venus?) and in 7 on agave leaves. In 1 and 3 his head is again surrounded by those dots suggesting stars, in 4 there seems to be a bird (quetzal?) seated upon it and in 2 it bears what may be the Kin sign. In 1 and 5 he has the pouch for incense in his hand, while in 3 alone he wears the gala mantle and is painted black, just as he appears in connection with the same hieroglyphs on page 29c. He carries a hatchet in repose in 2, 6 and 9, and raised for a blow in 1 and 7. In 7 he also holds the Imix sign.

The hieroglyphs form nine groups of four signs each. The first hieroglyph, as is always the case in this part of the Manuscript, is the sign which I have denoted by f, and the second is always B's hieroglyph. The cardinal points are everywhere specified by two signs each; in places 3 and 4 of group 1, the west comes first and beside it is the sign for the east, erroneously used for that of the west (a like error occurred in the preceding Tonalamatl); in group 2 there are two signs for the north; in group 3 that for the east with the sign for the west beside it erroneously given for the east, and in group 4 two signs for the south. In groups 5, 6 and 7 we find in the 4th place the head of C, and the same sign in group 7 in the 3d place, where it is joined to another head, which may be that of a woman. The 3d sign of group 5 is incomplete and cannot be determined. The 3d sign of group 6 displays a repetition of the astronomical signs represented below. There still remain the 3d and 4th signs of groups 8 and 9. Of these the 3d in group 8 is w, which is as yet unexplained. The 4th might be interpreted either as Oc (day 7) or as Xul (end). Its prefix is a Yax sign. Finally, in group 9 the 3d sign is Manik (day 4), the 4th the elongated head q with the Ben-Ik superfix, which Seler assigns to Men (day 12).

Pages 33c—39c.

The beginning of this Tonalamatl is indicated by a large red dot on page 33. It resembles the Tonalamatl almost exactly above it on pages 31b-35b, inasmuch as its arrangement is an unusual one. I will here, as I did above, give it the form in which it would present itself if it were set down in the usual order:—

XIII		9	IX 11	VII 20	I 10	XI 15	XIII
Ahau							
Chicchan							
Oc							
Men.							

In this passage as in the earlier one, instead of employing the above concise order, a preference has been shown throughout for carrying out the whole series in such a manner that the week days are set down each time and not merely in the left column. It, therefore, has the following form in the Manuscript:—

XIII Ahau (9)	IX Muluc (11)	VII Ahau (20)
XIII Chicchan (9)	IX Ix (11)	VII Chicchan (20)
XIII Oc (9)	IX Cauac (11)	VII Oc (20)
XIII Men (9)	IX Kan (11)	VII Men (20)

I Ahau (10)	XI Oc (15)
I Chicchan (10)	XI Men (15)
I Oc (10)	XI Ahau (15)
I Men (10)	XI Chicchan (15)

I have arranged the whole series in four parallel periods of 65 days each, for the 65 appears throughout the computation, although the entire Tonalamatl is written out in *one* continuous line. On the right of page 35 the scribe seems to have wished to erase an entirely incongruous 4, and in writing the last 15, on page 39, he began to use the red paint prematurely, so that the top one of the three lines is red.

Attention should also be called to the fact that the second of my vertical columns contains the year-regents, the others only the days following immediately after them, while 12 month days do not occur at all. Also the intervening periods 9 + 11 (= 20), 20, 10, 15 doubtless reveal some design.

In order to avoid repetition, I think it proper to mention first, that in the twenty groups of four hieroglyphs each, the sign *f* always stands in the first place, but the hieroglyph of B, who is represented 20 times, usually appears in the second place, in the first and second groups in the third place, and in the 18th and 19th his sign does not appear at all. I will discuss the remaining hieroglyphs in their place in each of the 20 groups.

1. B is sitting in a house and holding the Kan sign in his hand.

The second hieroglyph is apparently meant for the Ahau sign (referring to the 17th day), which usually does not belong to B. This hieroglyph, which certainly bears a resemblance to Ahau and with which we have become very familiar in the inscriptions, occurs again in this Manuscript on pages 46b, c, 50b, 54b, 65a and 66a. The fourth sign is a combination of Cauac and Manik.

2. B is seated on what may be a tree, below him is the cross *b*, and he holds the hatchet in his left hand.

The second sign with an emphasized 6 as a prefix (cf. the same sign with the 6 on page 48, bottom, left, below the gods), has the usual Ben-Ik superfix, perhaps to denote that a lunar month has now elapsed, for this passage extends from the 20th to the 40th day of the Tonalamatl. The rest of the hieroglyph is unintelligible. In the 4th place we see a vessel with Imix, probably denoting pulque.

3. B is sitting in water, the hatchet raised in his right hand and his face turned upward.

The 3d hieroglyph is again Imix and the 4th a compound of Ik and Muluc:—wind and clouds.

4. B is seated on a reproduction of his own head or D's, beating a drum with his hand.

The 3d hieroglyph denotes the serpent-god H with the number 3 as a prefix. The 4th hieroglyph is a Chuen with the sign for the south prefixed,—at any rate the upper part of that sign.

5. B is standing in the pouring rain and looking backward.

The 3d sign here is a Caban apparently in a vessel. Following this in 4 is the hieroglyph which I have proposed to interpret as the sign for *beginning* (Globus, Vol. LXVI, page 79). This sign occurs again in groups 7, 12, 15, 17 and 19, and must therefore be connected with the principal idea embodied in this Tonalamatl.

6. B with folded arms is sitting in a house.

Aside from the usual leaflike prefix, the third sign is composed of two parts. The upper part looks like a plaited mat and suggests that the word for the first month of the year (Pop) is expressed by mat. The lower part is the sign, which occurs frequently especially on pages 25-28, and which very much resembles the familiar sign for a year of 360 days. We shall meet it again in the continuation of this Tonalamatl on pages 36 and 38. The three passages refer to the 74th, 139th, and 204th days of the Tonalamatl, and hence are 65 days apart.

The 4th sign is the cross *b*, with possibly the sign of the east as a prefix.

7. B is seated on the cross *b*, which is here undoubtedly meant for an astronomical sign. He holds a Kan sign in his hand and there is an Ahau sign on his back.

The naked crouching personage, pointing upward, should have especial mention here. The same figure recurs above as a prefix to the 4th hieroglyph. We have already seen it in the 39th hieroglyph on page 24, and shall meet it with especial frequency in the second part of the Manuscript. It is placed sometimes, as in this case, *before* a sign, sometimes *after* a sign and again two of these figures are placed back to back as on page 22c, and one of them is even placed upside down before another sign, where it seemed to me to be a sign for Mercury ("Zur Entzifferung VII," p. 11). This figure is represented independently only on the right of page 58. In the passage under present consideration this personage appears again on page 38. The two figures are connected one with the 85th and the other with the 215th day, and are, therefore, divided by exactly half a Tonalamatl or 130 days. Here we find it as a prefix of the supposed sign for *beginning* of which mention was made in discussing the 5th group. The 3d sign is the same astronomical one, which we saw below under B. It might refer to the Moan and to the change of the year, and thus indicate that a Mercury revolution was coincident here with the beginning of the solar year.

8. B is walking in the rain, both arms are stretched upward, and the pouch hangs from his neck. At the left top there is a black spot suggesting those which usually occur beside the sun and moon.

The 3rd sign is Manik, with a prefix. The 4th is an indistinct head, which may be C's, with an Imix sign as a prefix.

9. B is walking with the pouch hanging from his neck, and the hatchet in his hand.

The 3d sign, which is unusual, is very obscure, but suggests the fish on page 44c or that on page 36b. The 4th sign with the prefix of the north is very indistinct.

10. B is standing in *water*, his face turned upward while water is pouring from a cloud. The third sign is very complex. The top, left, suggests a serpent, the right a hand, the bottom, left, a Chuen and the element at the bottom, right, may be intended for a bird's head. Exactly the same sign, with the 4th part merely indicated, occurs 65 days later on page 38. The 4th sign is the familiar compound Kin-Akbal.

11. B is sitting in a tent, on the roof of which there is a vessel containing food of some kind.

The third sign, which is very complex, is indistinct. The 4th sign likewise consists of four parts, the left, bottom, part is probably the vessel, above it is a spiral (which usually means serpent or time). The right, bottom, is again the sign resembling the year-sign which was spoken of in discussing group 6. The component at the right, top, is indistinct.

12. B is sitting here on no less than four astronomical signs, he has the hatchet in his hand and the design on his back may be a shield or the elaborately ornamented sun-glyph Kin.

The third sign (denoting *beginning*?) has already been discussed in connection with group 7, which is 65 days earlier. The fourth is the sign of the year of 360 days or the month Pax with the Ben-Ik as a prefix. These signs are here suggestive of the beginning and end of the year.

13. *Above* B are astronomical signs (Jupiter and Mercury?) and also the sun and moon. The rain is pouring down upon the god, and a fish is placed beside him. He seems to have the same chisel in his hand which we saw him using on page 41b in connection with the beginning of the year. This again would correspond to the date indicated in the preceding picture. The shield (?) also is the same here as in the preceding group.

The third sign ought to represent the fish; the drawing seems to have been unsuccessful and the sign looks more like a bird and also resembles the third sign in the ninth group on page 36. The fourth sign is a Kin-Akbal.

14. B is seated on the elongated head *q*, which has an ordinary prefix. He is pointing upward with his right hand and the left looks as if opened to receive something.

The third hieroglyph contains a *q* like the one under the god, the fourth is an indistinct head (C's?) with an unintelligible prefix.

15. B is standing in water while rain is again pouring down upon him. He holds the hatchet raised in his left hand, while the fingers of the right are extended upward in an unusual manner. This is repeated in the third hieroglyph.

The third hieroglyph, however, is the same as the third in the tenth group 65 days earlier, only here the hand is more distinct, while the element below it is vague. The fourth sign is again the one denoting beginning. Compare the fifth group (130 days earlier).

16. B with arms folded is sitting in a house with the Cauac sign below.

The third and fourth hieroglyphs contain the sign resembling that for the year, which was mentioned in discussing the sixth group (130 days earlier). In the third a Kin is prefixed to this sign, while the superfix of the fourth is what I take to be a mat, which also occurred in the sixth group. The prefix is a figure suggesting the serpent-deity, which we have already met with in the tenth and fifteenth groups.

17. B, holding the hatchet, is seated on a Moan head, and the third sign is probably intended to represent the same Moan head, in front of which we find the same crouching person met with in the seventh group, 130 days earlier.

The fourth hieroglyph is again the sign for beginning, which we have already often met with, as, for example, 65 days earlier in the twelfth group.

18. B is sitting in the pouring rain under astronomical signs (Mars and Mercury?) to which those of the sun and moon are added. The god's face is upturned and he holds the hatchet in his hand.

The third hieroglyph may be the vulture head, to which a part of the unintelligible second hieroglyph may also refer. This second sign stands in the place of B's hieroglyph, which is wanting here.

The fourth sign contains the enigmatical numeral 8, which we found on pages 36b and 37b, and has the Imix sign as a prefix, as in the first of these two passages. The same compound appears on pages 67a-68a.

19. B is seated here on his own head, as in the fourth group he is sitting on D's. His hands are empty.

The second sign is again the vulture head instead of B's hieroglyph. The third is probably the head of the lightning beast, and the fourth is again the sign supposed to denote beginning.

20. B is sitting in water and holding in his hands a vessel with a Kan sign upon it.

The water (with Imix prefixed) is denoted by the third sign, while the fourth represents a head (with what is probably a hand pointing to the right above it), which I should prefer to consider the grain-deity E.

In conclusion I would call attention to the remarkable fact that every four pictures, which are separated from each other by four of the other pictures, *i.e.*, after every 65 days, correspond in certain respects with one another, *viz:*—

1. Pictures 1, 6, 11 and 16. In all, and *only* in these, B is sitting in a house or tent, in 6 and 16 with his arms folded.

2. Pictures 2, 7, 12 and 17. In the first three the god is seated on astronomical signs and in the fourth on the Moan head, which I think refers to the Pleiades.

3. Pictures 3, 8, 13 and 18. Here in the last two B is sitting *beneath* astronomical signs. In all four pictures water, clouds and rain are represented.

4. Pictures 4, 9, 14 and 19. In the first and fourth the god is seated on D's head and on his own, and in the third on the elongated head *q*.

5. Pictures 5, 10, 15 and 20. Like the third of these five classes, these pictures are likewise distinguished by water, clouds and rain.

Now the first set of pictures is between the week days XIII and IX, the second between IX and VII, the third between VII and I, the fourth between I and XI, the fifth between XI and XIII, while the month days are quite different. Hence the conjecture is but natural that the pictures and week days bear some relation to one another, though that relation is still shrouded in obscurity.

Pages 40c—41c.

I   10   XI 10   VIII 10   V 10   II 3   V 9   I

Ahau

Eb

Kan

Cib

Lamat.

This is a Tonalamatl of the most ordinary kind, in which an unsuccessful attempt has been made to divide the subdivisions into equal parts.

In the groups of four hieroglyphs each, which belong to each of the six parts, the sign *f* always occupies the first place, and B the third. Let us now examine the six parts separately.

1. B is sitting in a boat and rowing (as on the top of the same page). Around his head there is again the suggestion of what may denote the starry sky, and in this picture his nose-peg is unusually large.

The second sign is an Imix, but it might also denote the thirteenth month Mac and therefore the Tonalamatl (13 × 20). The fourth sign is a fish forming a connecting link between the water represented below and the rest of the group.

2. B is seated on the Caban sign and his arms are apparently resting on an altar standing in front of him, on which fire is burning, indicated by the Ik sign, while the moon is placed below the altar.

The Caban sign below is repeated in the second hieroglyph, combined here as usual with a sign which may be Muluc.

The fourth sign is a head. I think the scribe meant to set down an 8 before it, but as there was not sufficient space for the heavy line *after* the three small circles, he indicated it by a black dot *below* the circles. Now, if we call the head D's, which of course cannot be asserted positively, this would be day VIII Ahau, and this, in fact, is twenty days from the beginning day I Ahau, as it is meant to be in this passage. There is no representation of food; can this have been a fast day?

3. B is seated on four astronomical signs. He wears the gala mantle and holds a serpent in his hand.

The second sign is *b*, and at the same time one of the astronomical signs. The fourth is the iguana prepared as food, recognizable by the spines on its back, as on page 25b. It is drawn in precisely the same curious fashion in Cort. 8 and 12c; hence it is represented in the picture by the serpent.

4. B is falling down from above headfirst. I believe that the numerous footprints below him are only intended to represent swift motion. The descent from above may only be intended here to bring the god into closer relationship with the head of the bird of prey in the fourth sign. That this head is again as usual joined to Kan, may refer merely to the fact that it was the Maya custom to eat bread with animal food. Compare page 27b. The second sign might be the abbreviation for the south.

5. B is seated on a mat with his hand extended as if to receive something. He is wet with water.

The second sign contains the mat, with what may be the sign below it, and the leaf-shaped prefix probably denoting the plant from which the mat is plaited. The very same combination is given on page 35c and a similar one on 38c. The fourth sign has the prefix of the west followed by two Kans, as if on this day (V Akbal) it had been the custom to eat tortillas without meat.

6. B is standing holding the hatchet. The fourth sign must denote venison, the fourth article of animal food. The second seems to represent the day Eb, with which the remaining 52 days begin, and if the prefixed 9 indicates nothing more than that the ninth day of the month is here meant, it is further evidence that the "Dresdensis" began the days with Kan and not with Imix.

In the discussion of this Tonalamatl I have omitted the mention of a very peculiar feature, which as yet does not admit of explanation. I refer to the numbers below the pictures. With the first picture we find 6 + 20, with the second 20, with the third 19 + 20, with the fourth 6 + 20, with the fifth 19 + 20, and with the sixth 6 + 20, *i.e.*, with the exception of the second, 26 or 39, two multiples of 13. Now the question arises, should not one of these multiples have been set down with the second picture? There was no space left for a prefixed 19. Therefore the idea suggests itself that what we took to be an altar with the sign Ik above it, is intended for nothing else than this 19, and Ik is the 19th day, if we count from Kan as the starting-point.

Pages 42c—45c.

This is a Tonalamatl consisting of 4 × 65 days. If written out in the usual way it would run as follows:—

XIII   17   IV 8   XII 8   VII 8   II 8   X 8   V 8   XIII

Akbal

Lamat

Ben

Ezanab.

Since, however, the subdivisions are divided and the individual month days also are given for all the parts of the whole Tonalamatl, the representation follows the order which we have already found on pages 31b-35b and 33c-39c. In this place, as in the two former ones, I will reproduce in four lines what is set down in the Manuscript in one single line extending over all four pages.

XIII Akbal (17)	IV Ahau (8)	XII Lamat (8)	VII Cib (8)	II Kan (8)
X Eb (8)	V Ahau (8)			
XIII Lamat (17)	IV Chicchan (8)	XII Ben (8)	VII Imix (8)	II Muluc (8)
X Caban (8)	V Chicchan (8)			
XIII Ben (17)	IV Oc (8)	XII Ezanab (8)	VII Cimi (8)	II Ix (8) X Ik (8)
V Oc (8)				
XIII Ezanab (17)	IV Men (8)	XII Akbal (8)	VII Chuen (8)	II Cauac (8)
X Manik (8)	V Men (8)			

Thus the days Chicchan, Lamat, Oc, Ben, Men, Ezanab, Ahau, and Akbal are repeated here twice, and the others occur but once. The 4 (17 + 48) strongly recalls the 4 (19 + 46) on pages 31b-35b. The repetition of six times eight days in each quarter of the Tonalamatl is closely connected with the fact that there are six Chuen signs on each page, two of which, however, are omitted on page 44. From this it follows, as we have already found on pages 25-28, that Chuen really denotes 8 days and that the count of the days in the "Dresdensis" begins with Kan. But the numbers 12, 15, 16 and 17 are entirely unexplained. They show no recognizable order and always stand near the bundle of Chuen signs. They recall the numbers on pages 25-28, which are equally irregular and unintelligible, and upon which, it is probable, light will break at the same time as it does upon these now under consideration.

We come now to the purport of this passage, which seems to be a further amplification of the contents of pages 29c-30c. The meaning is simply as follows:—every 65 days the god B discards a cardinal point and the deity presiding over it and installs another.

From this point of view let us now examine the four pictures.

1. Page 42. B is represented here as a warrior with the front of his body painted red. He is aiming a blow with his hatchet at a person sunk down before him, who, from the ornament above his head, seems to be the grain-deity E, the ruler of Kan and of the east, although the contents of this passage really demand a deity of the south, a ruler of Cauac. In a very similar way on page 27, E occurs with the completed Cauac years, instead of with the Kan years just beginning. Behind B's head is the sign of the discarded cardinal point, the south, while below it is a vessel with food, clearly a piece of venison with Kan.

2. Page 43 deals not with the removal of the old cardinal point, but with the introduction of the new one. Here B is rowing in a boat, as in other passages (29c),

and Muluc, the north, has certainly a close relation to water. We see here two kinds of food, while none is represented on page 45. The same bird's head, which we find at the bottom of the corresponding page 28, is placed in front of the canoe, and on 29c it is combined with the representation of rowing a boat. On the left is the picture of a vessel with Kan and the iguana. There is something resembling a net between the boat and the bird.

3. Page 44 likewise refers to the introduction of the new cardinal point, west, which is represented on page 26 by the tiger Ix. The two hieroglyphs in the middle of this passage must surely refer to an animal; the lower is the skeleton of an animal, which we so often find as the sign of the lightning-dog, but also as that of the month Kankin, and the upper I take to be a rather vague picture of the day Oc, which certainly denotes the dog. Below these two signs the fish is represented as the fourth species of animal food.

The picture belonging to these hieroglyphs is very remarkable. B stands opposite a seated personage wearing an animal's snout, which somewhat resembles that of the wind-beast on pages 44b and 45b and also the nose of the storm-god K, who occurs on the corresponding pages 25 and 26 both with the coming and the departing Ix years, as he does here with the coming years. In the picture before us, the two personages seem to be throwing something resembling a rope at each other, as if these ropes were to be tied together. Is this meant to suggest the casting of lots by means of the knotting of cords, as it is represented on page 2? Or of hunting with snares?

Page 45 refers to the displacement of the Ix period by the Cauac period, *i.e.*, of the west by the south. The end of the former is represented here. The lightning-beast, which occurred in the preceding period, here lies on his back and B sits astride his body brandishing in each hand a burning torch as an appropriate symbol of the south. On pages 29a and 30c we already saw the god riding on the lightning-dog.

Finally the six interesting hieroglyphs set down in a vertical row on the left of each of the four pages are still to be examined. I will give here in the following table what I think is a correct interpretation of them:—

Page 42.	43.	44.	45.
South (1)	East (7)	North (13)	West (9).
It ends (2)	(8)	(14)	(20)
B (3)	(9)	(15)	(21)
the time of the Cauac (4),	Kan (10),	Muluc (16),	Ix (22),
while Kan (5),	Muluc (11),	Ix (17),	Cauac (23)
begins (6)	(12)	(18)	(24).

If that which is actually set down in the Manuscript be compared with this, it will be seen that in 11 of the 24 places the Manuscript corresponds to my hypothesis:—1, 7 and 19 are the familiar signs for the three cardinal points, 8 and 20 are the sign Xul = end, which I have already frequently mentioned, 9 and 21 are the sign for B, 11 is Muluc, 23 is Cauac, where the scribe has added to the correct Kin-Cauac the sign for the year, as if the Cauac *years* were treated of here as on pages 26 and 27. Finally the two agree in 12 and 18, where the Manuscript has the compound Kan-Imix to denote beginning, *i.e.*, the two days beginning the series of twenty days, one of them according to this Manuscript, and the other according to the method resembling that used by the Aztecs.

The other cases have the correct signs, but set down in the wrong place, thus B is changed from 3 to 2, from 15 to 16, the north from 13 to 14, the Xul from 2 to 3, 14 to 15, the E (Kan) from 5 to 4 and 6 and Cauac from 4 to 5, *i.e.*, pushed along every time to the next place. This is all in favor of my theory. As one series began at the top, the scribe incorrectly placed the sign for beginning in the thirteenth place.

Strange to say in the tenth place we have the very general sign *a* in place of Kan. In the 4th, 17th and 22nd, and probably also in the half destroyed 6th sign, the scribe thoughtlessly put down a sign for E, which is proper only with Kan and should come after 5 or 10. Finally in the 24th place he put a sign for A, as if it were the intention that this passage should end exactly like its parallel on page 28. For, as a matter of fact, the two principal sections of the first part of the Dresdensis do end in a very similar way.

PART II.

PAGES 46—74.

The first glance at the form and contents of the second part of the Manuscript shows that it is very different from the first. The pages are no longer divided into the usual three parts and there are fewer pictures. The Tonalamatls, which form the principal contents of the first part, disappear wholly, and with them both the vertical columns of day-signs and the horizontal lines of numerals alternating between red and black. On the other hand, the large number series as well as the high numbers significantly increase and we note the appearance of the large vertical columns of hieroglyphs, which were impossible in the triple division of the earlier pages. We also find a large number of hieroglyphs which did not occur in the first part. The contents are essentially astronomical.

And yet the two parts are so closely connected with one another that the idea of two independent Manuscripts must be dismissed. Especially the front side of the second part as far as page 60 is nothing more than an amplification of page 24. The contents of pages 61-74 are of a more independent nature, but special attention should be called to the relation of 31a-32a to 62-63.

Pages 46—50.

The entire contents of these pages must be represented as a unit, for what is in the main true of page 24 is also true of these pages, namely that they treat exclusively of the period of 2920 days, in which five Venus years of 584 days each are brought into accord with eight solar or terrestrial years of 365 days each. Each page is a direct continuation of the preceding one. Each period of 2920 days is taken 13 times, the result being 37,960 days, which are equal to 146 Tonalamatls.

I will give here first a reproduction, as it were, of the left side of the five pages, omitting for greater clearness a few indifferent matters, which are intended only to fill the blank spaces, viz:—

1. The twenty hands pointing to the right, with a knife placed over them, in the middle of the pages, which mean nothing more than that these parts of the Venus year are to be read from left to right.

2. The Venus hieroglyph three lines below, repeated twenty times with the sign of the knife, to denote the *division* of the Venus revolution.

3. The *Akbal* sign occurring further down, four times on each page, except on pages 46 and 47. This is the last of the day-signs, again counting forward from the day Kan, and means only that henceforth the *close* of the four periods of the Venus

year is indicated below, as the beginning is indicated above.

4. The sixteen Venus signs also occurring below, except on page 48. This sign likewise occurs in a very similar form on Altar R of Copan.

With these omissions, the left side of these pages presents the following appearance: —

Page 46.

III Cib	II Cimi	V Cib	XIII Kan
XI Cib	X Cimi	XIII Cib	VIII Kan
VI Cib	V Cimi	VIII Cib	III Kan
I Cib	XIII Cimi	III Cib	XI Kan
IX Cib	VIII Cimi	XI Cib	VI Kan
IV Cib	III Cimi	VI Cib	I Kan
XII Cib	XI Cimi	I Cib	IX Kan
VII Cib	VI Cimi	IX Cib	IV Kan
II Cib	I Cimi	IV Cib	XII Kan
X Cib	IX Cimi	XII Cib	VII Kan
V Cib	IV Cimi	VII Cib	II Kan
XIII Cib	XII Cimi	II Cib	X Kan
VIII Cib	VII Cimi	X Cib	V Kan

4 Yaxkin	14 Zac	19 Zec	7 Xul
North.	West	South	East
Gods.			
236	326	576	584
9[1] Zac	19[2] Muan	4 Yax	12 Yax
Gods			
East	North	West	South
19 Kayab	4 Zotz	14 Pax	2 Kayab
236	90	250	8

Page 47.

II Ahau	I Oc	IV Ahau	XII Lamat
X Ahau	IX Oc	XII Ahau	VII Lamat
V Ahau	IV Oc	VII Ahau	II Lamat
XIII Ahau	XII Oc	II Ahau	X Lamat

---

[1] The Manuscript has incorrectly 8 and 18.
[2] The Manuscript has incorrectly 8 and 18.

VIII Ahau	VII Oc	X Ahau	V Lamat
III Ahau	II Oc	V Ahau	XIII Lamat
XI Ahau	X Oc	XIII Ahau	VIII Lamat
VI Ahau	V Oc	VIII Ahau	III Lamat
I Ahau	XIII Oc	III Ahau	XI Lamat
IX Ahau	VIII Oc	XI Ahau	VI Lamat
IV Ahau	III Oc	VI Ahau	I Lamat
XII Ahau	XI Oc	I Ahau	IX Lamat
VII Ahau	VI Oc	IX Ahau	IV Lamat

3 Cumhu	8 Zotz	18 Pax	6 Kayab
North	West	South	East
Gods.			
820	910	1160	1168
3 Zotz	13 Mol	18 Uo	6 Zip
Gods			
East	North	West	South
13 Yax	3 Pax	8 Chen	16 Chen
236	90	250	8

Page 48.

I Kan	XIII Ix	III Kan	XI Eb
IX Kan	VIII Ix	XI Kan	VI Eb
IV Kan	III Ix	VI Kan	I Eb
XII Kan	XI Ix	I Kan	IX Eb
VII Kan	VI Ix	IX Kan	IV Eb
II Kan	I Ix	IV Kan	XII Eb
X Kan	IX Ix	XII Kan	VII Eb
V Kan	IV Ix	VII Kan	II Eb
XIII Kan	XII Ix	II Kan	X Eb
VIII Kan	VII Ix	X Kan	V Eb
III Kan	II Ix	V Kan	XIII Eb
XI Kan	X Ix	XIII Kan	VIII Eb
VI Kan	V Ix	XIII Kan	III Eb

17 Yax	7 Pax	12 Chen	0 Yax[3]
North	West	South	East
Gods			
1404	1494	1744	1752
2 Pax	7 Pop	17 Mac	5 Kankin
Gods			
East	North	West	South
7 Zip	17 Yaxkin	2 Uo	10 Uo
236	90	250	8

Page 49.

XIII Lamat	XII Ezanab	II Lamat	X Cib
VIII Lamat	VII Ezanab	X Lamat	V Cib
III Lamat	II Ezanab	V Lamat	XIII Cib
XI Lamat	X Ezanab	XIII Lamat	VII Cib
VI Lamat	V Ezanab	VIII Lamat	III Cib
I Lamat	XIII Ezanab	III Lamat	XI Cib
IX Lamat	VIII Ezanab	XI Lamat	VI Cib
IV Lamat	III Ezanab	VI Lamat	I Cib
XII Lamat	XI Ezanab	I Lamat	IX Cib
VII Lamat	VI Ezanab	IX Lamat	IV Cib
II Lamat	I Ezanab	IV Lamat	XII Cib
X Lamat	IX Ezanab	XII Lamat	VII Cib
V Lamat	IV Ezanab	VII Lamat	II Cib

11 Zip	1 Mol	6 Uo	14 Uo
North	West	South	East
Gods			
1988	2078	2328	2336
16 Yaxkin	6 Ceh	11 Xul	19 Xul
Gods			
East	North	West	South
6 Kankin	16 Cumhu	1 Mac	9 Mac
236	90	250	8

---

[3] = 20 Chen.

Page 50.

VII Eb	VI Ik	IX Eb	IV Ahau
II Eb	I Ik	IV Eb	XII Ahau
X Eb	IX Ik	XII Eb	VII Ahau
V Eb	IV Ik	VII Eb	II Ahau
XIII Eb	XII Ik	II Eb	X Ahau
VIII Eb	VII Ik	X Eb	V Ahau
III Eb	II Ik	V Eb	XIII Ahau
XI Eb	X Ik	XIII Eb	VIII Ahau
VI Eb	V Ik	VIII Eb	III Ahau
I Eb	XIII Ik	III Eb	XI Ahau
IX Eb	VIII Ik	XI Eb	VI Ahau
IV Eb	III Ik	VI Eb	I Ahau

10 Kankin	20 Cumhu[4]	5 Mac	13 Mac
North	West	South	East
Gods			
2572	2662	2912	2920
15 Cumhu	0 Zec[5]	10 Kayab	18 Kayab
Gods			
East	North	West	South
20 Xul	10 Zac	15 Zec	3 Xul
236	90	250	8

Let us first examine the numbers which are regularly repeated in the lowest line:—236, 90, 250, and 8, and we shall find that the 584 days of the apparent Venus revolution are divided into these four periods.

The number 236 denotes the time of the western elongation, when Venus is the morning star, 90 the time of the invisibility of the planet, during its superior conjunction, 250 that of its eastern elongation, when Venus is the evening star, and 8 the time of its invisibility during inferior conjunction. The disproportion between 236 and 250 is somewhat striking. These periods which need not of course be exactly equal are usually computed at 243 days. The short period of eight days is only calculated for very sharp eyes; we actually find in the Anales del Museo Nacional de Mexico II, 341 (Mex. 1882), that the Aztecs calculated only eight days for the invisibility of Venus, and this period is also mentioned in the Anales de Quauhtitlan. The repetition of the cardinal points in the 15th and 20th lines of the extract given above refer to these periods; in the upper line to their beginning

[4] The sign denotes the end of the 360-day year.
[5] = 20 Zotz.

and in the lower to their close. Hence in the lower line the cardinal points must advance one place and the gods belonging to them in the 16th and 19th lines must follow the same course.

The numbers in the 17th line indicate to which day of the period of 2920 days the position has advanced.

But now we see that the indication of days in the lines 1-13, the indication of months in lines 14, 18 and 21, and the numbers in line 17 are separated from those directly to the right of them by a number of days equal to the numbers given in the lowest line.

From this it follows that each day of the thirteen top lines is joined to each of the month dates placed just below them, forming a complete calendar date. Therefore from the III Cib on the left upper corner of page 46 a III Cib 4 Yaxkin, a III Cib 8 Zac, a III Cib 19 Kayab must be formed.

All the $4 \times 13 \times 5 = 260$ day indications combined with three month indications each, show therefore that this whole passage is a huge abbreviation for 780 calendar dates and that the whole refers to $3 \times 37,960$ days $= 113,880$ days. But 37,960 which we already found on page 24, is equal to 146×260, 104×365, 65×584, 13×2920. I am inclined to think that I also found 113,880 on page 24.

But the $3 \times 37,960 = 113,880$ days do not form the entire period treated of here. For the three periods begin and end with the days:—

I Ahau 13 Mac (10 Muluc),

I Ahau 18 Kayab (3 Kan),

I Ahau 3 Xul (4 Cauac).

Hence these three dates, the second of which was found on page 24, prove that the three periods of 37,960 are not consecutive, but that there is an interval between them. Now between the first and second of the three dates the interval is 19 years + 85 days = 7020 days, and between the second and third, the interval is 26 years + 130 days = 9620 days. If these two periods be added to the 113,880 days, the sum is the whole period treated of here, viz:— $130,520 = 502 \times 260$ days.

But a truly surprising result is obtained, if, as must often be the case with series, we begin not with the upper of the three dates, but with the lower.

From I Ahau 3 Xul (4 Cauac) to I Ahau 18 Kayab (3 Kan) there is a lapse of 9360 days or 12 apparent Mars years of 780 days, such as we shall find as the principal subject of page 59. 9360, however, equals $25 \times 365 + 235$ days. We shall meet with this 235 again as a difference on page 63.

But from I Ahau 18 Kayab (3 Kan) to I Ahau 13 Mac (10 Muluc) there are 11,960 days, *i.e.*, the 104 Mercury years, which we found on page 24, and which we shall find again as the principal period on pages 51-58. But this is equal to 32 years + 280 or 33 years - 85 days. Now if 113,880, 9360, 11,960 are added together, we have for the entire period under discussion here, 135,200 days, and this is equal to $2 \times 260 \times 260$ days. Thus the Mayas seem actually to have had an idea of a second power.

Finally I would call attention to a singular double connection between the numbers occurring here:—

$$37,960 - 11,960 = 26,000 = 100 \text{ Tonalamatls,}$$

$$11,960 - 9,360 = 2600 = 10 \text{ Tonalamatls.}$$

But if we subtract $2 \times 11,960 = 23,920$ from $37,960$, the remainder is $14,040$, *i.e.,* an extraordinary number which often occurs and is equal to 54×260, 39×360 and 18×780.

In short, a Mars and a Mercury-lunar period are inserted in the two spaces between the three solar-Venus periods.

Now, let us try to gain a clearer understanding of this subject by approaching from another side.

As we have seen, the beginning of the middle one of the three equal periods of $37,960$ days, is the date I Ahau 18 Kayab (3 Kan). Now, however, page 24 furnished us with a day number for this date, $1,364,360$, and from this the beginnings of the other two periods may be computed in the following way:—

$$\text{I Ahau} \quad 3 \text{ Xul (4 Cauac)} \quad = 1,317,040,$$

$$\text{I Ahau} \ 18 \text{ Kayab (3 Kan)} \quad = 1,364,360,$$

$$\text{I Ahau} \ 13 \text{ Mac (10 Muluc)} = 1,414,280.$$

Between the first number and the second there are $47,320$ days $= 2^3 \times 5 \times 7 \times 13^2$, and between the second and third $49,920$ days $= 2^8 \times 3 \times 5 \times 13$ days.

But, according to what has been stated above, $47,320 = 37,960 + 9360$, and $49,920 = 37,960 + 11,960$.

The whole period is therefore divided as follows:—

It begins with a Venus-solar-Tonalamatl-period followed by 12 Mars years, then the great period again followed by $8 \times 13 = 104$ Mercury years, and lastly, apparently about the present time, comes the third great period, which, as already stated, ends $135,200$ days after the first date.

The case assumes a different aspect, if we insert between the three dates the other two from page 24:—

$$1,317,040 = \text{I Ahau,}$$

$$1,352,400 = \text{I Ahau,}$$

$$1,364,360 = \text{I Ahau,}$$

$$1,366,560 = \text{IV Ahau,}$$

$$1,414,280 = \text{I Ahau.}$$

Here we have again, as examination of page 24 showed, the difference $11,960$ between the second and third numbers, while there is no longer any connection with the periods of $37,960$ days.

Of the left halves of the pages we have now examined all except the twenty hieroglyphs of the gods. I shall mention them according to the upper place in line 16; the lower in line 19, where the hieroglyphs move forward only one place, is only referred to when the two signs differ. They offer many problems still unsolved.

The first sign on page 46 is an unknown sign, which, however, is repeated several times on the right side of the pages; the second is probably an Ahau (*i.e.*, D) with a prefix suggesting the snail, the symbol of birth; the third is a head also occurring elsewhere, which I have not yet determined; the fourth is A; compare page 24, hieroglyph 25.

Page 47. The first sign is probably K; compare the third picture on page 7a with its hieroglyph; the second is C's hieroglyph with an Akbal appropriate to it; the third sign is Moan with the 13 belonging to it; the fourth sign is N's with a prefixed 4; the year-sign in the lower series is replaced by Zac, which agrees equally well; compare page 24, hieroglyph 21.

Page 48. The first sign is Kin with the Ben-Ik superfix, perhaps denoting G; the second is a figure similar to the year-sign with a prefixed 6. This same sign in the line below has a 6, but is very different in other respects; the third is an Akbal with superfix and prefix, perhaps denoting D; the fourth is a head which might easily be F's; compare page 24, hieroglyph 22.

Page 49. The first sign is B's; the second, A's; the 3d, K's; compare page 24, hieroglyph 38; the fourth is H's with a prefixed 1; compare page 24, hieroglyphs 23 and perhaps 37.

Page 50. The first sign is E's; compare page 24, hieroglyph 38; the second is L, the black deity; compare page 24, hieroglyph 32; the third is an unknown hieroglyph with a prefixed 7, which also occurs on page 5a and 19b; the fourth is the bat-god; compare page 24, hieroglyph 24.

I find it impossible to discover any relation between these hieroglyphs and the periods and I have as little success with the hieroglyphs apparently belonging to the same cardinal point. Perhaps we should follow Seler here (Quetzalcoatl and Kukulcan, p. 403), who thinks these passages suggest constellations with which Venus is in conjunction; this question, owing to the retrogression of the planet, raises increased difficulties. It is curious that the fourth of these signs on page 46 is like the fourteenth on page 49 (A), and perhaps the two following refer to the same god K; the first two are separated by 1494 days and the latter by 1508 days.

We come now to the *right* half of the pages. Interpretation is rendered impossible by the destruction of the top part. For we do not even know whether the upper hieroglyphs occupied three or four rows each, the latter being the case at least in part, and there may have been a superscription over the day signs in the left half.

These upper signs are always followed by a picture, then three rows of hieroglyphs, then a second picture and next two rows of hieroglyphs and lastly a third picture.

Let us first examine the pictures: —

At the top of pages 46-49 there is on each page a deity, who with his right arm extended is offering or receiving something. He is seated on astronomical signs;

on page 46 B's head accompanies these signs. On pages 46 and 48 the deity is undoubtedly the old woman with tiger claws, who usually pours streams of water from a jug (compare pages 39, 43 and 74). I cannot identify the personage on pages 47 and 49. The object in the deity's hand seems invariably to be a cup of foaming pulque. On page 49 another object is placed above the cup, which I am unable to determine. The fifth, page 50, differs from the other four and forms the connecting link, as it were, between the upper row of pictures and the middle and lower ones. Here, too, a personage is represented sitting on astronomical signs and exhibiting symptoms of violent anger toward a second person opposite him holding the cup in his hands. Both personages are painted as warriors.

The middle pictures on all the pages represent a warrior in a half-kneeling, half-crouching posture, holding spears or a shield in the right hand and brandishing a hatchet in the left. The shield on page 46 is doubtless a representation of the sun-glyph; and on 47 the Venus sign is combined with the head ornament. The hieroglyphs of these deities occupy the first place in the middle line of the three lines above the pictures.

The five lower pictures represent a creature lying on the ground, pierced by arrows and spears. On page 47 it is a jaguar; at any rate it is the same animal found on pages 29a, 30c and 45c; a very similar creature pierced by arrows is given in the Cod. Vat. B.; compare also the pictures in Seler's "Venus-periode," page 371. On the other four pages this creature is in human guise. On page 50 where, differing from the other four pages, this figure is represented lying with the head to the right, it is plainly shedding tears. Seler takes this figure to be E on page 48 and the tortoise on page 49. The varying periods of time occupied by the revolution of the planets is plainly conceived of as contest. But who is the victor in this contest? The planet with the longer or with the shorter period of revolution? Owing to obliteration only a small part of the hieroglyphs of the top section is legible.

On page 46 we see the Venus sign and E's hieroglyph; on page 47 the sign c, which occurs frequently on these pages, and is probably always connected with Moan (the Pleiades and thus with the year). The numeral 1, prefixed to an obliterated sign on page 47, is still legible, and we find it repeated on the lower part of the same page. There is rather more to be seen on page 48:—first the elongated head q with the Ben-Ik superfix, then the sign a, beside it that for the west with a prefix, in the line below an Ahau, next, an Akbal sign with the prefix of the north, and lastly a Moan sign.

On page 49 we see sign c again occupying the first place, then o with Ben-Ik, and in the lower line the year sign with that for 20 or the moon as a superfix, and to the right of it the head with the Akbal eye, probably denoting D.

This top part of the page is best preserved on page 50. In the third line from the bottom we see the Venus sign and beside it the Moan sign, below, a Cauac, then a Kin with the Ben-Ik superfix, then a Kan-Imix. Finally, in the first place in the lowest row there is a Kin sign and in the second place a sign resembling the year-sign, both having the same superfix, the next sign is again c and the last is a half-effaced sign, of which only a Muluc is distinguishable.

Our knowledge of the middle section of these pages is somewhat more definite. There are twelve hieroglyphs on each page, which I will number in the following order:—

1 2 3 4

5 6 7 8

9 10 11 12.

Unquestionably these 5 × 12 signs refer to a Venus year, more exactly to the *beginning* of it, the period of the east. The first sign, which is a hand pointing to the right, merely refers here, as on the left side, to the direction in which this is to be read; the second sign is always the sign for the east, and the sixth invariably that for Venus.

Notice should be taken of the fact that the signs of the Moan and screech-owl or death-bird are recurrent, that of the Moan appearing on page 46, sign 7; 48, 3; 49, 11; 50, 11; and that of the death-bird on page 47, sign 3; 48, 11, 49, 3, 50, 3 and 7, *i.e.*, only in places 3, 7 and 11, which indicates that the 12 signs are divided each time into three times four.

It is further to be noted that the five gods, who are represented on page 24 by hieroglyphs 36-40, always recur in the ninth place in the order of the pages:—the god represented on page 24 by sign 36 is the 8th on page 49; the 38th on the same page is the 11th on page 46 and the 12th on page 50; the 39th is the 12th on page 47, and the 40th may be the 5th on page 49, though this is hardly possible. On page 49 the 9th hieroglyph seems to be the 39th on page 24 joined to the sign for the month Kayab.

Of the twenty gods on the left side of these pages, I have already remarked that E, who on page 24 occupies the 38th place, and the 11th on page 46, also occurs as the 9th on page 48 and the 12th on page 50.

It is doubtless of special significance that the sign of the first of the twenty deities on the left side of page 46 is repeated on the right as the tenth sign on all the pages (on page 47 also in the eleventh place where it has a prefixed 3). It seems as if this sign, which is otherwise quite unfamiliar, might be connected with the sun and regarded as a contrast to the Venus sign in the sixth place.

Also the 9th deity of the left side, the 1st of page 48, reappears in the 4th place on page 49; the 10th deity, the 2nd on page 48, in the 12th on page 49; the 15th deity, the 3d on page 49, in the 9th on page 46 and the 8th on page 49 (as already stated); the 18th, the 2nd on page 50, in the 5th on page 46.

The 2nd of these deities is suggested by the 8th on page 47, perhaps also by the 5th on page 50; the 3d and 13th seem to be A and to recur in the 3d place on page 46.

On the other hand C, the god who, as I believe I have proved, is connected with the day-sign Chuen, does not appear on the left side. Now the 4th sign on page 46 contains a Chuen, which in the 12th sign on page 48 is probably combined with a Muluc, in the 12th on page 49 with Yax and a prefixed 6, and in the 4th sign on page 50 with C's sign, *i.e.*, as a rule Chuen stands in the 4th place in a line.

As the gods E and K already mentioned also appear on pages 25-28 in connection with the change of the year, so we find the tiger on the top of page 26, and I believe this animal occurs again in the 7th sign on page 47.

Of the day-signs I take the 4th on page 47 to be Kan, the 7th on page 48 to be Caban, and the next sign, the 8th on page 48, to be Muluc. Now if we take into consideration the fact, that of the three periods of the month signs on the left side of these pages, the 18th (the middle) line is the most important, owing to its ending, 18 Kayab, alone, if for no other reason; furthermore, that in this middle period the second Venus year always ends with a Kan year and the third with a Muluc year, one is naturally led to suppose that the illegible sign 12 on page 46 is an Ix (for thus the first Venus year ends) and that the days Cauac and Kan might have been found among the obliterated day-signs on pages 49 and 50.

I shall examine the remaining signs in the order of the pages.

Sign 8 on page 46 is the same compound of Yax and Kin having as a superfix the sign assumed by me to be the numeral 18, which occurs again in the lower group on page 50 and also on page 27.

In the number 11 prefixed to the fifth sign on page 47, the 1 seems to be indistinct and may not belong here. If we correctly assume that this number is 10, then the sign is the same as the 34th on page 24, to the discussion of which I beg to refer my readers.

Sign 8 on page 47 is an indistinct compound, the first part of which I supposed above to be the sign of the second deity on page 46.

I cannot explain 4 and 5 on page 48.

As yet I do not understand sign 5 on page 49, which we seem to have met before on page 22c.

Sign 7 on page 49 is the moon, which is very curious here.

I would like to call special attention to signs 5 to 8 on page 50. I interpret the passage thus:—At the time of the summer solstice after the reappearance of the Pleiades, the change of the Venus year takes place (this time). I have already discussed the Venus sign in the sixth place and the screech-owl so closely connected with the Moan (Pleiades) in the seventh place. Sign 5 connects the sun (Kin) with the Ahau (lord) and the cross-hatching on the left of it, which I have assigned to the tortoise and thus to the summer solstice (Zur Entzifferung III, 3). Sign 8 is recognized as very appropriate to the change of year; compare the first sign of the middle section on pages 25-28. All this points to the day 18 Kayab, of one of the Kan years, if, as I stated above, we base our computation on the middle series of dates.

Now we have yet to examine the eight signs of the lower group, which we will do in the following order:—

1   2   3   4

5   6   7   8.

Regarding the beginnings of these groups, I will venture a bold surmise, which will, I hope, be improved upon by some one else. It concerns the first sign of four of these five groups, which seem to me to refer to the end of the Venus year, as those above refer to the beginning. This sign has the following form:—

I see in this the term of 73 days, which is the fifth part of the 365 days of the solar year and the eighth part of the 584 days of the Venus year:—

It is combined with Chuen in all four cases (pages 46, 48, 49 and 50). But I attribute the meaning of eight days to this Chuen sign, as I did on pages 25-28 and 42c-45c, though I am doubtful in these as in other cases.

Page 46 contains the sign for 73 with a Chuen under it, and a 1 prefixed to each sign; *i.e.*, 1 × 8 × 73 = expiration of the first Venus year.

On page 48 Chuen follows the sign for 73 and each sign has a 3 prefixed to it; *i.e.*, 3 × 8 × 73, expiration of the third Venus year.

On page 49 the two signs again stand side by side, but the prefix is a 7 instead of the expected 4. By an error this 4 has been added to the 3 of the preceding page, but, for a wholly unintelligible reason, prefixed to the crouching person below the Chuen, as if to correct the 7.

Page 50 again has the sign for 73 above and the Chuen below. A prefixed 5 would seem to be in order; instead of it, there is a 10, one 5 for the 73 and another 5 for the 8 days. In this connection let me say that I believe I have found on page 27, top left, the year of 365 days divided into 5 × 73.

Page 47 differs from the others. Above two oval bodies appears the cross-hatched figure resembling a clamp, like the one in the middle group of page 50 in the fifth place, which I ventured to refer to the summer solstice. There is a 1 prefixed to it. Is this equivalent to a union of two Venus revolutions?

Next we repeatedly meet here, as we did in the middle groups, with the Moan sign and that of the screech-owl belonging with it; the former is the 6th sign on page 46 and page 50, and the latter is the 3d and 7th on page 47, the 7th on page 49 and finally the 2nd and 4th on page 50.

The moon is represented in the 5th sign on page 48 and in the 3d on page 49 and indistinctly in the 4th on page 48.

The cardinal points occur here several times. The 3d and 7th signs on page 46 have at least the superfix of the south as a prefix; the 8th on page 47 apparently has the east, but with the familiar cross-hatched sign prefixed; the 7th on page 48 plainly has the east, the 3d on page 50 the prefix of the north prefixed to the cross *b*, and the 8th on page 50 the west, thus approximating the usual order and distribution.

Of the gods I note the Akbal head, perhaps intended for D, in the 4th place on page 46, also in the 3d on page 48, and lastly in the 5th on page 49, the first two times with the Ben-Ik superfix, and in the 2nd place on page 47 the sign for A.

In the 4th place on page 47 we have the tortoise as the sign of the month Kayab or of the summer solstice, in the 6th on page 47 the lightning-beast or the month Kankin with a Ben-Ik superfix; the beast itself is pictured below, and the same hieroglyph also with the Ben-Ik superfix is the 8th sign on page 49.

It is hard to decide whether the sign 4 on page 49 represents the god F owing to the line through the eye, or a female by reason of the prefixed lock.

Sign 7 on page 50 represents the deity whose sign began the series of twenty gods on the left of page 46 and which we have already met with several times in the centre of the right side. We recognize the prefix as having occurred in the middle group of the same page.

Sign 6 on page 48 is a Kin combined with an unfamiliar sign. Sign 5 on page 50 contains a Kin with a Yax and probably with 18 as a superfix (as on pages 27 and 46 middle).

Sign 6 on page 49 contains a crouching person with a 4 which is probably out of place here and to be regarded as a correction of the 7 above it.

Sign 5 on page 46 contains a Mac denoting the thirteenth Uinal or a Tonalamatl, and having the sign *p* as a superfix and a double Ik as a prefix.

Sign 3 on page 46 merits special attention, because it contains the duplication of the sign, which, at the end of the first part of the Manuscript, pages 29-41, always began the groups of hieroglyphs on the lower third of the pages.

I do not understand the second hieroglyph on page 46 and the 5th on page 47.

In conclusion I would call attention to the fact that the last hieroglyph on page 48 is very peculiar. As on pages 51, 52, 61 and 69 it has the meaning of 18,980 days and consists of an Imix with a comprehensive superfix; its prefix is a 7.

But what is the meaning here of 7 × 18,980 = 132,860? When we recall the statement made above that the whole section of pages 46-50 embraces 130,520 days, or, according to another calculation 135,200 days, it is a striking fact that 132,860 is exactly the mean of the two numbers, being separated from each by 2340 days = 9 × 260. Can it be an accident that on the next page (page 49) the fourth Venus revolution is reached, for 4 × 584 = 2336, *i.e.*, almost 2340? The hieroglyph discussed here would not be so extraordinary on page 50. I will not venture to assert as to the 511 in 132,860 = 511 × 260, that it is connected with the 511 which will appear as the difference on page 58.

Before leaving these pages, I will give a brief survey of the two signs of the screech-owl and the Moan (hieroglyph *c* and the lower part of *d*) which occur on these pages with such marked frequency.

In spite of obliteration, the first of these two signs is distinguishable in the top groups on pages 47, 49 and 50, in the middle groups on pages 47, 48, 49 and twice on page 50, in the lower groups on page 46, twice on page 47, once on 49, twice again on 50, making 14 times in all. A few additional cases might be added to these where the similar hieroglyph of the moon may have been set down instead of the one in question.

On the other hand the second sign, always provided with the same prefix and suffix as the first, occurs in the top groups on page 48 and 50, in the middle of pages 46, 48, 49 and 50, and in the lowest on pages 46 and 50, 8 times in all.

Since the subject here is astronomical, it is suggestive less of a deity or a sacrifice than of a period of time to which the allied page 24 has already referred (see page 110 of this book). The inner meaning of these pages is of course still enveloped in mystery.

Pages 51a—52a.

I shall begin the discussion of this very peculiar section with the remarkable fourth column on page 52, which, very possibly, the scribe ought to have placed at the beginning; for it looks like a repetition of the section on pages 46-50, while everything else on the left and right of it, apparently belongs together.

If we omit the two hieroglyphs at the top, which I regard as belonging to the two rows of hieroglyphs extending over these two pages, we shall have the following result, according to my point of view:—

1	5
Chuen	360
2	18,980.

Since, as is frequently the case, the Chuen will here have the value of 8 days and the 5 with the sign for 360 may be regarded as 365, this group might denote 8 × 365 = 2920, but actually be 2 × 18,980 = 37,960. Both numbers are the basis of the section included on pages 46-50. And in the same way the 13 repeated 13 times seems to me to refer to the 13 series of days on those pages, which begin with the 13th day of the Uinal.

The two rows of hieroglyphs are in the main destroyed. We can still recognize in the second and third columns of page 51 the signs for end and beginning, which we often find in the vicinity of numbers; in the second and third columns of page 52, the sun and moon; in the fourth column, the 8 days of such significance here and in the fifth and sixth, the normal date IV Ahau 8 Cumhu repeated twice.

As the problem on pages 46-50 was to bring into accord the solar year with the Venus year and consequently also the Tonalamatl, *i.e.*, to combine 365, 584 and 260, so the aim here is first of all to bring the Tonalamatl into unison with the Mercury year (115). For this purpose the number 11,960 is employed. This is equal to 46 × 260 = 104 × 115, including, therefore just as many Mercury years as there were solar years in the preceding section. 11,960 is also 8 × 1495, and this 8 is significant here, for, as we shall see directly, the day forming the basis of this calculation is XII

Lamat, which comes 8 days after the normal date IV Ahau.

The series given here is based, therefore, on 11,960 and consists entirely of multiples of this number, which, it is true, are recorded with the usual irregularity. The members of this series, representing the greatest values, which are set down in red numbers among the black, are the 31st and 39th multiples of 11,960, which are separated from each other by 8 × 11,960, viz:—370,760 and 466,440. All these numbers, of course, denote the day IV Ahau.

The day XII Lamat as the actual starting-point of the Mercury revolution is not introduced until we come to the dates placed below the series. Here we find the days XII Lamat, I Akbal, III Ezanab, V Ben and VII Lamat written one below the other, and repeated seven times. Each of these days is separated from the next by 15, and the last of one row and the first of the next on the left are 200 days apart, hence the whole is equal to 7 × 260 = 1820 days. From XII Lamat begins also the Peresianus, pages 21-22.

Now these dates are connected with the four large numbers, which we find on page 52, but between the third and fourth, one number corresponding to the day V Ben is omitted for lack of space.

These four numbers, to which I have added the corresponding dates, are as follows:—

$$1,412,848 = \text{XII Lamat I Muan (6 Muluc).}$$
$$1,412,863 = \text{I Akbal 16 Muan (6 Muluc).}$$
$$1,412,878 = \text{III Ezanab 11 Pax (6 Muluc).}$$
$$1,434,748 = \text{VII Lamat I Muan (1 Muluc).}$$

It is curious that while the first three are separated from each other by 15, between the 3d and 4th, or rather between the missing 4th and 5th, 84 × 260 days are inserted in excess of the required 15, *i.e.*, 21,855. This, however, is not accidental, but is due to the fact that between the first number and the last exactly 21,900 = 60 × 365 days have elapsed. This number is, however, = 18,980 + 2920, i. e., the sum of two very important numbers, in the first of which the Tonalamatl and the solar year accord, while both the solar and Venus years occur in the second.

I must here call attention to the fact that the four numbers are not obtained without slight corrections, since in the 20-place of the third, I have put a 11 instead of 10, while in the 360-place of the fourth, I have omitted the three dots, *i.e.*, set down a 5 instead of the 8.

Of these four dates, which were doubtless not far removed from the time of the scribe, the three last are only the result of the first. Day XII Lamat is the most important. As the beginning of a Mercury period it should be regarded in the same way as I Ahau of the Venus period and IV Ahau of the solar period; and the very next day, XIII Muluc, will subsequently be seen to be the beginning day of the Mars period.

The four dates XII Lamat, I Akbal, III Ezanab and VII Lamat are set down in the Manuscript directly below the numbers.

Now in the first column on page 51 we again find a day XII Lamat, as is expressly stated beneath it. It has the number 1,578,988 and the corresponding date is XII Lamat 6 Cumhu (6 Kan). This day, however, is separated from the same day on page 52 (1,412,848 = XII Lamat I Muan 6 Muluc) by 166,140 days, that is by 8 × 18,980 + 14,300 = 639 × 260, *i.e.*, by 8 so-called Katuns increased by 55 Tonalamatls. Here 58 × 260 = 15,080 seems to have been added to 252 (XII Lamat - IV Ahau) and the sum subtracted from 14 Ahau-Katuns = 1,594, 320. I could obtain this number only by substituting 1 for 0 in the 20-place.

In the Manuscript the sign XII Lamat is set down above and below this number. I must leave undetermined whether the 8 directly above the number and combined with Kin and the Katun sign refers only to the 8 Katuns or at the same time also to the 8 days from IV Ahau to XII Lamat.

It is also to be noted here that once before on page 24 of this Manuscript (which forms the basis of this section) 8 × 18,980 = 151,840 days was found to be the difference between 185,120 and 33,280, and that there, too, if my restoration is correct, it was the highest term of the series = 4 × 37,960.

Finally, in the first column of page 51, we have the complete normal date 4 Ahau 8 Cumhu (9 Ix). But below this, between red numerals denoting the 1,578,988 mentioned above, there is set down in black the number 1,268,800. This corresponds to the date IV Ahau 3 Zip (2 Cauac). It may have been formed by adding 16,120 = 62 × 260 to 11 Ahau-Katuns = 1,252,680. It is, however, not only equal to 4880 × 260, but also to 158,600 × 8, therefore also divisible by the interval between IV Ahau XII Lamat, as well as by 104 = 8 × 13, while on the contrary it is not as we should expect, divisible by 11,960. I have changed the 11, in the 20 × 11, to 8 by omitting one line and adding two dots, for otherwise the result would not be the one required.

The magnitude of the number recalls the one on page 31, which is only 260 less, and that on page 62.

Finally it should be noted that the two large numbers on page 51 are separated from one another by 310,188 days = 849 years and 303 days, which corresponds exactly to the dates given for each. One may be situated as far in the future as the other is in the past, but this does not necessarily mean that the present coincides exactly with 1,423,894.

Pages 51—58.

Thus far we have examined only the upper halves of pages 51 and 52 and have still to consider the lower, but not until we have finished the upper parts of pages 53-58 of which the former are the continuation. We have first to consider the series, then the pictures and lastly the hieroglyphs.

As on page 24 we found multiples of the number 2920 (= 8 × 365 = 5 × 584), while on pages 46-50 it was divided into four unequal parts, so on pages 51-52 we find multiples of the number 11,960 (104 × 115 = 46 × 260) while on pages 53-58 it is divided into 69 unequal parts. On pages 51-52 it was the aim to combine only the Mercury course with the Tonalamatl, but here we are confronted with the additional problem of bringing the lunar revolution into accord with these two.

The lunar revolution, which we assume to be 29.53 days, of course requires fractional computation, of which the Mayas either were ignorant or which they timorously avoided; like the ancient Egyptians, who were acquainted only with fractions having 1 as numerator, or beyond these at most with ⅔ (see Hultsch, "Die Elemente der ägyptischen Teilungsrechnung," 1895, page 16).

Now the Mayas had determined the lunar revolution so exactly that they perceived the incompatibility of the period of 11,960 days with a multiple of lunar revolutions. They found that 405 lunar revolutions amounted approximately to 11,958 days, which is, in fact, the largest number on the second half of page 58. In order not to drop the significant 11,960 altogether, they made use of a very shrewd artifice. They took as the starting-point the day XII Lamat, corresponding to the number 11,960, and set down XI Manik before it and XIII Muluc after it. Now if the count began with XIII Muluc and ended with XI Manik, it actually resulted in 11,958.

Therefore what the Manuscript presents here is, in the first place, the series, which is this time to be read from left to right. Below it are the three days belonging to each member of the series and then a number for each member stating the interval between it and the preceding one. The members, the days and the differences must correspond with one another. It is, therefore, no longer necessary to pay especial attention to the two latter. They will serve merely to control and to correct the manifold errors.

The entire period of 11,958 days was doubtless first divided into three equal periods of 3986 days. And in order still further to subdivide these shorter periods, the term of 177 days was employed as far as it would go; 177, however, is the half of a lunar year of 354 days, made up of 6 months of 30 days and 6 of 29 days, thus allowing 29.5 days in round numbers for each month.

Now 177 is = 3 × 29 + 3 × 30. The average, 29.5, however, is too short for the length of the lunar revolution. In order to raise it as nearly as possible to the exact time, two other numbers were introduced at certain points of the series, viz: — 148 = 2 × 29 + 3 × 30, 178 = 2 × 29 + 4 × 30. 148 = 5 months of 29.6 days, while 178 = 6 months of 29⅔ days. Now let us see in what *proportion* these 148 and 178 days were distributed among the periods of 177.

First we see that the period of 3986 days (*i.e.*, a third of the whole) was divided into 3 sections of 1742, 1034 and 1210 days, as follows: —

$$1742 = 8 \times 177 + 148 + 178$$
$$1034 = 4 \times 177 + 148 + 178$$
$$1210 = 6 \times 177 + 148$$
$$\overline{3986 = 18 \times 177 + 3 \times 148 + 2 \times 178.}$$

This is equal to 135 months of 29.526 days each. Now the question arises how did the Mayas express this fraction?

Perhaps some time in the future it will be found, that following their vigesimal

116   COMMENTARY ON THE MAYA MANUSCRIPT

system, they designated it approximately thus:—

$$29 + \tfrac{1}{2} + \tfrac{1}{40} + \tfrac{1}{800}.$$

The *whole* period of 11,958 days was divided as follows:—

$$3 \times 1742 = 24 \times 177 + 3 \times 148 + 3 \times 178$$
$$3 \times 1034 = 12 \times 177 + 3 \times 148 + 3 \times 178$$
$$3 \times 1210 = 18 \times 177 + 3 \times 148$$
$$\overline{3 \times 3986 = 54 \times 177 + 9 \times 148 + 6 \times 178.}$$

Thus for every 6 parts of 177 days there was consequently 1 of 148 and to every 9 parts of 177, 1 of 178.

Since 177 and 178 include 6 months each, while 148 equals 5 months, the entire length of the period is 405 months, which are divided into 69 periods.

It was necessary to discuss all this before I could introduce the entire series itself. In the following table I have set down the numbers and added to them the differences between each number and the preceding one (to the first, the interval between it and the zero point), just as they are given in the Manuscript. An asterisk is added to show that the number has been corrected by me and is wrong in the Manuscript, owing to a mistake either in writing or in computation. The three columns correspond to the three divisions of 3986 days, and the two horizontal lines divide the periods of 1742, 1034 and 1210 days.

	Page 53a:		24.	4163*	177	47.	8149	177
1.	177	177	25.	4340	177	48.	8326	177
3.	502	148		Page 58a:		50.	8651	177*
4.	679*	177	27.	4665	177		Page 55b:	
5.	856	177	28.	4842	177	51.	8828	177
6.	1034*	178*	29.	5020	178*	52.	9006	178*
	Page 54a:		30.	5197	177	53.	9183	177
7.	1211	177		Page 51b:		54.	9360	177
8.	1388	177	31.	5374	177	55.	9537	177
9.	1565	177	32.	5551	177	56.	9714	177
10.	1742*	177	33.	5728	177			
11.	1919	177	34.	5905	177	57.	9891	177
12.	2096*	177	35.	6082	177	58.	10068*	177*
13.	2244*	148	36.	6230	148		Page 56b:	
	Page 55a:			Page 52b:		59.	10216	148*
14.	24227	178	37.	6408	178*	60.	10394	178*
15.	2599*	177	38.	6585	177	61.	10571	177
16.	2776	177	39.	6762	177	62.	10748	177

17.	2953	177	40.	6939	177		Page 57b:	
18.	3130	177		Page 53b:		63.	10925	177
	Page 56a:		41.	7116	177	64.	11102	177
19.	3278	148	42.	7264	148	65.	11250	148
20.	3455	177	43.	7441	177	66.	11427	177
21.	3632	177	44.	7618	177	67.	11604	177
22.	3809	177	45.	7795	177		Page 58b:	
	Page 57a:			Page 54b:		68.	11781	177
23.	3986	177*	46.	7972	177	69.	11958	177

No one acquainted with the cursoriness of the Maya Manuscripts will be surprised that among 138 numbers I have declared 21 to be wrong. Furthermore the 21 errors are lessened by the fact that six of them are really only one, for in all 6 cases where the difference is 178, the scribe has overlooked this and written down the usual 177, although the numbers and the days of the series very correctly indicate 178. Again the three errors in groups 58 and 59 are also only one, for the author had confused the differences 177 and 148 and had, therefore, to write down 10,039 instead of 10,068. In group 4 the error is merely the omission of a line meaning 5. The scribe must have been at the same time the computer and therefore the actual author of the Manuscript.

Furthermore I must call attention to the regular position of the differences 178 and 148. In the three periods of 1742 days the 178 always occupies the 6th place and in the periods of 1034 it is always in the 4th place. This difference appears, therefore, in groups 6, 14, 29, 37, 52 and 60, *i.e.*, 8, 15, 8, 15 and 8 groups apart; but it is entirely lacking in the periods of 1210 days. And in all nine sections the 148 occupies the third place, *i.e.*, directly in front of the pictures, which will be discussed immediately, therefore in groups 3, 13, 19, 26, 36, 42, 49, 59, 65, *i.e.*, at intervals of 10, 6, 7, 10, 6, 7, 10 and 6 groups. But I must point out an error fraught with consequences. Groups 22 and 23 quite correctly have the difference 177, but in this single instance the scribe has written down 178 and hence has computed the three days belonging to it as VII Ix, VIII Men and IX Cib instead of VI Ben, VII Ix and VIII Men, and from here on to the close he is always one day in advance, so that on page 58 group 69 ends with the days X Cimi, XI Manik and XII Lamat, while it ought to have ended with IX Chicchan, X Cimi and XI Manik.

So much for the series. Vid. on this series my paper "Zwei Hieroglyphenreihen in der Dresdener Mayahandschrift" (Zeitschrift für Ethnologie, 1905, numbers 2 and 3). Let us turn next to the ten pictures which are inserted in this series, three of which appear at the end of each period of 2920 days as on pages 46-50. Let us attempt to advance a step further in the darkness which still surrounds us here.

One of these pictures, the 8th, which is on page 56b, is in the wrong place, owing to the error in computation in Groups 58 and 59 to which I called attention above. It belongs not *before* but *after* group 59, the first on page 56b. This is indicated in the Manuscript itself. For in group 59 the two hieroglyphs, usually placed above each group, are missing and we find instead of them the sign resembling a snail, which is doubtless a very much emphasized zero (compare my "Erläuterungen," page 29), which indicates that the section designated by a picture closes with this group.

Having corrected this error we see that the ten pictures are on the following pages and come after the following numbers of the series: —

1.	53a	502
2.	55a	2244
3.	56a	3278
4.	57a	4488
5.	52b	6230
6.	53b	7264
7.	54b	8474
8.	56b	10216
9.	57b	11250
10.	58b	11958.

From this it follows that a picture is assigned to each of the nine sections composing the series. They are placed, however, not at the beginning or end of the section, but always after the expiration of 502 (= 2 × 177 + 148) days. The pictures are thus separated from one another by 1742, 1034 and 1210 days, which intervals correspond exactly to the length of the nine sections. But the last picture is separated from the preceding one by 708 days, and as it has a character quite its own, it must be discussed separately. But these 708 days with the 502 days of the beginning quite regularly amount to 1210 days, and the series is therefore to be considered as a recurring one.

Now these nine pictures might very easily be regarded as forming a new series, which is inserted in the original one and which has the day 502 as its zero-point. In that case, we shall have to subtract 502 every time from the days set down in the Manuscript. This new series may be represented thus: —

1.	53a	0
2.	55a	1742
3.	56a	2776
4.	57a	3986
5.	52b	5728
6.	53b	6762
7.	54b	7972
8.	56b	9714
9.	57b	10748.

It is certainly remarkable that the last number, 10748, corresponds so closely to the time of the revolution of Saturn, which is computed at 10753 days. For owing to the slowness of its progress, the Mayas may have known not only the apparent but also the actual revolution of Saturn. Besides the apparent revolution of Saturn (378 days from one superior conjunction to the next) could not be made to coincide very well with the length of the solar year. I will immediately present a further confirmation of my theory.

All these pictures have rectangles above them, of which I have spoken in my "Erläuterungen," page 16, and which always enclosed two or three hieroglyphs in which, with due hesitation, I assumed to be the signs of the sun, moon, and planets. This theory has as yet called forth no serious opposition.

Now in the passages just mentioned, I indicated the following figures as the signs of Saturn:—

   or   

These figures actually occur in all the nine pictures with the exception of the first, which has no rectangle at all, and where in true Maya fashion, the zero-point is concealed.

I go still further in my bold hypothesis. The time of the apparent revolution of Jupiter has been placed at 397 days. The Mayas, I think, computed it at 398 days. In the passage alluded to I regarded the following as the sign for Jupiter:—

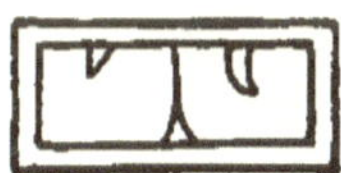   

We find these signs in pictures 4, 6, 7 and 9. The corresponding numbers reduced for the revolution of Saturn are 3986, 6762, 7972 and 10,748. I assume that the third picture, *i.e.*, the number 2776, is another zero-point, in consequence of which the sign is here suppressed, and that still another is the tenth picture with the number 11,958, which has no relation to the revolution of Saturn.

If we compare these numbers with the 398, *i.e.*, the apparent revolution of Jupiter, we have the following:—

$$3. \quad 2776 = 7 \times 398 - 10$$
$$4. \quad 3986 = 10 \times 398 + 6$$
$$6. \quad 6762 = 17 \times 398 - 4$$
$$7. \quad 7972 = 20 \times 398 + 12$$
$$9. \quad 10748 = 27 \times 398 + 2$$
$$10. \quad 11958 = 30 \times 398 + 18$$

The differences 10, 6, 4, 12, 2 and 18 are so small in comparison with 398, that the numbers 2776, etc., might very well have been regarded as approximate multiples of the revolution of Jupiter. And the remainders in the seventh and tenth pictures could be still further reduced. In the seventh picture, the first sign is very unusual and one which I do not remember having met with elsewhere. If it should be possible to regard it as the number of the thirteen week days, then it would follow (the Saturn sign being regarded as unimportant) that the contents of the rectangle meant:— 13 + a multiple of 398, by which this remainder would be reduced to -1.

The tenth picture has the cross b as the beginning of the rectangle. This is the sign for union, very often denoting especially the union of all the twenty days. Thus we have here (aside from the middle sign to be discussed later) the formula:— 20 + 30 × 398 - 2 = 11,958, or even 20 + 30 × 398 = 11,960.

The regular progression from the 7th multiple to the 10th, 17th, 20th, 27th, and 30th multiples in the above six equations is also somewhat in favor of my theory, while the four rectangles without the Jupiter sign are by no means multiples of the Jupiter revolution:—

1. 502 = 398 + 104
2. 1742 =   4 × 398 + 150
5. 5728 = 14 × 398 + 156
8. 9714 = 24 × 398 + 162.

Let us now try to interpret the meaning of the remaining rectangles (always omitting the Saturn sign as a matter of course.)

In pictures 2 and 8 the rectangle also contains the sign of the moon or of the twenty days. Beside it in picture 2 is the sign, which in my "Erläuterungen," page 16, I regarded as the sign for Mercury. Hence we have here 20 + 15 × 115 = 1745, *i.e.*, only 3 units more than the required 1742.

The rectangle with the eighth picture contains in addition to the moon a sign which looks as if it were intended for a whole divided into four parts. Until something better (perhaps the the sign of Venus) is proposed, I will assume that it is the quarter of the Tonalamatl, *i.e.*, 65, and I take the required number to be 9714 in the form of 20 + 149 × 65 + 9.

Above the third picture I see a Mercury and a Venus sign and I read 584 + 19 × 115 = 2769, which is only 7 units less than the required 2776.

The fifth picture still remains to be discussed, but I do not know how to unite the Mercury revolution here with the 5728. For the present, however, I am inclined to believe that there is a mistake in this passage.

We pass now from the obscure contents of the rectangles to the equally mysterious pictures themselves.

Aside from the tenth picture, I find human forms in four pictures.

Picture 1, page 53a, is the death-god (A) seated and pointing upward, an appropriate representation for the zero-point of the Saturn series, *i.e.*, for the end of the preceding revolution.

Picture 2, page 55a, contains the head of a deity, probably D's with the suggestion of a beard and the sun-sign on his forehead. The head is surrounded by a ring striped black and white.

Picture 3, page 56a, is the head of B, again with a beard and with the sign Kin (sun) above. The head is surrounded by a design, the left part of which is black and the right white.

Picture 6, page 53b, represents a hanged woman, which Schellhas, "Göttergestalten," page 11, takes to be the Maya goddess Ixtab, the goddess of the halter, *i.e.*, of the hanged.

The centre of picture 4 on page 57a, contains the suggestion of a face, perhaps in place of the Ahau sign, and on either side of it is a black and white surface.

It is further important to note that four times in this section Kin (sun) forms the centre of the picture, viz:—pictures 5, 7, 8 and 9, pages 52b, 54b, 56b and 57b. In all four cases there is on either side of Kin a black and white surface, such as we have already seen in picture 4 and similar to that in picture 3. Pictures 8 and 9 are vomited up, as it were, by a serpent placed below them, in the same way as B is represented on pages 34b and 35b. In pictures 5 and 8, four objects suggesting arrows extend from the Kin in four directions and probably denote the four cardinal points or the four Bacabs, of which we shall have more to say presently. Two of these arrow-like signs also appear in picture 7, page 54b, but only on the black and not on the white surface.

I will postpone discussing picture 10 until later and pass on to the hieroglyphs above the first nine pictures, about which it is true I have nothing satisfactory to say. There are always properly speaking ten of these hieroglyphs, among them the two signs for the sun and moon. But the scribe introduced the latter only in pictures 1-4, and also with the more elaborate last picture 10. With pictures 5 and 9 he omitted these signs in order to represent the other eight larger and with greater distinctness of detail. Among these hieroglyphs are several of gods, especially that of A with pictures 1, 5 and 9, and H with picture 5, and with pictures 1, 3, 5, 7, 8 and 9 there are other heads, some of them bird-heads, regarding which I am uncertain.

The Ben-Ik sign, to which I have assigned the meaning of a lunar month, belongs with pictures 4, 8 and 9 and occurs twice each with pictures 1 and 10.

I am inclined to see the sign for Mercury in the crouching figure belonging to pictures 9 and 10, which is drawn upside down and combined with the half Venus sign ($11958 = 104 \times 115 - 2$).

Hands grasping a hieroglyph (a sign for 20 days?) are represented in pictures 1, 7, 8 and 10.

The enigmatical numbers, prefixed to the hieroglyphs, occur several times, thus a 1 with pictures 1 and 10, and a 4 twice with picture 8 and a 6 with picture 3.

Now let us examine picture 10 somewhat in detail and also the signs standing above it, since both are of special significance here. This representation treats of the period of 11,960 days in which the Mercury and lunar revolutions meet. And this is proved by the ten hieroglyphs, which I will number as follows:—

1   6

2   7

3   8

4   9

5   10.

I can omit Signs 3 and 8, sun and moon, since they refer to a period of time only in a general way. Sign 1 seems to me, as I have already stated, to have reference to the revolutions of Mercury. Then follows sign 2, the upper part of which is a mat and the lower the Muluc sign. I believe this sign is intended to denote that the beginning of this period is in a Muluc year. Indeed, our examination of pages 51-52 showed that it was the year 6 Muluc. The mat (Pop) is very properly the symbol of beginning, since the first month of the year was likewise called Pop. Sign 7, it seems to me, indicates that this period should be divided into lunar months (denoted by Ben-Ik), and, as I have already demonstrated in my examination of page 24, the length of the period is stated here by Signs 4, 5, 6 and 9, but the dot before the fifth should be placed before the fourth, as is actually the case on page 24. Therefore:—

4 =   21

5 =   7200

6 =   4680

9 =   59

11960.

It is perhaps not accidental that the ninth sign is that of the fourteenth month, which signifies the expiration of the preceding lunar month, for here the month begins with the first day of the fifteenth month.

Sign 10 is doubtless Xul = end, as it so often is, for example, on pages 61-62 below. But I have not solved the meaning of the two prefixes. The end would be XII Lamat 16 Yax (13 Ix).

The picture represents a human form, which has in place of a head a design somewhat resembling the head of a lance. It is sitting with legs spread apart, and in this respect may be compared with god B of Cort. 9, who is represented in the same way. In the picture before us, the figure holds in its upraised hands the sun and moon signs, which are constantly repeated throughout the series. The Venus sign is placed between the outspread legs. In the rectangle above the figure, this sign is repeated in a more concise form, while on the left the cross *b* appears as the sign of union or multiplication, and on the right that of Jupiter, whose period of revolution is here multiplied by 30 (30 × 398 = 11,940). And the two Venus signs can mean nothing more than that this period of 11,960 also serves the purpose of filling up the gap between the two large Venus-solar periods of 37,960 days, like the similar process which we saw on pages 46-50.

We have examined first the series and then the pictures with the hieroglyphs belonging to them. Let us pass now, as the third step, to the examination of the two rows of hieroglyphs extending above the numbers throughout the whole section. First of all, I will again set down here the position of each of the sixty-nine groups:—

Page 51.	52.	53.	54.
31. 32. 33. 34. 35. 36.	37. 38. 39. 40.	1. 2. 3. 4. 5. 6.	7. 8. 9. 10. 11. 12. 13.
		41. 42. 43. 44. 45.	46. 47. 48. 49. 50.
Page 55.	56.	57.	58.
14. 15. 16. 17. 18.	19. 20. 21. 22.	23. 24. 25. 26.	27. 28. 29. 30.
51. 52. 53. 54. 56. 57. 58.	59. 60. 61. 62.	63. 64. 65. 66. 67.	68. 69.

Since each group contains two hieroglyphs, this makes 138. in all. Of these, however, about 24 on the upper halves of the pages, are wholly or almost wholly effaced which very materially hinders the trustworthy determination of the context.

Furthermore group 59 is entirely lacking or rather group 58, in the place of which the 59th has been set down. The eighth picture was probably already drawn, when the artist saw that there was not room enough left for the 58th and 59th groups. Hence he omitted the 58th, setting down in place of it the 59th and in the place of the latter he set down the zero mentioned above.

The question now arises:—Are these hieroglyphs dependent upon the days and numbers of the series and upon the pictures, or are they entirely independent of them?

I find but *one* point in favor of the first possibility, viz:—the Venus sign in group 4b (I will designate the upper hieroglyphs by *a* and the lower by *b*). It is placed in the period indicated in which 502-679 days elapse, and in which, therefore, Venus has finished a revolution of 584 days. It may be, that by way of exception, this significant date was intentionally recorded.

On the other hand, there are many things, which favor an entirely different interpretation of these hieroglyphs. Thus I am of the opinion that the ritual year of 364 days with its four Bacab periods of 91 days each is referred to here, as we have already found it referred to on pages 31a-32a and on page 45a, and shall find it again on pages 65-69 and 71-73. In that case the single groups would be separated from one another by one Maya week = 13 days.

I will now arrange the sixty-nine groups in the following order (the reason for which will become clear directly):—

I	4	11	18	25	32	39	46	53	60	67
II	5	12	19	26	33	40	47	54	61	68
III	6	13	20	27	34	41	48	55	62	69
IV	7	14	21	28	35	42	49	56	63	1
V	8	15	22	29	36	43	50	57	64	2

VI 9 16 23 30 37 44 51 58 65 3
VII 10 17 24 31 38 45 52 59 66.

The groups in a horizontal row are separated from one another by 7 or a multiple of 7. If now a hieroglyph is repeated in those places, which are in the same horizontal row, then this is a confirmation of the supposition that Bacab periods are meant to be represented here. Hence I will examine each row in turn. These rows extend over the long period of 69 × 13 days probably merely for the purpose of filling up the space.

I. In 39b, 46b, 53b and 60b, *i.e.*, after every seven groups, perhaps also in 18b, we find the following sign, which I identified as that of a Bacab, in Globus, Vol. LXXI: —

Hence this denotes the beginning of the Bacab period. In 4b the sign is replaced by that for Venus. In 11b, 25b, 32b and 67b we find other signs, it is true, nevertheless the regularity stated above cannot be accidental. The upper signs of groups 39a, 46a, 53a and 60a contain an Imix and corroborate the connection.

II. 5b and 26b (after 3 × 91 days) contain a head very like the preceding, which readily suggests the idea that it is merely a Bacab sign pushed one group ahead, but it also appears in 13b, 50b and 52b.

Then 12b, 54b and 61b correspond, *i.e.*, after six groups of 91 days and one more of the same length, but the same sign appears also in 34b, 48b and 56b.

III. 41b and 69a are Xul = end and are therefore separated by 28 × 13 = 4 × 91 days, *i.e.*, the length of a year. It is singular that both signs of 41 are like those of 47; if we assume that 47 was set down one group too soon, it would be in excellent keeping with the rest. The Xul also appears in 11b and 28b. 34b and 48b correspond after 2 × 91 days, as already mentioned under II.

IV. 42a and 49b both contain the sign for the sun between clouds.

V. 36b and 57b agree after 3 × 91 days; the same sign appears again in 10b and 20b.

15a and 36a correspond after 3 × 91 days; we shall continue the examination of this sign under pages 71-73.

VI. 37a and 65a agree, *i.e.*, after 4 × 91 days = a year. The sign contains a human figure stretching both arms aloft. The passing of a year was likewise indicated in III, but a year coming 52 days later than this.

VII. 10a and 31a agree, *i.e.*, after 3 × 91 days. The sign is composed of the crouching figure prefixed to the cross, which we also find in 12b, 35a and 65b; it is prefixed to a different hieroglyph in 30a. In 38b, 52b and 59b (58 in the Manuscript) we see bird-like heads resembling the Bacab sign. We should expect to find a familiar sign in 45, which is drawn between these, but a Moan appears there instead. These signs seem to indicate the end of the Bacab period. Does the Moan sign here, too, suggest the end of the year?

In 38a, 52a and 59a we again see an Imix, and I consider it a corroboration of my theory that all the four signs of groups 38 and 39 are repeated in 52 and 53 after 2 × 91 days.

I believe a further corroboration is the fact that though many of these hieroglyphs have no connection with these periods of 7 × 13, *i.e.*, with the divisions of the ritual year, they do correspond with the usual divisions of the Tonalamatl, *i.e.*, 4 × 13 and 5 × 13 days.

After 4 × 13 or a multiple of it the signs recur in 20b, 24b, 40b, 44b-12b, 48b, 56b-16b, 32b, 64b-26b, 50b-10a, 30a-37a, 65a-15b, 51b-11b and 47b.

As examples of 5 × 13 I would mention 3b, 63b-10a, 20a, 30a-5b, 50b-24b, 29b-35b, 65b-15b, 20b, 40b.

Finally, I must mention two more hieroglyphs, which are limited almost entirely to these pages: —

In the first sign, which occurred on page 10a, I thought I recognized the lunar month of 28 days. It occurs in this section in connection with the third picture on page 56, and besides in the following groups of hieroglyphs: — 16b, 32b and 64b, always combined with a Yax. The regularity of the intervals is striking, but as yet I can neither explain that, nor the crouching personage (Mercury?) in the 10th, 20th and 30th groups and again in the next, the 31st.

The second sign is found *only* on these pages and here not less than eleven times, possibly with the addition of the effaced sign in 6b and 27b which may have been the same hieroglyph. The eleven places in which it occurs are as follows: —3b, 15b, 17b, 23b, 24b, 29b, 40b, 44b, 49a, 51b and 63b. Two different prefixes are added to it; one in the first two and the last two places and also in the last but two joined with Kin, and the other in the six middle places. Of the eleven groups, 17 and 24, 44 and 51 are 7 groups apart, 3 and 17, 15 and 29, 49 and 63 are 14 groups apart, 23 and 44 are 21 groups apart, and hence 23 and 51 are separated by 28 groups or 1 year. Group 40 alone is not concerned with these intervals of seven or multiples of seven.

Now, how far may all these periods of time be due to accident and how far to design? Accident *alone* is quite out of the question. The frequent repetition of the sun-sign in groups 49, 50 and 51 on pages 54b and 55b, seems to me to refer to the conjunctions of the sun with certain stars, which occur at intervals of thirteen days.

Pages 58—59.

This section is also based on a series occupying the whole of page 59, which contains nothing but number and day signs. This series has the difference 78, which we found once before on page 44. There the starting-point was III Lamat, here it is the day XIII Muluc, probably coming in the year XIII Muluc, as in Cort. 40b, as I shall have occasion to suggest later. The series extends, with the usual errors and variations, in four divisions from top to bottom. The days, which are always two days behindhand, owing to the number 78, in 780 again reach the day XIII Muluc, at which point the succeeding members remain stationary, since from here on the difference is always 780 or a multiple of it. 780 days are, however, the apparent time of the revolution of Mars, which is the only planet now left to be discussed, the subject of pages 46-50 having been Venus and the sun, and of pages 51-58, Mercury and the moon with incidental treatment of Saturn and Jupiter. With 780 as its difference, the series ascends to 19 × 780 = 14,820, and then continues with this large number as its difference until the series is lost in the effaced passages.

Curiously enough, however, directly under the line containing the 14,820, there is a new series composed of nine members, or ten counting the suppressed starting-point. But this starting-point is again the day IX Ik, the difference, as proved by the annexed days, is again 78 and the series ends with 780. Thus the starting-point is the only difference between the two series. The principal series contains all the even and the secondary series all the uneven days. Can the starting-point of the revolution of Mars have been determined according to different principles? Is it possible that in one case the beginning of the planet's retrogression was adopted as the starting-point, and in the other case the date on which the planet, after completing its retrograde course, again reached the degree of right ascension at which it had begun its retrogression? This is a difficult matter to decide, since the period of the retrogression of Mars fluctuates between 62 and 81 days. The interval from IX Ik to XIII Muluc is 147 and in reversed order 113 days.

It can hardly be assumed that the 19 of the IX 19 or IX Ik is connected with the 19 × 780 mentioned above or with the 19 + 19 + 19 + 21 into which the 78 is divided on pages 44-45, or finally with the 19, which four times forms the principal part of the sub-divisions of 65 on pages 33-34.

Numbers amounting to millions accompany this series in the usual way. Two of these are on page 58, viz:—1,426,360 and 1,386,580; but with the sign of the sixth day, which is important here, between them. Below these numbers, however, are two month dates:—first the normal date IV Ahau 8 Cumhu and, if I have correctly restored the effaced number before the month sign, which in its turn is indistinct, the second is XIII Muluc 2 Zac, which would fall in the year VIII Muluc. The encircled numbers also occur here. They are set down beside the lower number of seven figures. We find here a red 12 with a black 1 inserted, below this a black 7 and below this again, enclosed in a red band, a black 11, which I regard as also representing the value of a red number. We shall find a similar instance among the serpent numerals. Then we have here 1. 7. 11. = 511 and 12. 11. = 251. But 511 = 260 + 251 and 251 is the interval between XIII Muluc and IV Ahau.

With the day XIII Muluc and the interval 9 between IV Ahau and XIII Muluc, numbers for XIII Muluc have been formed amounting to millions, which, however, have been suppressed in the Manuscript, just as they were on page 31 where, in like manner, numbers were first formed for day XIII Akbal.

I assume that to begin with, 76 Tonalamatls (= 19,760) were added to this 9 and then 228 Tonalamatls (= 59,280), the 228 being = 3 × 76 and the 59,280 including 76 revolutions of Mars.

The result in one case was 19,769 and in the other 59,289. If the 12 Ahau-Katuns, which are specified as 1,366,560 on page 24b be added here, we have the following numbers:—

$$1,386,329 = \text{XIII Muluc 2 Mol (3 Muluc)},$$
$$1,425,849 = \text{XIII Muluc 2 Zip (12 Muluc)},$$

and if the two encircled numbers of the Manuscript:—251 and 511 be added, the sums are 1,386,580 and 1,426,360, *i.e.*, the two large numbers of the Manuscript.

The dates corresponding to these numbers are as follows:—

$$1,386,580 = \text{IV Ahau 13 Muan (12 Muluc)},$$
$$1,426,360 = \text{IV Ahau 8 Muan (4 Ix)}.$$

If we compare the two numbers with the normal date, the curious result follows that:—

1) 1,386,580 - 1,366,560 = 20,020.

This number is equal to 55 × 364, including therefore the ritual year of 364 days.

2) 1,426,360 - 1,366,560 = 59,800.

This number is five times 11,960 days, which is assumed to be the time in which the lunar and Mercury revolutions accord. This 59,800 was found once before on page 24 as the suppressed difference between 68,900 and 9,100.

Thus the separate sections (of the book) are very closely connected.

If the two large numbers be compared with one another their difference will be found to be 39,780. This is equal first to 51 Mars revolutions of 780 days, and second to 4420 × 9, *i.e.*, a multiple of the interval between IV Ahau and XIII Muluc.

Now we must direct our attention to the seventeen hieroglyphs, which we find in the two columns on page 58, apart from the matter-of-course calendar date at the top, which is repeated at the bottom. One column contains 11 hieroglyphs and the other 6. I will here advance the following theory in regard to these hieroglyphs, which may serve until a better is found:—

Since, as a rule, the Tonalamatl is divided into 5 × 52 days, I believe that each group of three Tonalamatls treated of on page 59, is divided into 15 of these parts; that each hieroglyph, therefore, denotes 52 days and that the first three parts are separated from the others by the signs of beginning and end in the first and fifth places, so that three of these parts, which equal 156 days, always form a separate group. 156 is the 5th part of 780. With the omission of the first and fifth signs, the passage, I think, stands thus:—

		0	XIII Muluc	2	Kankin (13 Muluc).
1)	0-52		XIII Imix	14	Pax.
2)	53-104		XIII Ben	1	Pop (1 Ix).
3)	105-156		XIII Chicchan	13	Zip.
4)	157-208		XIII Caban	5	Xul.
5)	209-260		XIII Muluc	17	Mol.
6)	261-312		XIII Imix	9	Zac.
7)	313-364		XIII Ben	1	Kankin.
8)	365-416		XIII Chicchan	13	Pax.
9)	417-468		XIII Caban	25	Cumhu.
10)	469-520		XIII Muluc	12	Zip (2 Cauac).
11)	521-572		XIII Imix	4	Xul.
12)	573-624		XIII Ben	16	Mol.
13)	625-676		XIII Chicchan	8	Zac.
14)	677-728		XIII Caban	20	Mac.
15)	729-780		XIII Muluc	12	Pax.

If we adopt this arrangement for the present we cannot fail to see that the author had an aim in view, when we consider the following:—

1. The zero-point lies 15,609 days later than the normal date IV Ahau 8 Cumhu (9 Ix). This is equal to 20×780 or 60×260 increased by the interval between IV Ahau and XIII Muluc = 9. There are 86 days between 2 Kankin and 8 Cumhu *i.e.*, $15,609 = 43 \times 365 - 86$, and from 9 Ix to 13 Muluc it is 43 years.

2. The same zero-point, 13 Muluc, lies in the year with the same name, that is, the very point where a Tonalamatl of the year ends.

3. In this arrangement the first as well as the last day of the year 1 Ix is exactly reached in the second and ninth groups. While the meaning of the second is as yet unintelligible to me, the end of the year is appropriately indicated by the ninth with its compound of Kin and the year-sign, above which there may be an Ix as a superfix, but misshapen for want of room.

4. Also the fact that it is the first of the two columns, which closes with this year-end, seems to show a purpose.

5. Several instances of similarity appear among the hieroglyphs in these groups of three:—an Akbal sign in 1 and 4 suggests the god D, the superfix and prefix of 2 and 14 the god K and 5 and 11 the screech-owl and therefore A.

Little else is to be said of these hieroglyphs.

C might be denoted by 3 (13 Zip) and 10 (12 Zip). Group 8, the central point of the series, has on the left and right the signs for the north and south as if the time between the north (Muluc) years and the south (Cauac) years were meant to be indicated here.

I am inclined to consider the crouching personage in 12 as the revolution of Mercury, which requires 115 days: — 573 is 5 × 114 + 3 or 5 × 115 - 2.

Is 7 a sign, as yet unknown, for the year of 364 days?

15 looks like two signs for the month Mac, placed back to back, which here designates the Tonalamatl as it does on page 24. The superfix of three parts might denote three Tonalamatls = 780 days. The familiar sign in the fifth place in connection with the expiration of the first Tonalamatl is striking; it is the one usually identified as that of the screech-owl or death-bird.

Page 60.

This is the last page of the front of the second part and is divided into four sections: — at the top we find hieroglyphs, below these a picture, then hieroglyphs again and in the lowest section another picture.

The upper picture contains first a rectangular elevation like a platform. Enclosed in this rectangle is the picture of the animal resembling a dog lying down, which we have often met with, the last time on page 47. In front of the dog is a hieroglyph, which, I regret to say, is still unknown and which occurred six times as a heading on page 23b. On the platform two personages are fighting; one is in war-dress holding in his left hand the throwing-stick or atlatl, and in his right probably arrows; the other figure, whose back is somewhat indistinct owing to obliteration, is apparently unarmed and is making a defensive gesture with one hand. Beside the platform, and therefore on a lower level, is a second person walking behind the armed person as if to help him. He too is in war-dress and likewise holds an atlatl. A black 3 is set down between the two combatants, and there may also have been a red 2, which is indistinct owing to the red background of the picture.

Let us next examine the lower picture. A blindfolded personage is kneeling on the left. A serpent's head rises from the ground in front of him. A second serpent rises in several coils on the shoulders of the blindfolded personage and on the serpent's neck sits enthroned another personage, who is rather indistinct, holding a spear and a shield. On the right, opposite this group and facing it, is a second. A personage with arms bound and bowed head is sitting on the ground. There is a black ring around his eye. Behind him stands the victor in war-dress and again equipped with spear and shield. There is a red 11 and a black 2 between the two groups.

We see that the reference here is to combat, just as it was on the right side of pages 46-50. And since the subject of these pages like that of 46-59 is confined to the revolutions of the planets, it is natural that the pursuit of one by the other, their periodical disappearance, the crossing of their orbits and the variation in the length of their revolutions should be looked upon as a contest. Therefore, since the sun, the moon and the five planets have hitherto been treated of on these pages, I look for these seven heavenly bodies in the seven personages pictured here on page 60. I will attempt to explain them, hoping that my interpretation may be replaced by a better one.

The sun and moon stand on the platform in the upper picture; their combat is equivalent to the eclipses to which they at times succumb. The moon is the assailant and the sun makes only a proud defensive gesture. The person behind the moon must be Mars. The animal under the two persons is the embodiment of the eclipses, which the Aztecs interpreted as the act of being devoured by the jaguar. The hieroglyph in front looks very much like the meeting of two circles. Does it refer to the day Lamat (Aztec tochtli = rabbit)?

At the left, bottom, the powerful Venus triumphs over the weak Mercury. The two planets are real chronometers by reason of the regular alternation of their appearance as morning and evening stars, and also by their disappearance twice in each revolution and finally even in the variation in the length of the two periods of invisibility. Hence they are each accompanied by a serpent as the usual symbol of time.

On the right, on the other hand, Jupiter as the stronger has vanquished Saturn, whose bound arms symbolize his slowness of motion and the fact that he is confined to the same region of the sky. Should not the ring around his eye have a very special meaning? But we must guard against an excess of imagination. Jupiter and Saturn are the last to be represented, as they were of but secondary importance, on pages 51-58 and perhaps also in the 2200 on page 24.

I will not deny that yet another interpretation of this page is possible. The top picture may be Venus and the moon opposing one another, and the bottom picture may represent the sun as victor over Mercury. There are some things in favor of this point of view.

The correct order of the twenty-four hieroglyphs is the following, in my opinion, which is borne out by the different colors of the four groups:—

1	2	7	8
3	4	9	10
5	6	11	12
13	14	19	20
15	16	21	22
17	18	23	24

These signs can have no relation to mythology. There is not a hieroglyph of a god among them, for if sign 6 could be taken for B's hieroglyph, the resemblance to the sign of the fist, familiar from the inscriptions, as well as the Imix and the cross-hatching as a prefix, makes this doubtful. The latter component would rather suggest the summer solstice. If sign 12 were intended to denote the Bacab, then it would refer to chronology rather than to mythology. Also the Cimi in 17 might equally well mean the day as the god. Indeed several things refer here to chronology and astronomy, among them the unmistakable union of numbers and month signs, which occur here repeatedly. Thus from what remains of the almost obliterated signs 1 and 2, they might denote the normal date IV Ahau 8 Cumhu, which always occupies the first place. Signs 7 and 20 are plainly the same, 9 Xul (sixth month) and sign 14 is 10 Yaxkin (seventh month). Sign 5 might be Caban combined with Uo (second month) and a ten. In sign 19 we again see Yaxkin without a number. Signs 9 and 23 are Zec (fifth month) and signs 21 and 22 may be Kankin (fourteenth month). The days occur in the same manner as the months. It is true that Kin is only a part of hieroglyph 10, the rest of which is effaced, but the familiar compound of Caban and Muluc appears in 18 and 24 and Cimi is in 17, as we have seen. In sign 13, Ahau is combined with a red number, which must lie between X and XV. But this should not be regarded as forming a calendar date with the 10 Yaxkin near by, for Ahau is never the tenth day of a month. Can 16 be the sign of the twelfth month, Ceh, combined with that for 7200? Hieroglyphs 3 and 8 are effaced and I do not understand 4, 11 and 15.

There are no parallels in the kindred passages 46-50, unless it be 7 Zec on the bottom of page 49 and here in signs 9 and 23, but without a number. Cf. my paper on this page 60 in the "Weltall," year 6, pages 251-257.

Page 61—64.

On examining the reverse of the second part of our Manuscript, *i.e.*, pages 61-74, we find an empty page on the left, the back of which is occupied by page 60. This may be explained by assuming that the scribe wrote pages 61-64 and possibly even pages 61-74 from right to left, the great series having occasioned such a proceeding, and that his material came to an end when he had finished page 61. Nevertheless, it is advisable to continue with the original numbering in order to avoid confusion.

Aside from the concluding (or beginning) page 74, this whole section of pages 61-74 consists of three parts:—61-64, 65-69 and 70-73. Let us first consider the first section, which I have already discussed in my treatise "Zur Erläuterung der Mayahandschriften II."

The basis of this section is a series, the beginning of which is on the bottom, right, of page 64. Its primary difference is always that which we found on pages 31-32, viz:—the Bacab period of 91 days, the quarter of the ritual year of 364 days = 7 weeks of 13 days each. It ascends by 91 until it reaches 1820, which number is a multiple of both 364 and 260 and is also divisible by 28, the number of weeks in a year. Just as on page 32 the series continues with the new difference 1820 as far as 7280, its fourth multiple, which then becomes the third difference. Indeed, I believe that even the partially effaced numbers could be so restored as to carry the series to the number 36,400 = 400 × 91, which would then become the fourth difference and the series would close at the top of page 63 with 145,600 = 1600 × 91, *i.e.*, with the numbers 1. 0. 4. 8. 0. of which the 1 is entirely and the 0 half effaced. The series on pages 31-32, however, closed with 29,120 = 320 × 91, but there is still room for a higher series.

Under this largest number (1600 × 91) there is on page 63 a large red number consisting of 19. 0. 4. 4. which is crowded into a very small space between the figures of 1820. I can only understand it by replacing the first 4 by a 3, for then it is

136,864 = 1504 × 91 or by addition of a zero. We shall return to this number in the examination of the serpent numerals.

The series is accompanied in the regular way by five days. At the beginning of this series, page 64, right bottom, are the days III Cib, III Men, III Chicchan, III Caban and XIII Ix; the III is set down only with the first of these days and is to be supplied with the next three. Hence the actual zero point is to be found 91 days back in the days III Chicchan, III Kan, III Ix, III Cimi and XIII Akbal, the last of which is also the beginning of the corresponding series on page 32. From 1820 on, these last-named days, of course unchanged, accompany the numbers. The most important of these days are the first and last, but we shall see later in connection with the serpent numbers that the other three, which are separated from one another by 39, 130 and 52, *i.e.*, 3 × 13, 10 × 13 and 4 × 13, are likewise not set down here by mere accident.

We come now to the five columns, three on page 63 and two on page 62, which join this series on the left. They contain the large numbers, which invariably accompany these series. Here there are six numbers, four of which, in my opinion, refer to the past and two to the future. Two of these numbers, the two largest, are set down together in the third column on page 63, one with red numbers and the other with black. Of these black numbers, I take the second from the top to be not 8 but 13, assuming that a line is omitted. The normal date IV Ahau 8 Cumhu from which, as the starting-point, all these numbers are to be computed, is set down below at the end of each of the five columns.

I now give the six numbers, first the two highest, then the other four from right to left, adding in each case the calendar date and the year in which they should be situated:—

> 1,538,342; IV Ik   15 Zac (12 Muluc).
>
> 1,535,004; VII Kan   2 Chen (3 Kan).
>
> 1,268,540; IV Ahau   8 Mol (1 Ix).
>
> 1,234,220; IV Ahau   18 Kayab (11 Kan).
>
> 1,272,544; IV Kan   17 Yaxkin (12 Muluc).
>
> 1,272,921; IV Imix   9 Mol (13 Ix).

The first, third and fifth numbers are already known from page 31a, and hence they need no further discussion here.

As these three numbers depend on the day XIII Akbal, so the other three all proceed from the day III Chicchan in the following positions, which are again suppressed in the Manuscript:—

> 1,483,585 = III Chicchan   8 Zac (5 Cauac).
>
> 1,233,985 = III Chicchan   8 Kankin (10 Cauac).
>
> 1,272,465 = III Chicchan   18 Zip (12 Muluc).

The second date in the manuscript is 13 Kankin and the third is 13 Zip; hence there is one line too many in the former number and one too few in the latter. While on page 31a the origin of the numbers belonging to the day XIII Akbal seems to be quite clear, here their relation to one another is entirely concealed. I must, therefore, refrain from expressing any conjecture in regard to them.

Now the numbers set down in the Manuscript are formed only by the addition of the encircled numbers also found there. The encircled number for the first expressed number is 51,419, which is the same number we found with the corresponding day XIII Akbal; the second has 235 and the third 456 = 260 + 196. The 51,419 was 197 × 260 + 199; but 199 is the interval from III Chicchan to VII Kan, just as it is from XIII Akbal to IV Ik. The 235 is the interval between III Chicchan and IV Ahau and the 196 that from III Chicchan and IV Imix.

By the addition of these differences, the numbers written out in the Manuscript are obtained:—

$$1{,}483{,}585 + 51{,}419 = 1{,}535{,}004 \text{ (VII Kan)}.$$
$$1{,}233{,}985 + 235 = 1{,}234{,}220 \text{ (IV Ahau)}.$$
$$1{,}272{,}465 + 456 = 1{,}272{,}921 \text{ (IV Imix)}.$$

Keeping in mind what was said in reference to page 31a, let us now examine the six numbers and dates collectively.

The fact that the days IV Ahau and XIII Akbal occur here and consequently also III Chicchan is not surprising. Nor is the choice of VII Kan and IV Ik an accident, for the interval between these days is exactly the same as that between III Chicchan and XIII Akbal, viz:—218 days.

Hence the distance from III Chicchan to VII Kan is also exactly equal to that between XIII Akbal to IV Ik, viz:—199 days.

Finally, the distance from VII Kan to III Chicchan is exactly equal to that between IV Ik and XIII Akbal, viz:—61 days.

IV Imix and IV Kan are separated from the normal date IV Ahau by 3 × 13 = 39 and 8 × 13 = 104 days.

Regarding the encircled numbers, so far as they are independent of 260, I would note the following:—

$$17 = \text{XIII Akbal to IV Ahau}.$$
$$121 = \text{XIII Akbal to IV Kan}.$$
$$196 = \text{III Chicchan to IV Imix}.$$
$$199 = \text{III Chicchan to VII Kan and XIII Akbal to IV Ik}.$$
$$235 = \text{III Chicchan to IV Ahau}.$$

In addition let me remark that 36 = VII Kan to IV Ahau, 39 = IV Imix to IV Ahau and 104 = IV Ahau to IV Kan.

The following arrangement will prove that these numbers were as usual also employed to form the large numbers by multiplication:—

$$17 \times 74{,}620 = 1{,}268{,}540 \text{ (IV Ahau)},$$

$$235 \times 5{,}252 = 1{,}234{,}220 \text{ (IV Ahau)},$$
$$36 \times 42{,}639 = 1{,}535{,}004 \text{ (VII Kan)},$$
$$39 \times 32{,}639 = 1{,}272{,}921 \text{ (IV Imix)},$$
$$104 \times 12{,}236 = 1{,}272{,}544 \text{ (IV Kan)}.$$

But the highest number, 1,538,342, was formed in a different way; it = 59,167 × 26; but the interval from IV Ahau to IV Ik = 182 = 7 × 26, and from IV Ik to IV Ahau = 78 = 3 × 26.

If in conclusion, we now examine the twelve numbers of seven figures given in this section, we will clearly see that by twos and twos they plainly belong together in pairs: —

The three pairs of numbers found by computation are as follows: —

1,486,923, XIII Akbal.

1,483,585, III Chicchan.

Difference 3338 = 12 × 260 + 218 (VII Kan to IV Ik, III Chicchan to XIII Akbal).

1,268,523, XIII Akbal.

1,233,985, III Chicchan.

Difference 34,538 = 132 × 260 + 218 (as above).

1,272,423, XIII Akbal.

1,272,465, III Chicchan.

Difference 42 (which is 260 - 218); 42 = IV Kan to IV Imix.

On the other hand the three pairs specified in the Manuscript are as follows: —

1,538,342, IV Ik.

1,535,004, VII Kan.

Difference 3338 = 12 × 260 + 218 as above, by reason of the encircled number 51,419 which is common to both numbers.

1,538,342, IV Ik.

1,535,004, VII Kan.

Difference 34,320 = 132 × 260, on account of the same day.

1,538,342, IV Ik.

1,535,004, VII Kan.

Difference 117 = IV Kan to IV Imix; strictly speaking 377 = 260 + 117.

The upper part of the five columns just now under discussion still remains to be examined. Here are five vertical rows of hieroglyphs, the first four each containing seven, and the fifth only six owing to lack of space.

The two rows at the top are as usual much obliterated, which is the more to be deplored since they consisted of five calendar dates, which would have contributed materially to the comprehension of the entire section. Fortunately, however, one of these dates is preserved complete, and we are able to see in what relation it stands to the rest. Thus we find in the third column of page 63 the date XIII Imix 9 Uo. It comes in the year 12 Ix and represents the number 1,523,921 (or a number separated from it by a multiple of 18,980). Now 1,523,921 = 4175 × 365 + 46 and = 5861 × 260 + 61. This agrees with the lower number inserted in red: — 1,538,342 = IV Ik 15 Zac (12 Muluc), which comes later by 14,421 = 39 × 365 + 186 and = 55 × 260 + 121. 121, however, is the difference between both XIII Imix and IV Ik and the days XIII Akbal and IV Kan in the last column of page 62. If we set down with these two numbers, those of the normal date just preceding and the normal date next following, we have

$$1,518,400 = 80 \times 18980.$$
$$1,523,921,$$
$$1,538,342,$$
$$1,556,360 = 82 \times 18980.$$

This is a period of 37,960 = 2 × 18,980 days. It is possible that at some future time an indication of such a transition from one Katun to the other will be found in the writings. Now these two top lines contain two dates; on page 62 we find 13 Ceh, and on page 63, 13 Xul, but nothing further is to be learned from this than that one or the other of the day-signs, 2, 7, 12, 17, must have been set down in the effaced indication of the position in the Tonalamatl. All else is obliterated. From the third to the seventh row of these five columns it is all extremely simple. The third row consists only of five signs for beginning, the fourth, of five for end, the sixth of B's sign five times and the seventh of the elongated head q four times. But in the fifth, two deities alternate, one is apparently male and the other female; the god is in columns 1, 3 and 5 and the goddess in 2 and 4; the god probably belonging to the days III Chicchan and the goddess to XIII Akbal.

If we look upon this series as the first story of a structure and the large numbers just now discussed as the second, then we find the third story here, as we shall find it again on page 69. In the passage on page 31, which is so closely related to the present one, a timid attempt has already been made with the number 2,804,100 to erect a third story of this kind, which however barely attained to a quarter of the height of the one which now engages our attention. If the numbers hitherto examined refer to a time not very far from the present, we now come to numbers which lie in so remote a future that they can hardly suggest anything else than the destruction of the world or a sort of twilight of the gods. Nevertheless the starting-point of the whole, the series, which is built up with the number 91, *i.e.*, the Bacab period or the quarter of a ritual year, continually comes to view. Indeed, the number of serpents is suggestive of this.

There are four large serpents, which fill most of the space on the left half of page 62 and the right of page 61. The two outer ones are bluish and the two inner ones white. They rise in several coils, their tails below and their heads above. A deity is represented above the gaping jaws of each of the four serpents, having apparently been vomited up. Above the first and third serpents B is represented in a fashion very similar to that which we have already seen on pages 33-35. Above the first serpent B has the pouch hanging from his neck and his hatchet is held downward; above the third he wears the pouch and the gala mantle and his hatchet is raised. Above the second fourth serpents, on the other hand, there are four-footed animals, but of a species not represented elsewhere. They might suggest a (four-footed?) walrus and a bear. We have here a double contrast, apparently referring to the four cardinal points.

The veil enveloping this representation would be lifted to a considerable extent, if all the eight hieroglyphs written above each serpent, were still legible. But, unfortunately, the second group is wholly and the third almost wholly effaced, while the first is partially effaced and only the fourth is preserved in its entirety. I read these groups in the following order:—

1 2

3 4

5 6

7 8.

Of these 7 and 8 in the first and fourth groups form the date IX Kan 12 Kayab, which is in the year 4 Ix; this same date probably occurred also in the other two groups. That it is of special importance here, is shown by the two columns of hieroglyphs on the left side of page 61, where this date occurs again in the lowest place. The last three large numbers are not computed from the normal date IV Ahau 8 Cumhu, but from this very date and the other five from a similar one. The sixth hieroglyph in the first group seems to correspond to the fifth in the fourth, since both contain the elongated head *q*, though with different accompaniments.

In the first group the fourth hieroglyph is the Bacab sign familiar to us from pages 51-58, suggesting that the series here is closely connected with the one which had the difference 91. The fifth sign of the same group is that for *beginning*, probably to confirm the fact that this section begins here. The third sign of the first group is probably an Imix, as it is in the first and fourth of the fourth group, combined here with the woman's head, which we saw repeated on pages 62 and 63 at the top; and over it in the second place of the fourth group is B's hieroglyph, which is also repeated on pages 62 and 63 at the top. The third place of the fourth group is occupied by a head, which may be C's and which is distinguished by the same kind of circle which on page 9b surrounded the Ahau.

Eight complete dates are set down below the serpents, among which are the XIII Akbal already found with the previous large numbers, and III Chicchan (repeated three times), and then III Kan (twice), forming the beginning and end of the series (page 64), and also III Cimi and III Ix. As we shall see directly these are the end dates of the large numbers, and Xul = end repeated eight times at the extreme bottom corresponds with this. On the other hand, the starting-points must be found by computation, with the exception of the date IX Kan 12 Kayab, which is actually written down and is the point of departure for three of the numbers.

I will designate the black numbers by *a* and the red by *b*. Seven of the eight numbers are undoubtedly absolutely correct; but I must alter the number 1b, the red number belonging to the first serpent. I assume that a line is wanting in the lowest figure, *i.e.*, it should be 8 instead of 3, and that the conspicuously large 1 further down on the page serves also as the red number, which belongs here. Only one slight change is necessary in the dates on the bottom of the pages, which were mentioned above. To the 16 in the date 4b I add a dot, and read it 17.

I will now give a table of the numbers, the starting-points of the periods obtained by computation, and the ends of the latter which are indicated below the serpents: —

1a: 12,489,781; XI Kan 12 Kankin (1 Ix); III Chicchan 18 Xul (4 Muluc).

1b: 12,388,121; XI Kan 12 Muan (7 Ix); III Chicchan 13 Pax (4 Ix).

2a: 12,454,761; IX Kan 7 Kankin (4 Cauac); III Chicchan 13 Yaxkin (2 Ix).

2b: 12,394,740; IX Kan 2 Chen (5 Kan); III Kan 12 Ceh (7 Ix).

3a: 12,438,810; IX Kan 12 Xul (3 Ix); III Ix 7 Zac (9 Muluc).

3b: 12,466,942; IX Kan 12 Kayab (4 Ix); III Cimi 14 Kayab (9 Ix).

4a: 12,454,459; IX Kan 12 Kayab (4 Ix); XIII Akbal 1 Kankin (1 Kan).

4b: 12,394,740; IX Kan 12 Kayab (4 Ix); III Kan 17 Uo (7 Muluc).

See my treatise, "Die Schlangenzahlen in der Dresdener Mayahandschrift" (Weltall, year 5, pages 199-203).

Several details show how this number-structure forms a definite, closely connected whole.

1. The beginning day in each case is the day Kan, which thereby indicates its position as the first.

2. The last three starting-points are the same; the first three end dates, at least, are the same in the Tonalamatl, though not in the year.

3. The two numbers 2b and 4b are exactly the same.

4. The first three numbers are each divisible without a remainder by 17, the interval from XIII Akbal to IV Ahau, which was true also of the 1,268,540 in the second column on page 63, although only this last number has anything to do with these important days, of which the other three numbers are independent.

On the other hand, a notable difference between the first serpent and the other three is, that the day XI Kan is the starting-point of the first and IX Kan of the others. There are, however, 80 days between IX Kan and XI Kan. Hence the numbers 2a and 1b are separated from each other by 66,640 = 256 × 260 + 80, although they have the same end III Chicchan.

Further it is to be noted that the largest of the eight numbers, 12,489,781, is separated from the lowest, 12,388,121, *i.e.*, the black number from the red one of the first serpent, by only 101,660, *i.e.*, by not a full one per cent of the entire magnitude. 101,660 = 5 × 18,980 + 26 × 260 or 391 × 260 or 7820 × 13.

It is to be noted also that the differences between the black and red numbers in the second and third serpents (60,021 and 28,132) are divisible by 13 (4617 × 13 and 2164 × 13). They *must* be, since all six numbers refer to the day III.

Finally the question naturally arises, how did the computer obtain these values, *i.e.*, how was the whole structure built up? On page 63 we found a 136,864 (not 136,884) set down in strikingly small characters and crowded between the other numbers, which would remain a mystery unless one assumed that it was reserved there for this structure; it is 91 × 1504. At first I thought it possible that this 136,864 had been again multiplied by 91, the real basal number of this section; for we had found a second power once before (on pages 46-50) by computation, viz:—2 × 260 × 260. The result of multiplication in this case would be 12,454,624, and the differences between the eight numbers in the serpents would be as follows:—1a + 35,157, 1b - 66,503, 2a + 137, 2b and 4b - 60,884, 3a - 17,814, 3b + 12,318, 4a - 165. But these differences are doubtful, inasmuch as they bear no relation to the dates beginning and ending the serpent numbers.

On the other hand, another number contains the desired properties. I refer to the 12,412,920, *i.e.*, it is 109 times the so-called Ahau-Katun of 113,880 days, and I believe I have found that the Ahau-Katun and its multiples were mostly used in the formation of the large numbers. In the following table I have placed this number beside each of the serpent numbers, have then found the difference between the two and have added to it the interval between the first and last day of each serpent number:—

1a) 12,489,781
    12,412,920
        76,861 = 295 × 260 + 161
        XI Kan - III Chicchan = 161.

1b) 12,388,121
    12,412,920
        -24,799 = 95 × 260 + 99
        III Chicchan - XI Kan = 99.

2a) 12,454,761
    12,412,920
        41,841 = 160 × 260 + 241
        IX Kan - III Chicchan = 241.

2b) 12,394,740
    12,412,920
        -18,180 = 69 × 260 + 240
        III Kan - IX Kan = 240.

3a) 12,438,810
    12,412,920
        25,890 = 99 × 260 + 150
        IX Kan - III Ix = 150.

3b) 12,466,942
    12,412,920
        54,022 = 207 × 260 + 202
        IX Kan - III Cimi = 202.

4a) 12,454,459
    12,412,920
        41,539 = 159 × 260 + 199
        IX Kan - XIII Akbal = 199.

4b) = 2b

Where the serpent number is less than 12,412,920, I have had to place the last day before the initial day.

The work of the Indian computer was, therefore, as follows:—

He took the days for granted. First he determined the differences between them; then he added to each difference a multiple of 260; and the choice of the multiple seems to have been quite arbitrary. The number thus obtained he added to 12,412,920, unless it was the smaller, in which case he subtracted it from 12,412,920, and the result he wrote down in the serpents.

We shall find the same process, only somewhat amplified, with the serpent on page 69.

Are the seven numbers intended to denote the destruction of the seven planets? I hope this question will be answered in the near future.

There now remains of the contents of these pages only the two columns on the left of page 61, which we will now examine and at the same time compare them with the corresponding column of page 69, the upper part of which is exactly the same, and the lower very nearly so. Each column consists of 18 hieroglyphs, which I count from the top downward, designating those of the first column by *a* and those of the second by *b*.

At the first glance these double columns remind one of the inscriptions in the temples and on the stelae, especially of their beginnings, the so-called initial series. Here, in the second column, we find the statement of the usual periods:—144,000, 7200, 360, 20, 1, but in the first column we find faces belonging to them. In his work "The Archaic Maya Inscriptions," 1897, which, on the whole, contains more of imagination than of science, J. T. Goodman unqualifiedly declares these faces to be numbers by which the periods indicated beside them are to be multiplied, and this theory has already found considerable recognition; we will therefore try to follow where he leads.

1a and 1b are effaced on page 61; they probably contained a sort of superscription as on the inscriptions. 2a is effaced on page 61, but the sign may be recognized from page 69 as that with which on page 46 the series of the twenty deities begins after 236 (4 × 59) days. On pages 61 and 69 it takes the place of a face, to which I am inclined to assign the numerical value 4. In 2b, which is C's head, I am inclined to look for the value 2,880,000 = 20 × 20 × 20 × 360 days, which is not at all inappropriate for C, as the sign of the north pole around which everything revolves. I therefore propose to read 2ab as 4 × 2,880,000 = 11,520,000. 3b, it seems to me, resembles the sign for 144,000, which I found in the inscriptions and which is repeated in 12a. It must, however, be left undecided by what this same number in 3a is to be multiplied; 3a is repeated besides in 8a and 13b. 4a contains the head of E, and 4b that of the Moan. 4a seems to refer to 5a, and 4b to 5b. But 5a and 5b are the same sign, which, inserted between the 144,000 and the 7200, can scarcely mean anything else than the so-called Ahau-Katun of 6 × 18,980 = 113,880 days. Have we two such periods here? Were they designated by consecutive numbers? Now comes the 7200 in 6a, and the number 8 with E's head and the inserted sign for 360 days in 6b (on page 69 without E's head), therefore 8 × 360 = 2880. Seler also thinks 7a has the numerical value 16 (Einiges mehr über die Monumente von Copan, etc., page 217); 7b belongs to 7a. 7b, a Kin with a I and a suffix and a leaf-shaped prefix, is inserted between the 360 and 20. What can it mean? Hardly the 260, for this is represented elsewhere (*e.g.*, page 24) by the thirteenth month Mac. Or can it possibly refer to the month Yaxkin (days 120-140)?

8b is a Chuen sign, which, with its prefix (superfix on page 69) always denotes twenty days in the inscriptions. It is multiplied with the same unknown head in 8a, which we have already met with in 3a. 9a contains H's head, and 9b is an unknown head with inserted Kin; the two signs must of necessity indicate the single days still to be added to the period, though as yet we do not know how.

The normal date IV Ahau 8 Cumhu then follows in 10ab. If it refers to the signs just now discussed, then they must denote a number of about the same magnitude as the serpent numbers. 653 or 654 times 18,980 seems to suggest itself, but we shall have more to say later on this subject. My efforts to reach a definite result here have failed.

Nor does the lower part of the two columns lead me to the desired goal. As it seems to consist of several groups, I will first combine 11ab and 12ab. I look upon 11a as denoting 20, and with regard to 11b I have already expressed the surmise in the Zeitschrift für Ethnologie XXIII, page 153, that it may mean $8760 = 24 \times 365$, *i.e.*, three Venus-solar periods. That would be $20 \times 8760 = 480 \times 365 = 175,200$. The Moan in 12a may have the value 13, for this number is so often combined with the Moan. As we saw under page 51, 12b is $= 18,980$; $13 \times 18,980 = 246,740$. Accordingly the four signs taken together may mean $421,940 = 1156 \times 365$.

The second group, from 13a to 15b, refers, on the other hand, to the year of 360 days. First 13a $= 144,000$, having in 13b the unknown multiplier, which we have already seen in 3a and 8a. Then follows in 14a, $15 \times 7200 = 108,000$; in 14b, $9 \times 360 = 3240$; in 15a, a 20 with a prefixed 1 (21?); and in 15b, three days. It would be more correct to place the 1 beside the following 3. The whole sum would then end with the number 4, which would agree with the day Kan, the date specified below.

In the third group the 16a $= 19 \times 18,980 = 360,620$, remains a mystery; an empty outline of a sign is added in 16b.

17ab also forms a group by itself. 17a contains a sign, which rather suggests the Bacab, upon whose period of 91 days the series belonging here is based. The Imix in 17b with a superfix is still unintelligible.

The columns end in 18 with the date IX Kan XII Kayab, the starting-point of the serpent numbers.

Pages 65—69.

I think it very likely that this section bears the same relation to pages 61-64 as pages 46-50 do to 24 and as 53-58 to 51-52. For here, too, a period of time forming the basis of the earlier section seems to be divided into smaller parts. On page 64 we recognize as the basis of the series the number 91, the quarter of the ritual year of 364 days; here we have to do with the fourfold division of 91 into 13 unequal parts. And the real starting-points on these pages, as on the previous ones, are the days III Chicchan and XIII Akbal.

The four series of numbers, the top one of which I have probably correctly restored from what still remains, are as follows:—

9 XII, 5 IV, 1 V, 10 II, 6 VIII, 2 X, 11 VIII, 7 II, 3 V, 12 IV, 8 XII, 4 III, 13 III.

11 I, 13 I, 11 XII, 1 XIII, 8 VIII, 6 I, 4 V, 2 VII, 13 VII, 6 XIII, 6 VI, 8 I, 2 III.

11 XI, 13 XI, 11 IX, 1 X, 8 V, 6 XI, 4 II, 2 IV, 13 IV, 6 X, 6 III, 8 XI, 2 XIII.

9 IX, 5 I, 1 II, 10 XII, 6 V, 2 VII, 11 V, 7 XII, 3 II, 12 I, 8 IX, 4 XIII, 13 XIII.

The first two lines, forming together a single period of 182 days, refer to a day III, as we see by the ending, and the last two to XIII, which undoubtedly refers to the III Chicchan and XIII Akbal, the days so significant in the preceding section. Hence an interval of 218 days (III Chicchan to XIII Akbal) is to be assumed between the second and third lines, with the addition of which interval each of the two periods extends over 400 days.

The first and fourth series have the same difference; and the second and third correspond with one another in this respect. In the first and fourth the differences follow a rule, viz:—as if one were walking in a ring having on its edge the numbers 1 to 13, and kept stepping backward four numbers. The differences of the second and third series apparently do not follow any rule. Hence I think that the fourth series follows the third by mistake and ought rightfully to precede it. Only the fifth member in the first and second series has the same day VIII and the day V in the third and fourth series, otherwise the week-days of each series differ from those of the others.

As I regard III Chicchan and XIII Akbal as unquestionably the starting-points, I will here give a table of the days on which each of the twenty-six members of each series must fall and at the same time I will indicate for each day its number from the beginning of the series. Accordingly the first 182 days present the following appearance:—

III 2.

1.	9.	XII Ix	14.	102.	I Manik
2.	14.	IV Cauac	15.	115.	I Ahau
3.	15.	V Ahau	16.	126.	XII Chuen
4.	25.	II Oc	17.	127.	XIII Eb.
5.	31.	VIII Cib	18.	135.	VIII Ahau
6.	33.	X Eznab	19.	141.	I Cimi
7.	44.	VIII Muluc	20.	145.	V Oc
8.	51.	II Cib	21.	147.	VII Eb
9.	54.	V Cauac	22.	160.	VII Chicchan
10.	66.	IV Chuen	23.	166.	XIII Chuen
11.	74.	XII Cauac	24.	172.	V Caban
12.	78.	III Akbal	25.	180.	I Chicchan

13.   91.   III Cib   26.   182.   III Manik

In the same way I will tabulate the second group of 182 days, but in this case I shall place the fourth line before the third, which is probably correct, and which shows for the first time parallelism of the two rows: —

XIII 20.

1.	9.	IX Eb	14.	102.	XI Chicchan
2.	14.	I Caban	15.	115.	XI Ezanab
3.	15.	II Ezanab	16.	126.	IX Muluc
4.	25.	XII Lamat	17.	127.	X Oc
5.	31.	V Ix	18.	135.	V Ezanab
6.	33.	VII Cib	19.	141.	XI Kan
7.	44.	V Manik	20.	145.	II Lamat
8.	51.	XII Ix	21.	147.	IV Oc
9.	54.	II Caban	22.	160.	IV Akbal
10.	66.	I Muluc	23.	166.	X Muluc
11.	74.	IX Caban	24.	172.	III Men
12.	78.	XIII Imix	25.	180.	XI Akbal
13.	91.	XIII Ix	26.	182.	XIII Chicchan

It would be very essential now to know what place these days occupy in the year, and what year is meant; the answer to one of these questions would at the same time solve the other.

Now I think I come nearer to the solution of this problem by assuming that the pictures and hieroglyphs refer here only to the more important of the two days, XIII Akbal, and that III Chicchan is represented only by the numbers of the series. Thus both the pictures and the hieroglyphs of the two sections connect without the interval of 218 days, which must be assumed in the case of the numbers.

Here, as is usually the case of series, we have to begin at the bottom. Now the first group of the lower half of page 65 contains the sign 9 Kan. If, as it seems, this actually denotes the year, then the day XIII Akbal must be the first of the eleventh month, *i.e.*, the 201st day of the year. Hence I will again set down the twenty-six dates, but add to them the position in the year.

0.		XIII Akbal I Zac (9 Kan)	14.	102.	XI Chicchan 3 Pax
1.	9.	IX Eb 10 Zac	15.	115.	XI Ezanab 16 Pax
2.	14.	I Caban 15 Zac	16.	126.	IX Muluc 7 Kayab
3.	15.	II Ezanab 16 Zac	17.	127.	X Oc 8 Kayab
4.	25.	XII Lamat 6 Ceh	18.	135.	V Ezanab 16 Kayab
5.	31.	V Ix 12 Ceh	19.	141.	XI Kan 2 Cumhu

6.	33.	VII Cib 14 Ceh		20.	145.	II Lamat 6 Cumhu
7.	44.	V Manik 5 Mac		21.	147.	IV Oc 8 Cumhu
8.	51.	XII Ix 12 Mac		22.	160.	IV Akbal 21 Cumhu
9.	54.	II Caban 15 Mac		23.	166.	X Muluc 2 Pop (10 Muluc)
10.	66.	I Muluc 7 Kankin		24.	172.	III Men 8 Pop
11.	74.	IX Caban 15 Kankin		25.	180.	XI Akbal 16 Pop
12.	78.	XIII Imix 19 Kankin		26.	182.	XIII Chicchan 18 Pop
13.	91.	XIII Ix 12 Muan				

Let us now prove the correctness of my theory by an examination of groups 22 and 23. In 22 the 160th day of this period, the 361st day of the year is reached, *i.e.*, the first of the five Uayeyab days. The year 9 Kan is ended and the year 10 Muluc is not yet reached. In the corresponding picture we see B occupied in conveying in a bag the image of God K to whom belongs the next year. B is armed with the official staff and the bag also contains water (rain). In the 23d group the 166th day has passed and the second of the year 10 Muluc is reached, which gives the name to this year. The first hieroglyph shows two personages sitting back to back. This representation is repeated on a larger scale below in the Janus picture of B who is sitting on signs of planets. The second hieroglyph, with equal fitness, represents a clamp, which is intended for fastening two objects together, and which is repeated twice over the Janus picture, black in one case and white in the other. Rain is pouring over the second half of the picture, for it has long been known that Muluc and rain belong together, and in our examination of page 7a we saw that K is the ruler of the day Muluc (6).

Now, before I begin the examination of the separate pictures and the groups of six hieroglyphs belonging to each picture, I wish to mention three things which are often repeated here.

First, B's picture, which appears in all the twenty-six pictures with the exception of 20, 24 and 25, and represents the god in the most varied positions and activities. These pictures are very similar to those on pages 29-46 and we shall therefore make frequent reference to the section there represented.

Second, the first hieroglyph in groups 1 to 13, strange to say, is not found in the second half. It is hieroglyph *f*, which appears in exactly the same way in close combination with B in two sections, which differ from each other but are placed side by side on pages 30c-39c. In the present passage it has a distinct prefix resembling the beak of a bird or tortoise, but in the former passage it has rather a stunted appearance. It seems to refer to the eagle in B's hands in group 13.

Third, the head with no underjaw, which is the sixth hieroglyph in groups 1 to 13, but does not occur in groups 14 to 26. It is repeated in a very similar fashion in the last hieroglyph but one on page 23b. I propose to attribute to it the meaning of fasting.

Now for the single groups:—

1. B is seated rowing in a boat, as he is represented also on pages 29c, 36b, 40c and 43c. A creature is swimming beneath him, which may be a crocodile. The fifth hieroglyph is the important 9 Kan already discussed, the fourth is *a* and the second the cross *b* combined with Caban. The day is the 210th of the year.

2. B is walking with the atlatl in his hand, and armed with javelins. Hieroglyph 5, Manik, denotes the chase, but has a prefix, which often seems to have the meaning of 20. 2 is the elongated head *q* with the prefix of the east belonging to the Kan years. 4 is a Moan sign (c) with the leaf-shaped prefix. Does this perhaps denote the slaying of game in the forest? It is remarkable that B's feet are hidden, as if he were walking in sand or in a bog.

3. B is walking, carrying a large stick like that for tilling the field, as on pages 38b and 39b, and he bears a carrying-frame; there are footprints below him. Hieroglyph 2 is the compound of the signs for south and east, 4 (*r*) may denote rain, and 5 is two elongated heads with an unknown prefix.

4. B, is seated on astronomical signs as on page 37c. The copal pouch is hanging from his neck and he is brandishing his hatchet. Sign 2 is *b*, 4 is *a* and 5 is *r*, but all three signs have unusual prefixes; the first of these prefixes appears again in the tenth group, 41 days later.

5. B is seated on a head, probably that of D, which, however, is peculiar owing to the ornaments resembling bunches of grapes in place of both the eye and the ear (compare pages 39c and 41a). I do not venture to decide what he holds in his hand nor what are the other objects which he carries. Sign 2 is *r* with a prefix, 4 is Imix perhaps with a knife as a prefix, 5 is the skeleton which sometimes belongs to the lightning beast, but also to the 14th month; its prefix is unknown.

6. B is seated on a support, which contains two cross-bones, down to which he points with his right hand, while his left hand holds the hatchet on his knee. Sign 2 is the crouching naked personage, with the cross *b* prefixed, 4 is the elongated head with a prefixed Yax, and 5 is Kan with a vessel as a prefix (instead of Imix) from which steam or froth is rising. The day is the 234th of the year, *i.e.*, the end of a week of 18 × 13 days.

7. B is sitting on a tree at the root of which his own head appears (compare with this the representations on pages 31c, 33c, and especially 40a, and also 41b and 42b). The second sign is Yax with a prefix; 4 is Kin within which there is a 1, as is several times the case, for example, on pages 61 and 69. The fifth sign is still a mystery to me. The day here is V Manik. Do the hieroglyphs suggest that the interval from the day IX Kan, which gives the name to the year, to V Manik is exactly the same as that from the normal date IV Ahau to the true starting-point of our passage, the day XIII Akbal? Both intervals are 243.

8. B is seated in a house, on the roof, wall and floor of which are several Caban signs, just as on page 30a; he seems to be pointing forward. Sign 2 is Caban with a prefix, the 4th and also the 5th is Kan with two unusual prefixes.

9. Water is pictured at the bottom of this picture, and in it are a fish, a mussel and a snail (possibly page 37b may be compared with this). There seems to be a

suggestion of footprints on the margin of the water, back of which B is walking, his legs hidden as far as the knees. He holds the hatchet uplifted in his left hand and his right holds what may be a long-stemmed aquatic plant (compare page 42b). Sign 2 is composed of *b*, Imix, the mouth and nose of C and the object which apparently is a beak, previously met with in sign 1. 4 is Kan-Imix, and 5 is Kan with prefix and suffix.

10. B is seated in an expectant attitude, his hands resting on his knees. We see a very similar representation of him on page 38a, where he faces himself, and in general the remaining pictures of that passage furnish a striking parallel to the present one. Sign 2 is a head (E's?) with a call seemingly issuing from its mouth. 4 is the elongated head *q* with the Ben-Ik superfix and an unusual prefix, which we found on page 66c prefixed to the cross *b*; 5 is Kan with the same prefix, which I regarded as denoting a call in sign 2, and which is probably answered here by an affirmative cry.

11. The expectation has been fulfilled. B is seated on a mat holding a woman in the same position as on page 38a. Sign 2 is the cross *b* with the prefixed beak as in 1, and also with another prefix, which seems sometimes to denote the number 20. 4 is exactly the same Kin with 1 and the leaf-shaped prefix, which occurred in the same place with the seventh picture. 5 contains the sign for 73 days; a new period of this length begins here on the 74th day.

12. As in the parallel passage on page 38 B seems to be offering a Kan, so here his gift consists of a kind of wreath, like the one in the fifth picture; he is seated on astronomical signs, which contain the cross *b* twice as does also hieroglyph 2. 4 is Kin-Akbal, and 5 is a Kan with the prefix which generally belongs to the south as a superfix.

13. B is seated on the elongated head *q* with a superfix and a prefix, exactly as on pages 37c and 40a, and this sign is repeated in the hieroglyphs (in 2) just as it is in the two former places. He holds the eagle on his lap and we see him connected with the same bird in a different way on page 43c. Is B represented here as the preventer of evil? Hieroglyph 4 is *a*, while 5 is Kan, apparently with the sign of the south as a prefix. A Bacab period of 91 days ends here. We come now to the upper series of pictures.

14. B is walking in the rain, with the copal pouch around his neck and the hatchet uplifted in his left hand. An unknown object, possibly held in his right hand, is hanging in front of his legs. Hieroglyphs 1 and 3 are effaced, 2 is indistinct, 5 seems to be a Xul (end, close) and 6 is E's head.

15. B is walking, brandishing the hatchet in his left hand, and holding in his right an object resembling a cornucopia filled with fruit; below this hangs what appears to be a flower. The god wears the copal pouch. Hieroglyph 1 is a hand holding K's head; it is curious that this sign should also occur in the next group as an indication of the approaching Muluc year. 3 is a sign still undetermined; but the prefix is the crouching naked personage with dots suggesting stars around its head. I have often thought that similar figures represented Mercury; it is remarkable that exactly the 115th day of this section is reached here, corresponding with

the apparent revolution of Mercury = 115 days. Similarly sign 2 invites computation; it is a face resembling an Ahau sign, with a 3 as a superfix and a 9 as a prefix; compare the other places containing the same face, with 33c. After the fashion of the inscriptions this would denote 9 + 3 × 20 = 69, which by the way is three fifths of the Mercury revolution. 5 is a compound of Akbal and Imix and 6 a compound of a Moan sign (*c*) with *a*.

16. B is in a half sitting position and holds a strange object before himself. On top of his own head is K's, which is repeated in sign 2. I do not know how to explain 1, unless it is the bat-god; 3 is a Xul = end (but of what?) combined with Imix, and 5 is the usual Kan-Imix. 6 is a Kin with an 8 back of it (as 36b, 37b, 67a, 68a) and over it is a hand pointing to the right, just like those in groups 20 and 25. This looks as if we ought to count forward 8 days, but what can be the purpose of doing so?

17. B is walking armed with spear and shield. Sign 1 is *b*, 2 the face resembling an Ahau, which occupied the second place in group 15, 3 is probably Xul again, but with an effaced prefix; of 5 also only an Imix remains; while 6 is the usual compound of Muluc-Caban.

18. We have now reached the day 16 Kayab, a day very close to the day 18 Kayab, which on page 24 we recognized as an especially important day, while in my article "Zur Entzifferung III" I regarded it as the day of the summer solstice. Computed from the normal date IV Ahau 8 Cumhu it may also have denoted the end of a lunar year, as on pages 51-58 where it is the basis of the series. The picture here agrees with this. B is sitting in the pouring rain of the rainy season and gazing upward at the planets, as on page 36c and particularly on 39c; the sun and moon are also represented, but below the planets. The hieroglyphs likewise contain the sun and moon in 1 and 2, in 3, Ahau and Xul with a prefix, as if this were the end of the increase of the sun's power; 5 is Kin-Akbal, day and night, and 6 is Caban with the cross *b*.

19. B is walking armed with hatchet and shield. He holds a serpent in his hand as on page 40c, but here with the head downward. Hieroglyphs 1 and 2 are destroyed, 3 is the cross *b* with a suffix and the horse-shoe prefix *e*, known to us from pages 5 and 6. 5 is Imix combined with Chuen and probably with Yax, and 6 is E's head.

20. This is the old red woman with the tiger claws, whom we saw on pages 39b and 43b and shall see again on page 74; she reinforces the water falling from the planets by pouring a stream from her jug. The first three hieroglyphs are effaced, 4 is the elongated head *q*, 5 is Kin-Akbal, 6, as in group 16, is again the enigmatical 8 with a hand pointing to the right.

21. B is walking and bears pouch, spear and shield. Hieroglyph 1 is a hand holding the sign of the rising Moan, just as in 15 a hand holds the head of K; 2 is again K, whose sign is probably effaced several times in the last groups of this series. 3 is E with the sign of the east; 5 is compounded of Imix, Chuen and *b*, and 6 is Kin with the sign of the north. Here the day of the normal date is reached, but this may be significant only for the year 9 Ix.

22. We come now to the representation of the change of the year, which we

have already mentioned. Hieroglyph 1 is curious, consisting of the moon with a stripe running around it like a strap; 3 and 5 are not clear to me and are doubtless closely connected with one another; 3 also contains a trace of K and is perhaps a determinative of the same. 6 is again E, and suggests the tilling of the fields.

23. This picture as well as the first two hieroglyphs have already been discussed above. The crouching personage, repeated again in 3 as a prefix to the cross *b*, is curious. 5 is again E and 6 is Imix, referring to grain and honey.

24. The picture and three of the hieroglyphs plainly correspond. The grain deity E holds food and drink in his hand. Rain is pouring from the planets, and the wind-beast plunges down, as on pages 44 and 45. Sign 3 is E's hieroglyph, 6 is Kan-Imix and 2 is the wind-beast. B is superfluously added in 4 and the same is true of the cross *b* in 1, while Kin-Akbal in 5 seems to fit almost everywhere. Pages 29a, 30a and 45c show the lightning-beast in a different form.

25. As is usually the case, rain is pouring from the stars and below them are the sun and moon as before. This time C is sitting in the rain, clad in the gala mantle and holding Kan. Hieroglyphs 1, 2 and 4, the latter apparently representing C, are effaced. The other three are enigmatical, 3 is again Xul with a prefixed 9, 5 a Caban, but with an unintelligible prefix, and 6 is again the mysterious 8.

26. B is sitting on a tree or sacrificial stone, which is colored half blue and half red, and may denote the ceasing of the rainy season; he is brandishing his hatchet. Hieroglyphs 1, 2 and 3 are effaced; 4 is B's sign, 5 might be Xul and 6 is *a* with *c* added and thus referring to the Moan. And here the half of the ritual year ends with the 182nd day, which is XIII Chicchan 18 Pop (10 Muluc); and it is left to the reader to imagine or to find hieroglyphs and pictures for the other two series of numeral signs.

I am troubled about the five naked crouching figures of this section, which I am inclined to regard as the sign for Mercury with its apparent revolution of 115 days, which, however, seems sometimes (as on pages 54, 56 and 58 in the upper sections) to be raised to the value of half a Tonalamatl = 130 days. This may be explained by the fact that it is difficult to determine exactly the length of the revolution of Mercury. In group 15 this figure appears exactly on the 115th day of this section, but in group 6 on the 234th day of the year, *i.e.*, approximately at the expiration of two Mercury periods after the beginning of the year. But now for group 23. Here there are three of these crouching figures. The two upper ones leaning back to back must serve the purpose of indicating the change in the year. But they would hardly do so, if the third personage were not added, which may indicate that the solar year consists approximately of three Mercury periods. I look upon this view of the matter merely as the first attempt at an explanation.

Pages 69—73.

The chief subject of the last great section of this Manuscript is two of the usual series, from which large numbers are developed in the usual way and the largest of all is finally recorded in a serpent. This section thus forms a parallel to the contents of pages 61-64, but is somewhat more composite.

Before I begin the discussion of these series, I wish to examine two passages, which I think are not connected with these series, but are independent, like the instance on pages 51-58, where the hieroglyphs were found to be quite independent of the numerals. The Mayas took advantage of space wherever it presented itself, which is admissible in ideographic writing.

The first of these two passages is at the top of pages 71-73. Here there are four horizontal rows of twelve hieroglyphs each. Since, however, the top row is entirely effaced and none of the other three are perfectly preserved, it is quite impossible at present to judge of the interconnection of the whole. But I must point out a certain resemblance to the passage on pages 44b-45b, where a period of 78 days is considered with reference to the wind-deities. The first and sixth columns of pages 71-72 likewise contain the signs for wind and the pierced ears. The fact that the Bacab sign occurs in the eighth column, and in no other, must attract 'attention; if we knew it to be effaced in the first column, then each column might refer to 13 days, though 12 × 13, it is true, does not form a natural whole. C's sign is the only hieroglyph of a god to be found in both passages. E also occurs on pages 44b-45b and may be one of the effaced signs on pages 71-72. There is no trace left of the others. The fact that some hieroglyphs occur in both the passages referred to proves nothing with regard to signs in frequent use and I can find no cases of correspondence among those occurring more rarely. Hence this passage must be left for the present as an almost complete mystery.

I have discussed the second passage in detail in my article "Zur Entzifferung der Mayahandschriften V," of the year 1895, and from it I will borrow the following. This second passage fills the middle and lower thirds of pages 71-73, occupying the same space as the first passage in the upper third, and offering far more reliable material than the latter.

That these hieroglyphs are not connected with the numerals above and below, can be deduced from the fact that the numbers follow one another from right to left and the hieroglyphs in the reversed order. This is proved by the hand pointing to the right, which occurs here at least eight times like the one occurring twenty times on pages 46-50.

But the scribe, misled by the direction of the numeral series, began on page 71 to write the *first* of these hieroglyphs from the right instead of from the left, but after the first four groups he corrected his mistake. Hence I read the groups of three hieroglyphs each, in the following order:—

		Page 71.		Page 72.								Page 73.			
2	1		5	6	7	8	9	10	11	19	20	21	22	23
4	3		12	13	14	15	16	17	18	24	25	26	27	28

The number 28 shows that we have to do here with 28 weeks of 13 days each, *i.e.*, with a ritual year of 364 days, as was the case on pages 31-32, 63-64 and 65-69. This year, however, is divided into four parts of 7 x 13 = 91 days, *i.e.*, into four so-called Bacab periods. This is very plainly indicated here, for groups 4, 11, 18 and 25, *i.e.*, those separated by seven groups each, are exactly alike, but in group 4b (I will designate the three hieroglyphs of each group from top to bottom by *a*, *b* and *c*) there is a prefixed 4 which refers to the four Bacabs as does the same 4 prefixed to the Bacab sign at the top of page 72.

Now the question arises as to when this ritual year began. Undoubtedly its beginning day was very different from that of the civil year (360 days) and from that of the astronomical year (365 days).

In this matter I follow Mrs. Zelia Nuttall, who has rendered such estimable service to Aztec science. At the Congress of Americanists at Stockholm in 1894, she submitted an article entitled "Note on the Ancient Mexican Calendar System," in which with keen discernment she pointed out a year beginning with the spring equinox and including in its centre the sacred Tonalamatl, *i.e.*, 260 days, which were preceded and followed by 52 days. I recognize this ritual year also in the present passage of the "Dresdensis," as the one current in the Maya country. It probably began about the 10th of March, at that period about the time of the vernal equinox, according to the Julian Calendar.

Beginning with this date, I will now attempt to tabulate the chronology of this passage. In the first column I will place the number of the group of hieroglyphs in question, in the second I will set down to what day of the Maya year each group refers; in the third, the corresponding day of our year, and finally in the fourth, the 20-day periods which agree in general with the dates.

1.	1-13	March 10-22	Ceh.
2.	14-26	March 23-April 5	Mac.
3.	27-39	April 6-18	Kankin.
4.	40-52	April 19-May 1	
5.	53-65	May 2-14	Moan.
6.	66-78	May 15-27,	Pax.
7.	79-91	May 28-June 9	Kayab.
8.	92-104	June 10-22	
9.	105-117	June 23-July 5	Cumhu.
10.	118-130	July 6-18	
11.	131-143	July 19-31	Pop.
12.	144-156	August 1-13	Uo.
13.	157-169	August 14-26	
14.	170-182	August 27-September 8	Zip.
15.	183-195	September 9-21	Zotz.
16.	196-208	September 22-October 4	
17.	209-221	October 5-17	Zec.
18.	222-234	October 18-30	Xul.
19.	235-247	October 31-November 12	

20.	248-260	November 13-25	Yaxkin.
21.	261-273	November 26-December 8	Mol.
22.	274-286	December 9-21	
23.	287-299	December 22-January 3	Chen.
24.	300-312	January 4-16	
25.	313-325	January 17-29	Yax.
26.	326-338	January 30-February 11	Zac.
27.	339-351	February 12-24	
28.	352-364	February 25-March 8	Ceh.

In the following I will call attention to a few points by which this arrangement is justified.

Hieroglyph 1a admits of explanation. It consists of four parts:—the left top is Kin, meaning sun or day, the right top is the sign of the year, the right bottom is the knife as symbol of separation or division, and the left bottom, which is especially decisive, is the month Ceh. Hence I read 1a thus:—the day of the change of year in the month Ceh. The sign 1b is the familiar Kin-Akbal signifying either the beginning day or the day Akbal. If the year should be named from this sign, then this would mean a Kan year, as in the preceding section the beginning lay in the year 9 Kan. If the year in the latter section had been as equally divided as the one in question here, it would have furnished us with some very remarkable parallels.

Again the four groups:—4, 11, 18 and 25, which are alike, are important. The cross in sign *a*, combined with the three dotted lines passing from top to bottom, may refer to the wind and this meaning is further confirmed by the Ik sign (wind) in *c*. Further the sign *b* between them is that for the Bacab, the wind deity itself.

The most important events of the year are obviously the sowing and harvesting of the maize together with the beginning and end of the rainy season. Now we find the first two in connection with the god E, the maize-god, who is represented in 6c and 13c, 91 days apart, corresponding to the end of May and the beginning of August. Generally speaking, sixty days only were reckoned as the time between sowing and reaping, but here a quarter of a year may have been taken as a round number and it may also have reference to a more elevated region.

I am inclined to think that the beginning and end of the rainy season are referred to in signs 8c and 16c, where, as it seems to me, three lines of drops are falling from a rectangle denoting the sky (as is usual) like the representation of rain dropping from a cloud at the bottom of page 36 (second picture). The serpent 8b as symbol of water may also refer to the same thing, especially as it is combined with an Akbal (often denoting beginning). The sign, which I think denotes the rainy season, is very similar, but not the same as another one, which is common to the Dresdensis and Tro-Cortesianus, the significance of which is certainly very close to the idea of the week of 13 days.

I have some other ideas on this subject, which, however, are mere conjectures, advanced with some hesitation. If the Chuen sign in 7a is actually a serpent's jaw, then it might refer to the beginning of the astronomical year in May, since the serpent so often designates that time.

In 9b we find a crouching figure with the sign which is usually considered that of the death-bird. In another place (Zur Entzifferung IV, 12) I have regarded the naked human figure placed upside down on page 58 as the sign for Mercury, and on page 60 at the bottom, left, I also regarded the crouching figure as representing Mercury vanquished by Venus. But in 9b, which belongs to the 105th-117th days of the year, a 115 day revolution of Mercury is computed. A crouching figure, like that in 9b, likewise appears on page 65a in the second series of 91 days after 11 + 13 = 24 days of this series have elapsed, *i.e.*, directly after the 115 days of the apparent revolution of Mercury.

In 10b, and it is the only place in this passage, we find the hieroglyph of B, the leading god of this Manuscript. This corresponds with the time of the greatest power of the sun and of the change in the civil year (July 16th). In Group 12, do *a* and *c* mean the year and is *b* the head with the Akbal eye, thus denoting the beginning of the civil year? It ought really to have formed group 11, but there was no room for it, since it was necessary that the signs for the period of 91 days should be set down there.

Signs 14a and the combined signs 15bc are almost alike and suggest 1a. Is it intended to designate here the ritual year, the time of the autumnal equinox (September 10th?). In 15a two hooks, turned in opposite directions proceed from one side of the sun-glyph. Do they signify two halves of the year and does the 3 in front of them signify the third quarter of the year?

20b is the sign of the death-god A, probably not placed accidentally here at the end of the month Xul, which denotes the end; but the end of what?

The hieroglyph in 23a is a black bird, with two hooks, one pointing up and the other down, projecting from its head. Usually these hooks belong to K, and by means of them this bird becomes the storm-bird; the year symbol is below. Does this hieroglyph signify the time of the shortest day, when darkness predominates?

A peculiarity of this passage is the striking frequency of the sign looked upon as that of the death-bird as well as of the cognate sign, which is commonly considered as that of the rising Moan. The first bird is in the 14th group, in the 9th it is combined with the apparent Mercury sign, and in the 17th with the year sign. The second bird with the prefixed Yax is in the 2nd group. But it is especially striking that several times both signs, and this is the case nowhere else, are combined into a single sign in groups 9, 13 and 26 and also probably in 19 where, however, the Moan sign seems to be effaced.

This is all I have to say at the present time in reference to this calendar. Some of my statements are positive and some are only conjectures. Compare my treatise "Zwei Hieroglyphenreihen in der Dresdener Mayahandschrift" (Zeitschrift für Ethnologie, 1905, 2 and 3).

Having disposed in this way of the two supplementary subjects of this section,

I will now proceed to consider the principal theme, viz:—the two series and whatever is connected with them.

1. The 54-Series of the Day IX Ix.

As with the other series, we begin here at the right, *i.e.*, with page 73. There in the last column we find the superscription as it were. It is true that nothing positive can be gathered from the top part consisting of five hieroglyphs, which are mostly destroyed. The third hieroglyph seems to be the sign in group 2a discussed above. The fourth is an Akbal with a prefixed arm as on pages 8a, 36a, and the fifth is an Ik with a prefix.

Below these are three numbers:—14,040, 702 and 54, which are in the proportion of 260, 13 and 1, so that the 14,040 is a Tonalamatl, as it were, of 260 periods of 54 days each. The fact that 54 is chosen here as the difference of the following series is curious, because usually only parts of 260 or of 364 are selected. But 54 is probably only a secondary matter, while 14,040, with its marvellous property of divisibility into the most varied and important periods, is the chief subject.

There is a 9 in a red circle under the three numbers. It is meant to denote the starting-point of the series, the day IX Ix. Perhaps these two as well as the 54 are connected with the 9 "señores de las noches."

In passing on to the left, I shall not consider the hieroglyphs and numbers in the next two columns in the upper third, since they are only set down here in order to secure space for them. They will be discussed later.

The series itself begins in the upper third of page 71, in the next to the last column; it is continued on page 72 and on page 73 as far as the third column. The first twelve numbers are written from left to right contrary to the usual practice, doubtless occasioned by the passage above the series, which has already been discussed. And below, again contrary to rule, we find not the week and month days, but only the week days and they are in red circles. If written in the usual way, the series would have the following form (with the usual omission of the initial day IX Ix):—

54	108	162	216	270	324	378
XI Lamat	XIII Ik	II Cib	IV Oc	VI Kan	VIII Ezanab	X Eb

432	486	540	594	648
XII Cimi	I Ahau	III Ix	V Lamat	VII Ik.

The series must now continue with the 702 already specified on page 73, which it proceeds to do from right to left in the middle of page 71, and continues from there on with regularly added dates and with the 702 itself as the difference. At the same time, since 702 = 54 × 13, the week-days are forced to come to a standstill on the IX, while each of the month days ascends by two (702 = 35 × 20 + 2). The 4914 = 7 × 702 is obtained in the next to the last column of page 70. On page 71 the 702 is incorrectly set down as 1. 15. 2. instead of 1. 17. 2. The series continues on page 71 in the same way beyond the 702, until in 7020 a number is obtained which is also divisible by 260, so that now the accompanying day must be IX Ix. Now we ought to expect to see here the double of 7020, the very 14,040 abovementioned, but it is omitted just because it was set down on page 73. Nevertheless this very number forms the new difference with which the series returns from page 70 to the top line of page 71, where the numbers are mostly effaced, but enough remains to enable us to assume that the last number on page 71 is the 10th multiple of 14,040, and this may be followed by the 11th and 12th multiples, the last number being 168,480.

2. The 65-Series of the Day IV Eb.

This series begins in the middle of page 73 with the day IV Caban, the zero-point therefore being IV Eb. It then advances to the left across 28 members, until on page 71 it reaches the number 1820 = 5 years of 364 days = 7 Tonalamatls. From there on, 1820 itself is the difference, and the accompanying day therefore remains IV Eb. Then, in the two lowest sections of pages 71 and 70, the fourth multiple of 1820, *i.e.*, 7280, is the third difference and thus the series advances to 15 × 7280 = 109,200 on page 71, after which on page 70 the omitted 8 × 7280 = 58,240 is written out. Close beside this number are the figures 1. 0. 12. 3. and a 0 below the latter, which was not successfully erased; this would be the number 7443 of which I can make nothing at all.

The initial dates of the two series, IX Ix and IV Eb, are 138 days apart and reversely 122 days.

3. The Groups of Hieroglyphs.

The transition, as it were, from the series to the large numbers is formed by a few groups of hieroglyphs.

The first of these groups is at the top of pages 69-70; its first top line is completely effaced. The remainder I will designate by the following numbers:—

1	2	5	6	9	13
3	4	7	8	10	14
				11	15
				12	16.

The date IX Kan 12 Kayab, set down under 3 and 4 does not belong there but to the serpent below and will be discussed later.

I take sign 1 to be that of a Bacab, 2 I do not understand and it is half obliterated; it seems to occur again on page 73 in the column to the extreme right. 3 and 7 are the elongated head *q* with an unusual superfix, 4 and 8 correspond with one another, but I cannot explain them. 5, 10 and 14 denote the beginning, 6, 11 and 15, the end. 9 and 13 both designate the 8th day of the month Kayab and over them IV Ahau must have been set down twice. 12 and 16 are two heads of gods, 12 is probably D's with the sign for west and 16, B's with that of the east.

On page 70, in the middle of the third and fourth columns, the day IX Ix occurs twice. In one case it ought to have been IV Eb and the scribe has really changed the

IX to IV, but he omitted changing the Ix to Eb. Directly below these dates we find the second group, consisting of two rows of four hieroglyphs.

I think these eight hieroglyphs can be interpreted as follows:—

1) 13 Pax	2) 20 Pop or 25 Cumhu
3) VIII Ahau	4) 13 Yaxkin
5) 10 Muan	6) 37,960
7) 20	8) 1 Zec.

The following is to be noted in this connection:—

3 is really set down X Ahau, but an VIII is written above the Ahau by way of correction. The day VIII Ahau will presently prove to be important.

6, a compound of Imix and the superfix denoting multiplication, is the sign for 18,980, and its prefix seems to me to denote duplication. We have long known how important the $37,960 = 146 \times 260 = 104 \times 365$ is, and, if my theory is correct, we shall see directly that it occurs again here.

8 seems really to be 1 Zec, but the composite prefixes demand further examination.

Impenetrable darkness still shrouds the meaning of the whole group. Though it is clear that in several cases certain days are specified according to their position in the year, their distance apart does not agree with the interval between days IV Eb, IX Ix and IV Ahau under discussion here.

If signs 3 and 4 ought to be read together as VIII Ahau 13 Yaxkin, then this date would come in the year 7 Muluc. In the Zeitschrift für Ethnologie I explained the five hieroglyphs in the third column at the bottom of page 70 (the third group) as civil years of 360 and astronomical years of 365 days:—

$$
\begin{aligned}
1) \quad & 8,760 = 24 \times 365 = 15 \times 584 \\
2) \quad & 2,920 = 8 \times 365 = 5 \times 584 \\
3) \quad & 7,200 = 20 \times 360 \\
4) \quad & 18,720 = 52 \times 360 = 72 \times 260 \\
5) \quad & \underline{360} \\
& 37,960.
\end{aligned}
$$

This, it is true, is a striking explanation and certainly a surprising one!

Now the date IX Ix 12 Kayab is at the very bottom of the fourth column. This, without apparent reason, would refer to the year 4 Kan. Should it not be read IX Kan 12 Kayab (4 Ix), thus indicating that the entire passage is only the preparation for the date from which the serpent numbers proceed? The scribe may have had in mind the IX Ix of the series.

The fourth and last group on page 73, above the two numbers 83,474 and 34,732, consists of four hieroglyphs. The two upper hieroglyphs on the left are effaced, and the top one on the right. I think it probable that the day VIII Ahau, which will be discussed later, may have stood in the top line, and possibly with a month date. Of the two remaining signs of the fourth group, the upper is the moon and the lower Imix, probably with the hieroglyph of the east as a prefix; but there is nothing to be done with it owing to the obliteration of the sign above it. In the Zeitschrift für Ethnologie, 1891, page 153, I have endeavored to explain these three signs on the right above 34,732, by suggesting for them the values

$$18,980 = 52 \times 365$$
$$8,760 = 24 \times 365$$
$$7,200 = 20 \times 360$$
$$34,940$$

and calling special attention to the fact that between IV Eb and IV Ahau there are 208 days, and that the 34,732 placed below them in the Manuscript, increased by 208, is equal to 34,940. This group then seems really to belong to the day IV Eb and to the 65-series, while manifold problems are still to be encountered in interpreting the other groups.

4. The Large Numbers.

The Manuscript offers material with which to work, beginning on page 70:—

1,394,120	1,437,020	1,567,332	1,520,654
(606)	(1646)	IV Eb	IX Ix
IV Ahau	IV Ahau	VIII Ahau; 13 Yaxkin (7 Muluc).	
8 Cumhu	8 Cumhu		
IX Ix	IV Eb		
1,201,200	1,202,240	111,554	101,812
(86)	(208)		
IV Ahau	IV Ahau		
8 Cumhu	8 Cumhu		

This is followed at the right top of page 73 by

83,474	34,732
IX Ix	IV Eb.

Two of the numbers and two of the dates are conjectural:—

I read the 1,202,240 as 8. 6. 19. 10. 0. while the Manuscript has 16 instead of 6. I read the 101,812 as 14. 2. 14. 12. the Manuscript has 16 instead of the second 14. And in two places in the third column of page 70, I have restored the day IV Eb, where the Manuscript incorrectly repeats the IX Ix, and does the same thing on page 73.

Let us now first consider the construction of those large numbers, which are connected with the day IX Ix and thus with the 54-series. These numbers are the two upper ones of columns 1 and 2 and the lower one of column 1 on page 70.

174 is the starting-point, the number of the day is IX Ix, which seems to have been chosen because it divides the Tonalamatl approximately in the proportion of 2 to 1. (IV Ahau - IX Ix = 174.)

The 5359th, 5520th and 4619th multiples of 260 have been added to 174; why precisely these multiples were chosen remains a mystery. In this way were obtained the following numbers, which the Manuscript suppresses. I will give them with their corresponding dates:—

$$1,393,514 = \text{IX Ix 12 Muan (5 Kan).}$$

$$1,435,374 = \text{IX Ix 17 Chen (3 Cauac).}$$

$$1,201,114 = \text{IX Ix 7 Mac (11 Muluc).}$$

When we add to the above the three encircled numbers 606, 1,646 and 86, the resulting sums are the three numbers found in the Manuscript:—

$$1,394,120 = \text{IV Ahau 8 Chen (7 Ix).}$$

$$1,437,020 = \text{IV Ahau 23 Cumhu (7 Cauac).}$$

$$1,201,200 = \text{IV Ahau 13 Kayab (11 Muluc).}$$

I am placing the first two not far from the present and the third in the past.

As multiples of 260 these three numbers have the following form:—

$$1,394,120 = 5362 \times 260.$$

$$1,437,020 = 5527 \times 260.$$

$$1,201,200 = 4620 \times 260.$$

Some curious facts come to light with regard to their magnitude and their mutual relation.

The two largest numbers are $165 \times 260 = 660 \times 65$ apart; this recalls the 65-series. The third lowest number is 165×7280 and thus contains not only the 65 but $= 165 \times 65 \times 112$.

The ritual year (364) and its excess over the Tonalamatl (104) is likewise contained in these numbers, at least in the first and third:—

$$1,394,120 = 3830 \times 364 = 13,405 \times 104.$$

$$1,201,200 = 3300 \times 364 = 11,550 \times 104.$$

The three encircled numbers are connected with one another because the first $= 2 \times 260 + 86$, the second $= 6 \times 260 + 86$ and the third is 86 itself. The larger encircled numbers are, therefore, $1040 = 4 \times 260$ apart, and this is also the interval between the two numbers near the bottom. 1040, however, also $= 5 \times 208$, and 208 is the interval from IV Eb to IV Ahau. Now it is curious that the two numbers below are 5775×208 and 5780×208, though the third belongs to day IX Ix and the fourth to IV Eb. One result of this is that $1,201,200 = 1155 \times 1040$ and $1,202,240 = 1156 \times 1040$.

As these three numbers relate to day IX Ix and the 54-series, so the fourth relates to IV Eb and the 65-series.

Here the starting-point is the number 52, which belongs to day IV Eb and this is separated from IV Ahau by 208 days *i.e.,* it divides the Tonalamatl in the proportion of 1 to 4.

To the number 52 then, for unknown reasons was added 4623 × 260 = 1,201,980, and thus the number 1,202,032, suppressed in the Manuscript, was obtained for the day IV Eb. To this sum the encircled number 208 was then added and the result was 1,202,240, the number in the Manuscript.

The number = 23,120 × 52 = 4624 × 260, which is self-evident, but it also = 5780 × 208, *i.e.,* it is a multiple of the encircled number. It consequently also = 11,560 × 104, and thus it is related to the first and third numbers just now discussed.

The position of this number is IV Ahau 18 Kankin (1 Kan) and the position of the suppressed number is IV Eb 10 Zotz (also 1 Kan).

We ought now to discuss the last two numbers of this section amounting to millions:—1,567,332 and 1,520,654, which are in the third and fourth columns at the top of page 70. But before going further, we must examine four other numbers, two of which, 111,554 and (with my correction) 101,812, are in column 4 on the lower part of page 70, and the other two, 83,474 and 34,732, are on the top of page 73. Although these four numbers are not ornamented with circles, they all have the significance of the numbers enclosed in circles and are designations of differences between suppressed and specified numbers.

Let us first of all examine their curious relation to one another:—

The Manuscript should have set down under these numbers the day IX Ix twice and IV Eb twice, from which days the numbers in question must be computed; but here the two errors already mentioned were made. 111,554 - 101,812 is 9742, the very same number which we shall afterward find as the difference of the serpent numbers on page 69.

83,474 - 34,732 = 48,742. If 9472 be subtracted from this, the remainder is exactly 39,000 = 150 Tonalamatls = 50 revolutions of Mars. I have already found this number on page 31a, and also the double of it, 78,000, on page 24, and this I found by using 68,900 + 9100 for my computation.

111,554 - 83,474 = 28,080, *i.e.,* exactly the double of the important 14,040, which is recorded on page 73.

101,812 - 34,732 = 67,080, *i.e.,* = 258 Tonalamatls or 86 revolutions of Mars.

111,554 - 34,732 = 76,822; if 122, the interval from IV Eb to IX Ix be subtracted from this, the remainder is 76,700 = 295 Tonalamatls.

101,812 - 83,474 = 18,338; if 138, the interval from IX Ix to IV Eb, be subtracted from 18,338, the remainder is 18,200 = 70 Tonalamatls = 50 ritual years of 364 days each, *i.e.,* exactly the double of the 9100 specified on page 24.

Now we also have the following equations for the four numbers:—

$$111,554 = 429 \times 260 + 14.$$

$$83,474 = 321 \times 260 + 14.$$

$$101,812 = 391 \times 260 + 152.$$

$$34,732 = 133 \times 260 + 152.$$

A day VIII Ahau is 14 days back of the day IX Ix, and another VIII Ahau is 152 days back of IV Eb.

Thus a day VIII Ahau hitherto unmentioned is introduced into the computations. This day has no doubt been chosen, because it divides the Tonalamatl beginning with IV Ahau into two parts of 160 and 100 days, which are in the proportion of 8 to 5, *i.e.*, the same proportion as the Venus year to the solar year.

This day VIII Ahau may also figure in the large numbers of the first two columns on page 70, for 1,394,120 and 1,201,200 are both divisible by 14, the interval between VIII Ahau and IX Ix.

Now I believe that the large numbers were constructed in the following two-fold manner (I add the corresponding dates):—

$$
\begin{aligned}
&160 \\
&\underline{1,408,940 = 5419 \times 260} \\
&1,409,100 = \text{VIII Ahau 3 Yax (9 Cauac).} \\
&\underline{111,554} \\
&1,520,654 = \text{IX Ix 7 Zip (3 Muluc).}
\end{aligned}
$$

$$
\begin{aligned}
&160 \\
&\underline{1,437,020 = 5527 \times 260} \\
&1,437,180 = \text{VIII Ahau 18 Mol (8 Kan).} \\
&\underline{83,474} \\
&1,520,654 = \text{IX Ix 7 Zip (3 Muluc).}
\end{aligned}
$$

$$
\begin{aligned}
&160 \\
&\underline{1,465,360 = 5636 \times 260} \\
&1,465,520 = \text{VIII Ahau 8 Uo (8 Ix).} \\
&\underline{101,812} \\
&1,567,332 = \text{IV Eb 5 Pop (1 Muluc).}
\end{aligned}
$$

$$
\begin{aligned}
&160 \\
&\underline{1,532,440 = 5894 \times 260} \\
&1,532,600 = \text{VIII Ahau 13 Pax (9 Muluc).} \\
&\underline{34,732} \\
&1,567,332 = \text{IV Eb 5 Pop (1 Muluc).}
\end{aligned}
$$

The last record of the date of VIII Ahau seems to throw light on the date 13 Pax (page 70, column 3), which is directly above the date VIII Ahau, and which I have already mentioned in the discussion of the groups of hieroglyphs.

Indeed, it seems as if a day VIII Ahau occurred a fifth time in that passage, for in consequence of the correction made by the scribe we read here VIII Ahau 13 Yaxkin. This would point to a year 7 Muluc, the position of which between the other four is, of course, undetermined.

If the two large numbers in the Manuscript were treated in the same way as the other large numbers, they would not be recorded at all, but instead of them there would have been two numbers belonging to the day IV Ahau and under them would have been the encircled numbers 208 and 86, or these numbers increased by a multiple of 260. This passage would then read about as follows:—

$$1{,}567{,}540 \quad \text{(IV Ahau)} \quad 1{,}520{,}740 \quad \text{(IV Ahau)}$$
$$208 \quad \text{(IV Eb)} \qquad\qquad 86 \quad \text{(IX Ix)}.$$

These two numbers for IV Ahau are equal to 6029 and 5849 Tonalamatls. If 5549×260 be subtracted from these, the remainders are 480 and 300 Tonalamatls respectively, *i.e.*, 124,800 and 78,000, and these are in the proportion of 8 to 5.

Now the two large numbers have the difference $46{,}678 = 179 \times 260 + 138$; the latter is the interval from IX Ix to IV Eb.

The four numbers of the days VIII Ahau seem to stand in very irregular relation to one another and yet they show the following striking results, if the first and third and also the second and fourth numbers be combined (as I combined them under page 24):—

In the first case we see the following:—

$$1{,}465{,}520 - 1{,}409{,}100 = 56{,}420 = 3 \times 18{,}980 - 520.$$
$$3 \text{ Yax (9 Cauac) to 8 Uo (8 Ix)} = 18{,}460 = 18{,}980 - 520.$$
$$56{,}420 - 18{,}460 = 37{,}960 = 2 \times 18{,}980.$$

While in the second case:—

$$1{,}532{,}600 - 1{,}437{,}180 = 95{,}420 = 5 \times 18{,}980 - 520.$$
$$18 \text{ Mol (8 Kan) to 13 Pax (9 Muluc)} = 520.$$
$$95{,}420 - 520 = 94{,}900 = 5 \times 18{,}980.$$

5. The Serpent.

As in the section occupying pages 61-64, the single series is crowned by four serpents with eight large numbers, so in this section the two series end in a single serpent with two numbers, one for each series, but both bear some obscure relation to the day VIII Ahau, which has made its appearance here. The two sections also correspond, inasmuch as the numbers in both are computed not from the normal date, but from the date IX Kan 12 Kayab (4 Ix).

The serpent pictured here is different from the previous ones, inasmuch as it is partly black. The god B is sitting on its opened jaws, and this time he, too, is painted black (as on page 31c); there is an animal's head upon the god's head, in which we again recognize that of the animal with the fourth serpent in the preceding section. The god is armed with spear and shield and recalls his picture at the bottom of page 74.

There are eight hieroglyphs above this picture, just as there are over each of the first four serpents. The two top hieroglyphs are obliterated. Of the legible hieroglyphs, the one at the left top is the Bacab sign, which also occurs over the first of the four serpents. In the third line are the same two hieroglyphs, which are in the third line of the first and second columns on page 70. The first of the two also occupies the same place on page 62 above the fourth serpent. But here at the bottom we find the date IX Kan 12 Kayab (4 Ix), the same date which we found over the fourth serpent, which is thus again brought into closer connection with the single serpent.

There can be no doubt here regarding the two numbers in the serpents, but notice should be taken of the fact that the figure 1 is barely visible in the red number.

The black number here has the figures 4. 5. 19. 13. 12. 8. and the red 4. 6. 1. 0. 13. 10. The black is therefore 12,381,728, and the red 12,391,470. The black number is somewhat less than the eight numbers in the four serpents, and the red is somewhat larger than the least of them.

The difference of the two is 9742 = 37 × 260 + 122; but 122 is the interval between days IV Eb and IX Ix. Now this is the same 9742 which we found on page 70, as the difference between 111,554 and 101,812.

In order not merely to examine these numbers, but also to understand them, we will again make use of 109 Ahau-Katuns = 12,412,920, as we did in the first four serpents, and we shall have the following: —

Black	Red
12,381,728	12,391,470
12,412,920	12,412,920
-31,192 = 119 × 260 + 252	-21,450 = 82 × 260 + 130
IV Eb - IX Kan = 252	IX Ix - IX Kan = 130

The date given for both numbers was the day IX Kan, which was likewise the starting-point for six of the eight numbers in the previous serpents.

Besides this the day IV Eb, the starting-point of the 65-series, is given for the black number, and therefore also the interval between IV Eb and IX Kan = 252.

To this 252 was added a multiple of 260, not an arbitrary choice, but one which combined with 252 resulted in a number divisible by 8, the interval from IX Kan to IV Eb. 31,192 = 3899 × 8 = 119 × 260 + 252 was thus obtained.

The subtraction of this number from 12,412,920 resulted in the serpent number 12,381,728.

In addition to all this the day IX Ix, the starting-point of the 54-series, is given for the red number; consequently also the interval between IX Ix and IX Kan = 130, which, at the same time, is reversely the interval from IX Kan to IX Ix.

To this 130 was added a multiple of 260, which *must* in every case be a multiple also of 130. Thus we obtain the 21,450 = 82 × 260 + 130.

The subtraction of this number from 12,412,920 results in the serpent number 12,391,470.

Reckoned from the starting-point IX Kan 12 Kayab (4 Ix) the black number corresponds to the date IV Eb 5 Chen (10 Muluc) and the red to IX Ix 12 Zip (11 Kan), and these two dates must certainly have been under the serpent; the months unfortunately are effaced.

It is self evident that the black number is exactly divisible by 8 and the red by 130.

The two events indicated by the two numbers must be to some extent coincident with the beginning of the seven events recorded in the previous four serpents. These large numbers pertaining to the destruction of the world are a reminder of the numbers, which on page 24 we believed were connected with the creation of the world. Thus here, too, we have the genesis and the apocalypse of all the mythologies.

6. The Columns of Hieroglyphs.

The last portion of this section is formed by the two middle columns of hieroglyphs on page 69. They bear an extraordinary resemblance to those discussed under page 61 even in regard to the fact that each column contains 18 signs. Besides, the upper 10 lines, *i.e.*, the upper 20 signs, are exactly alike on the two pages, aside from slight variations, and differ only in so far as the passage on page 69 is written on blue ground and the one on page 61 on white.

But also the lower part, with eight signs in each column, shows many points in common with page 61. Here as there the whole is divided into several groups.

With the four signs 11ab and 12ab, which formed the first group there, I can compose only the two signs 11ab here. In the cross 11a, as on pages 24 and 58 of the Manuscript, I see the sign for 20 with the prefixed 5 making 25. In 11b we find the sign for 18,980 days, which we have already met with several times. Hence 11ab would have the value of 25 × 18,980 = 474,500 days, as on page 61 the corresponding four signs seemed to form 421,940. And as the number there was 1156 × 365, so on page 69 we have 1300 × 365.

I believe there is a disarrangement in what follows, inasmuch as I assume that the two signs 12b and 13a ought to be placed *before* and not *after* 12a. Assuming that the two little crosses on either side of the 1 are meaningless, we should assign the value of 61 to the 3 Chuen, 1 Kin. Here, in the first place, the intention seems to be to establish some connection with the two days VII Kan and IV Ik specified with their numbers on page 63, column 3, as well as with the days most important there, III Chicchan and XIII Akbal, *i.e.*, a connection with the previous section of the four serpents in general; for the interval from VII Kan to III Chicchan, as well as that between IV Ik and XIII Akbal is 61 and on pages 70-73 the two most important days, IV Eb and IX Ix, are 122 days apart, and 122 is the second multiple of 61. I can now put the 144,000 of 12a in the place of the 13a. Then, secondly, the four signs from 13a to 14b in the one section are exactly like those in the other section, and therefore need not be discussed here. Only 15ab differs from the signs in the other passages inasmuch as on page 69 we find 4 × 20 + 4 × 1. The last 4 agrees even better than it does there with the distance from IV Ahau to the day Kan with which the serpent numeral begins.

Nothing on page 69 corresponds to the signs in 16ab and 17ab of page 61. On the contrary, the initial date of the serpent IX Kan 12 Kayab, which on page 61 does not appear until 18ab is set down in 16ab. On the other hand on page 69 the four signs 17ab and 18ab are added, 17a being a sign as yet unknown with 13 as a superfix. I feel inclined, though with many misgivings, to treat 17ab like 5a and b of page 61 and to assign to them the value of an Ahau-Katun of 113,880 days. For then they would denote the 13th Ahau-Katun, which extends from the day 1,366,560 (page 24) to 1,480,440 and which contains the two large numbers on page 70, left, top, while the two lower numbers in the first and second columns of that page belong to the 12th Ahau-Katun, and the two in the third and fourth belong to the 14th Ahau-Katun. The 13th would be the present and the 12th and 14th the past and future; but all this could only be confirmed by further research. At all events, the signs for beginning in 17b and for end in 18a refer to past and future. Unfortunately, 18b is entirely effaced.

Page 74.[6]

Besides the picture, this page contains only 15 hieroglyphs in three horizontal rows. Only about six of these signs are decipherable. The second, third and fourth of the lower line are three different heads; the middle is the familiar head of god B, the one on the left has the Akbal eye and the abbreviated sign for the south, which is repeated in the affix; the head on the right has the sign for the west as a prefix. Very little more is to be said of the other hieroglyphs than that the second and third of the second line have the sign for the east; the first of the second line, however, was the one which we found on pages 71-73 as the constant companion of the Bacabs and which suggested the wind. The last sign of the second line must have contained that for north, so that the four cardinal points all came together here.

The picture begins below these signs. Astronomical figures, apparently Venus, Mars, Mercury and Jupiter, end in the fore part of a crocodile. Below the astronomical signs are the signs for the sun and moon. Streams of water are falling from the jaws of the crocodile and also from the sun and moon. And a fourth stream is being poured from a jug by the old woman with the tiger claws, and with the serpent on her head, whom we saw on pages 39, 43 and 67 engaged in the same occupation. Cross-bones are represented on her skirt as the symbol of death. The sign of the ninth day, Eb, appears on the jug; this is the day which was avoided in the Tonalamatls, for not a single Tonalamatl begins with Eb in the Dresdensis, nor does one begin with the week-day IX; does Bolon meaning nine suggest Balam, the jaguar?

Still further down on the page sits a black god, who may be the same as the

---

[6] Compare the Peresianus, page 20.

god on pages 7a and 16b, with a bird of prey on his head. There are two arrows in his right hand and his left hand holds what may be an atlatl, but it is very much longer than is usually the case; at the same time it can be regarded as a spear.

This page can denote nothing but the end of the world, for which the serpent numbers have prepared the way. Perhaps what looks like a zero above the sign Eb in the stream of water may likewise point to this calamity.

INDEX.

The numbers in the first column refer to the pages of the Manuscript, and those in the second column to the pages of the Commentary.

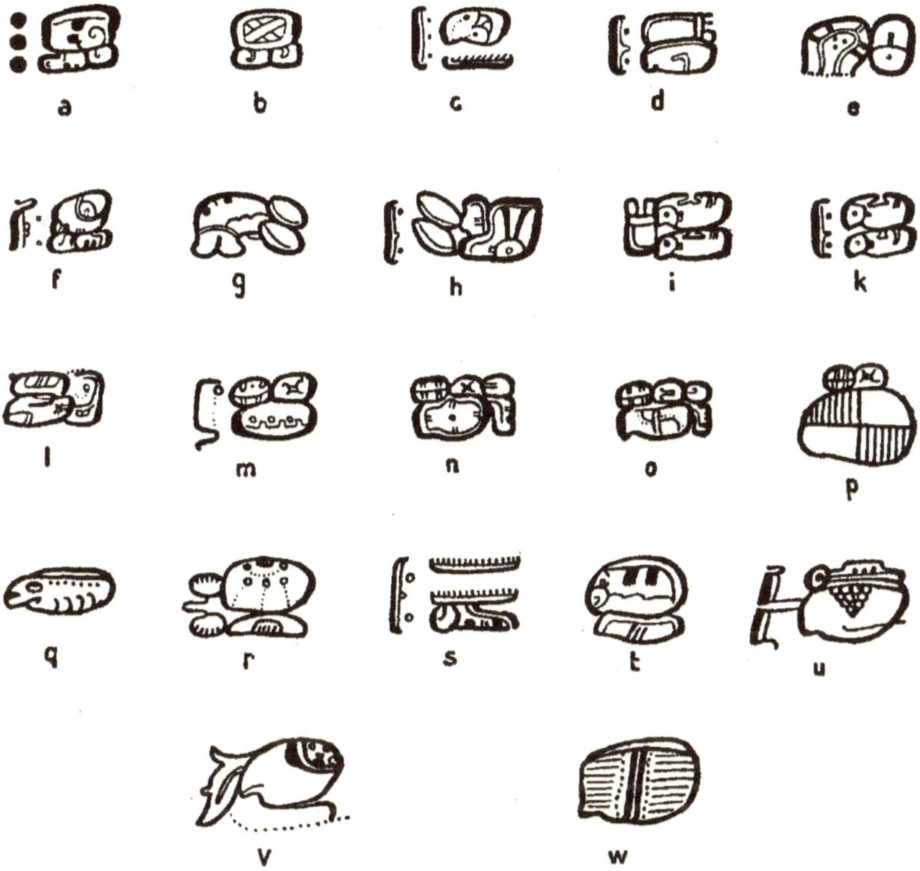

a
b
c
d
e
f
g
h
i
k
l
m
n
o
p
q
r
s
t
u
v
w

GLYPHS REFERRED TO IN THE TEXT.

EAST
NORTH
WEST
SOUTH

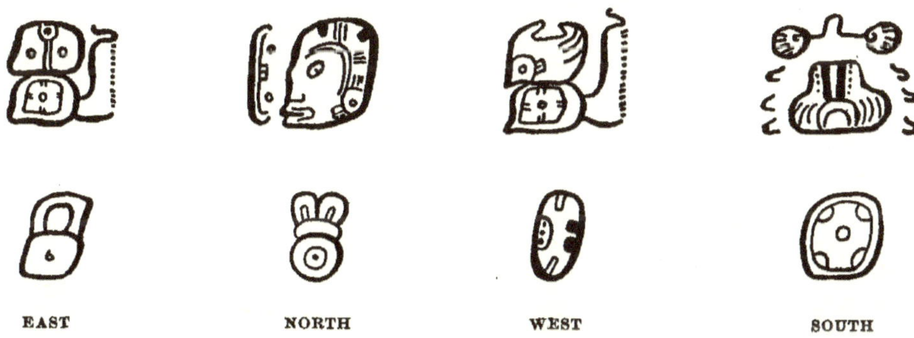

CARDINAL POINTS.

Lector House believes that a society develops through a two-fold approach of continuous learning and adaptation, which is derived from the study of classic literary works spread across the historic timeline of literature records. Therefore, we aim at reviving, repairing and redeveloping all those inaccessible or damaged but historically as well as culturally important literature across subjects so that the future generations may have an opportunity to study and learn from past works to embark upon a journey of creating a better future.

This book is a result of an effort made by Lector House towards making a contribution to the preservation and repair of original ancient works which might hold historical significance to the approach of continuous learning across subjects.

HAPPY READING & LEARNING!

LECTOR HOUSE LLP
E-MAIL: lectorpublishing@gmail.com